EVE'S BIBLE

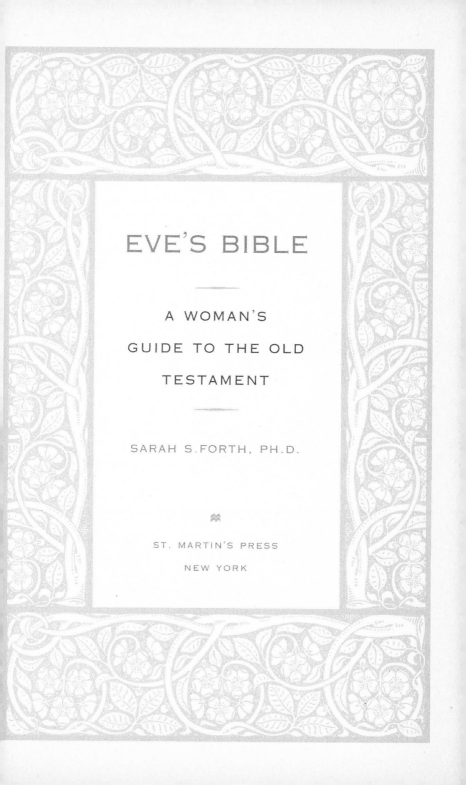

EVE'S BIBLE

A WOMAN'S GUIDE TO THE OLD TESTAMENT

SARAH S. FORTH, PH.D.

ST. MARTIN'S PRESS

NEW YORK

www.stmartins.com

Grateful acknowledgment is made for permission to reprint the following:

"Miriam's Song" reprinted from *Shulamith,* poems by Julia Stein, copyright © 2002. Used by permission of the author and West End Press, P.O. Box 27334, Albuquerque, NM 87125. All rights reserved.

New Revised Standard Version Bible, copyright © 1989, Division of Christian Education of the National Council of the Churches of Christ in the United States of America. Used by permission. All rights reserved.

Scripture taken from the Holy Bible, New International Version® Copyright © 1973, 1978, 1984 International Bible Society. All rights reserved throughout the world. Used by permission of International Bible Society.

The Message by Eugene H. Peterson, copyright © 1993, 1994, 1995, 1996, 2000, 2001, 2002. Used by permission of NavPress Publishing Group. All rights reserved.

Library of Congress Cataloging-in-Publication Data

Forth, Sarah S.
    Eve's Bible : a woman's guide to the Old Testament / Sarah S. Forth. —1st ed.
        p. cm.
    Includes bibliographical references.
    ISBN-13: 978-0-312-34103-9
    ISBN-10: 0-312-34103-2
1. Bible. O.T.—Feminist criticism. I. Title.

BS1181.8.F67 2008
221.6—dc22   2007043067

First Edition: March 2008

10 9 8 7 6 5 4 3 2 1

TO JOE

איש חיל רב ימשא

CONTENTS

ACKNOWLEDGMENTS

I had the good fortune to begin my study of the Bible at a Quaker institution that valued truth above dogma. Frederick C. Tiffany and Judith Applegate taught me how to ask open-ended questions and to have the patience to wait for answers.

Two women who guided my work in the Garrett Seminary–Northwestern University Joint Ph.D. Program showed me what it meant to be a scholar. Rosemary Radford Ruether demonstrated that activism and scholarship coexist quite nicely; Barbara Newman's intellectual rigor was matched by her kind encouragement.

My classes in Bible at the Immaculate Heart College Center's M.A. Program in Feminist Spirituality were populated with students who helped me develop the ideas that form the backbone of this book. A deep bow to all of them and to the memory of the program's founder, Patricia Reif, IHM.

The National Writers Union, and especially the members of the Book Division, helped me to find my way in the publishing industry. The

NWU has been a source of knowledgeable advice and companionship in what is otherwise a very lonely pursuit.

Fellow writers Peter Levitt, Cathy Curtis, Donna Frazier Glynn, Terry Wolverton, and members of Women at Work have helped to shape my writing in felicitous ways. Many thanks.

Jane, George, Mike, Kathy, Sara, Ray, and all the other members of my dear family, as well as my friends Paul and Nancy: I always felt your support, even when it came in the form of that dreaded question, "How's the book coming?"

Until I met June Clark of the Peter Rubie Literary Agency, I did not fully understand why authors thanked their agents so heartily in their acknowledgments. Now I know. Thank you, June! You would not hold this book in your hands were it not for the enthusiasm of Nichole Argyres and Diane Higgins of St. Martin's Press. I am grateful to them for shepherding *Eve's Bible* into print.

This work is built on the shoulders of many bright and articulate women, some of whom I have met in person and others whom I know only through their writings. Their names are salted throughout the pages of this book and in its bibliography. Please buy their books, read their articles, and invite them to speak to your group. Their scholarship deserves a wider audience.

And lastly, thank you, Joe—my matchless "man of valor"—for making it possible to do the work I felt called to do.

AUTHOR'S NOTE

Eve's Bible is hands-on. It takes thought, imagination, and openness to develop the kind of intimate relationship with the Bible that will transform it into a fresh source of inspiration and wisdom for your life. As you read this book, or afterward, when you find yourself wanting to go more deeply into the Bible's stories, history, and wisdom, consult the appendices at the back of the book. You'll learn how to approach any passage in the Bible to extract its deeper meanings; how to buy a Bible that's right for you; and what's in the Bibles of various religions.

Enjoy the journey, and consider sharing it with other women in study, discussion, or reading groups. The insights that come from close reading are multiplied when many minds come together to learn and share their discoveries.

EVE'S BIBLE

BEGINNING THE
JOURNEY

The Bible is a dangerous book.

Written by men for men, it has been used for thousands of years to keep women in their place.

The Bible also vigorously challenges the powers that be and demands justice, compassion, and care.

How are we to reconcile these competing messages?

By reading with Eve's eyes, not Adam's.

One of the Bible's well-known stories says that God made a man, Adam, and from his rib fashioned a female whom the man named Eve. For millennia, this story has driven the belief that women are not quite as good as God's first creation, man.

In this book, we are going to institute a new understanding of where Eve stands in the order of creation. We will find the story behind the Bible's stories, reclaim what nourishes, discover new understandings of God, and let go of the rest. Hand-me-downs no longer suffice.

The Bible Transcends Religious Labels

If you come from a religious tradition that claims the Bible as its foundation, this work is imperative. But the Bible is not just for Christians or Jews. It offers enrichment that transcends religious labels, in the same way that the Dalai Lama's writings have inspired many who are not Buddhists. The Bible offers you:

- Strong women and admirable "bad girls"
- Triumphant underdogs
- Wisdom to live by
- Ancient tales of power politics
- Erotic poetry and verses that support and comfort

Eve's Bible does not assume that you know anything about the Bible or that you subscribe to the religious doctrines based on it. It gives you the tools and information you need to read with insight, regardless of your religious affiliation—or lack of one.

You Know More Than You Think You Do

Eve's Bible helps you feel comfortable with the Bible by drawing on reading skills you already possess. As unlikely as it sounds, reading the Bible is much like reading the daily newspaper. A newspaper contains a wide variety of writing—news stories, features, editorials, book reviews, the crossword puzzle, comics, and so on—yet you take that in stride. You intuitively read an op-ed piece differently than you read a movie review.

The Bible, too, is a mixture of different types of writing. Genesis, for example, contains stories, legal documents, poetry, and genealogies—among other forms of material—all wrapped together and presented as history. It can seem an impenetrable mishmash, especially if you try to read it like a modern novel, as most of us have attempted to do.

Once you learn to distinguish the Bible's basic genres of writing—histories, stories, laws, poetry, prophecy, and wisdom—as *Eve's Bible* shows you how to do, you will know when to switch gears, just as you do with a newspaper. You will find that each of these is more familiar than you would think; it's all a matter of knowing what you're looking at.

Eve's Bible also tells you about real women's lives during the biblical era and how politics and history determined the final composition of the Bible. If you've been wondering why the biblical Deity sometimes comes across as such an unlovable character, you will learn the reasons. On the practical side, you'll get tips for how to read through a passage and how to buy a readable Bible.

Not for Yourself Alone

When you grapple with biblical texts, you do not do it for yourself alone. Although I sometimes feel as if men really are from Mars, in today's gender war it's not men versus women. Rather, it's advocates of equal rights for all versus religious traditionalists who believe that women and men have distinct, "biblically defined" roles. Wielding power disproportionate to their numbers, traditionalists promote policies that harm women and families—from abstinence-only sex education to laws that permit pharmacists to refuse birth control prescriptions—based on their reading of the Bible.

Using *Eve's Bible*, you, too, will be able to lay claim to biblical authority. You will learn how to challenge those who would use the Bible against you and where to find the words to articulate your aspirations for justice and equality.

How I Came to Write *Eve's Bible*

I had been living in an ashram for about four years when I picked up the Bible and was startled by how familiar it sounded. The rebellious followers of Moses in the wilderness and the dim-witted disciples of that rabbi, Jesus: I knew those guys! They were all around me in the ashram. In fact, I was one of them: anxious to touch the Divine, falling short in my efforts, whining, miffed, mystified.

As much as I liked the ashram, I decided it was time to check out my own religious tradition and see what more it had to offer. Eighteen months later, I was enrolled at a tiny Quaker seminary, taking my first course in the Hebrew Bible. That was more than twenty-five years ago.

I wish I could say that first moment of recognition was the start of a long, satisfying love affair with the Bible, but honestly? I've been more than a little ambivalent about this relationship.

To me, the Bible's stories about women nestle inside one another like Russian matreshki dolls. My most immediate response to the Bible's focus on men was, "Unfair!" But when I looked closer at the women who were there, I got excited. There were women prophets, a queen or two, pious and spunky heroines, and protective mothers.

But wait a minute. Some of these women are less than ethical—they lie, trick, steal, and deceive—and too many are victims. Something felt terribly wrong.

Then I realized that even the "good" women were valued primarily for their capacity to bear children. And those tricksters? They, too, were merely part of the plan to continue the male line.

But that still wasn't the whole story. Looking yet again, I discerned something subversive about some of these women. They may have played their part in the patriarchal game plan, but at times they turned it on its head. Ultimately I concluded that if I read cautiously, there was enough to salvage and use.

These contradictory feelings prompted me to write *Eve's Bible:* to help other women re-vision biblical traditions and empower readers to decide what meaning the Bible has for them. If our spiritual lives are of any value at all, we need the best sustenance available, and the Bible, if read intelligently, can nourish us.

THREE FALLACIES ABOUT THE BIBLE

Both religious traditionalists and nonbelievers have perpetuated fallacies about the Bible that lead otherwise intelligent, educated people to ignore its wisdom. Let's look at three misguided propositions that might keep you from moving ahead.

Fallacy #1: The Bible is the inerrant "Word of God."

Traditionalists claim that everything in the Bible is literally true (or, true except in matters of science), dictated by God to willing scribes.

Yet the great majority of scholars view the Bible as a compilation of writings by humans who were inspired by Divine promptings to greater or lesser degree. Politics, economics, cultural trends, and assorted worldly fixations influenced biblical writings.

The best motive for reading the Bible is not belief but engagement. The texts are there for you to ponder and wrestle with.

Fallacy #2: With the Bible, it's all or nothing; you can't accept some of it and ignore the rest.

Traditionalists argue that the early rabbis and church fathers [*sic*] determined the Bible's contents once and for all. We must accept the entire *canon,* or collection of scripture, without picking and choosing.

For starters, although we call it "The Bible" as if everyone knew what that meant, Jews, Protestants, Roman Catholics, Greek Orthodox, and Russian Orthodox each have accepted a different collection of works as its Bible. The Old Testament is not identical to the Jewish Bible. (Appendix 3 explains these peculiarities.) And even the most devout believers have made accommodations for modern circumstances. (No one nowadays is sacrificing bulls to atone for sin, for example.)

Furthermore, successive generations of biblical scribes augmented and commented upon received tradition—additions that then became part of the canon. When we use life experiences to gauge whether something in the Bible is valid and meaningful, we join a line of biblical interpreters stretching back more than 2,500 years.

Fallacy #3: The Bible is Western literature's greatest work of fiction.
Folks who don't care for the Bible repeat this fallacy, often to counter Fallacy #1. Yet as you explore what is really in the Bible, you will discover this: The Bible is not fiction—yet neither is it nonfiction. It's true but not necessarily factual, historical but not a history book. Rather, it is "sacred history," a story about the origins of a tribe and its relationship with the Deity that maintains a somewhat tenuous connection to actual events. And as we enter its stories, you'll find that what appears to be the past becomes an ongoing story in which we can participate.

Touring the Bible

Touring the biblical world is a lot like traveling in the wider world. You'll journey across distance and time to encounter a world both like and unlike your own. And as you travel into new knowledge, you'll be changed by the experience.

Eve's Bible will be your companion in this new land to keep you from getting lost or overwhelmed, encouraging you to rely on your sense of adventure, and to draw satisfaction from the self-discovery that is certain to result.

You are welcome to be an armchair traveler and simply read and learn from *Eve's Bible*. But at the back of the book, in the first appendix, I've outlined the methods you can use to find your way more deeply into a passage from the Bible, and I invite you to explore along with me as we go. I describe how to choose a passage, what to look for as you read, how to pace yourself, and ways to make sense of what you read.

"Making sense" has two parts: First, we have to grasp what the biblical author was trying to get across. Second, we figure out what it means in our lives. The first task requires a certain amount of analytical, left-brained activity, but your heartfelt intuition is needed at all times.

For each of the six genres I have identified within the Bible, I've included a "tutorial" that walks you through a passage. I also provide lists of where to find the women in each genre. A half dozen passages in each list are starred. These are good selections with which to start. My secret wish is that by reading *Eve's Bible*, you will feel inspired to explore further and will eventually become confident interpreting the Bible for yourself. That brings with it a wonderful sense of empowerment.

Travel Advisory

I have just one caution for the road ahead: Please be careful about what you designate as holy and authoritative in your life—even the Bible. While it is called the "Holy Bible," the Bible is holy only to the degree that we allow it to have authority in our lives. The book called the Bible is not, by itself, holy, any more than are the sun or the stars. Holiness is what happens in our lives through dynamic encounters that let us hear the voice that guides us. Whether you call that voice God, or a Higher Power, or your own consciousness is up to you. But this holy wisdom is only potential until we complete it by recognizing it as our own.

Don't let the Bible become another domineering voice. "Authority" comes from the Latin word *auctōritās*, from *auctor*, or "author." Who is the author of your life? Who makes the decisions that shape your story? I hope it is you.

DATES, NAMES, AND SOURCES IN *EVE'S BIBLE*

All religious traditions have their own calendars, numbering the years according to their understanding of history. The West has adopted the Christian schema (AD and BC), but in this book I'm trying for something a bit more neutral. I use Common Era (CE) and Before Common Era (BCE), which refers to time without referring to the Christian messiah.

Biblical writers called the Deity by many different names, but the designation that appears most often in English versions of the Bible—LORD—was not one of them. LORD is a stand-in for the four Hebrew letters YHWH, traditionally considered too holy to pronounce. Chapter 13 tackles the question of what this name might mean and chapter 2 explains its significance to understanding how the Bible was composed—particulars that argue against a circumlocution such as LORD.

Some scholars and Bible versions write this name out as Yahweh. I've chosen instead to use the four letters (printed as Yhwh) to promote historical accuracy *and* allow readers to pronounce it or not as they wish. I hope this middle way will be acceptable to all concerned.

One of the things you will learn in *Eve's Bible* is that not all Bibles are created equal. In fact, there is no single collection of materials that everyone agrees is *the* Bible. Jewish and Christian Bibles are ordered and categorized differently, and the contents of Christian Bibles differ depending upon whether they're intended for use by Protestants, Anglicans, Roman Catholics, Greek Orthodox, or Russian Orthodox.

In *Eve's Bible,* I've included for the sake of discussion all of the books that form the Jewish Bible—often called the *Tanakh*—as well as the collection used by Christians that is called, variously, the Apocrypha or Deuterocanonical books. Whether you consider all of these "Holy writ" is up to you, but this more generous selection mirrors the compilation of Jewish scriptures that was translated into Greek late in the first millennium BCE. Appendix 3 tells you all about it.

Most of the quotations from the Bible in this book come from the New Revised Standard Version, unless otherwise noted. In certain places, for clarity's sake, I've used excerpts from the translation by the Jewish Publication Society (designated JPS). Appendix 2 tells you about the many different translations now on the market (only they're not called translations; they're *versions*) and how to shop for a modern edition that can significantly improve your pleasure in reading the Bible.

Companions for the Road

If you still have doubts about taking on the Bible, know that you join a long line of remarkable women who have felt empowered to interpret the Bible for themselves and who can be companions for your journey.

One of them was Sojourner Truth, who was born a slave in New York during the American Revolution. Freed after thirty years, Truth became an ardent campaigner for women's rights and the abolition of slavery. Although she never learned to read or write, she drew upon the oral tradition of her African heritage to memorize scripture, which she quoted at length in her public speeches. Truth interpreted critically what she memorized based on her own, intuitive relationship with God.[1]

Truth challenged literal interpretations of the Bible by comparing them with her own experience of God and everyday life. In her famous 1851 "Arn'n't I a Woman?" speech she said:

> *If the first woman God ever made was strong enough to turn the world upside down all alone, these women together ought to be able to turn it back, and get it right side up again! And now they is asking to do it, the men better let 'em.*[2]

This is a clever bit of interpretation. Truth took the standard patriarchal criticism—that Eve upended God's plan for creation by eating that apple—and said it testified to women's power. To refute her assertion that women have the capacity to make the world right again, it would be necessary to deny that Eve caused a major upheaval.

And by warning that "the men better let 'em," Truth issued a veiled threat that played upon the same patriarchal proposition: If Eve was so powerful that she thwarted God, just watch out what her daughters might do to you!

I hope that you will join other daughters of Eve in reading the Bible with her eyes. I know you'll derive pleasure and benefit from its pages. You'll also find a renewed sense of your place in the world as well.

2

HISTORIES: PIOUS FRAUDS AND SACRED TRUTHS

Your Bible looks like other books on the shelf, with a cover, title page, table of contents, and numbered chapters. All in all, a typical, modern book, albeit a bit thicker and heavier. But the tales it contains were first told with awe and gratitude in the vastness of an ancient desert, and the distance they've traveled to your shelf spans more than three thousand years.

Imagine this:

Nighttime in an arid land. A fire pushes back the inky darkness but, beyond the shadows, you feel deep space all around you. Look up: Tiny pinpricks of light mass together in a silver band across the dome of the sky.

You yawn and settle closer on the blanket to your sisters. The evening chill creeps down from the scrubby hills beyond the tents and you seek warmth. So sleepy! But you won't go to the tent, not yet. These new moon nights are too few and too precious, nights when your whole clan gathers at the tents of your father. For food, yes, but even better, for stories, the stories of how you came to be—you, your family, and your

family's family, words gathered across the ages that tell you why you be-
long here and where you are going. Words that feed you like the warm
food your mother and aunties make. Stories you have heard before, many
times, that dwell in your heart even when you aren't thinking about
them.

    You begin to doze, then your ears prickle and you jerk awake. One
of your uncles is speaking, and you've never heard the story he tells.
This is no story about sheep and goats and shepherds, but a tale about
your father's god, the one he calls Yahweh. You follow the rising and
falling voice, sometimes uncertain of the words but sure of the truth
that lies beneath them. Your uncle finishes his story and your mother
begins a joyous song to which the other women add their voices. When
the singing fades away at last, no one moves; the earth under you, and
the stars in the sky, and all your family seem to breathe together in the
chill night air. Without even thinking about it, you feel confident that
you are safe, deep in the shelter of each other and your God.

The chronicle of how these desert tales became the book we call the
Bible contains many twists and turns. The Bible did not just happen; it
was created—the work of many hands and minds, each with a distinct
perspective on the world and the Divine.

The Bible is not a history book, although many treat it that way.
Rather, the Bible recounts a "sacred history" compiled from historical
sources embellished with distinctive religious viewpoints. Much of it
was written by powerful men to serve their political and religious interests.

You might wonder where truth lies in this sort of account. Should
we take what we read at face value? How do we know what is fact and
what is embellishment? Can we believe what we're told about women
in the Bible's sacred history?

In this chapter you will find answers to these and other questions
raised by the Bible's curious mixture of history, politics, and theology.
We'll start with the "official history"—as the Bible tells it—then

question that version of events. We'll find out who actually wrote this sacred history and why. Then, in chapter 3, we will explore strategies for reading biblical history as if women mattered.

History According to the Bible

This is how the Bible tells the story of the tribes that became known as Israel.

In the beginning, God created the heavens, the earth, and everything on the earth including women and men, whom God made "in His image." The Bible also tells us that a deity named Yhwh formed a creature from dust, set him in a beautiful garden called Eden, then made a woman from the earth creature's rib to be his helpmate. When the woman and man, at the behest of a serpent, ate forbidden fruit from the tree of the knowledge of good and bad, Yhwh sent them out of Eden forever. [GENESIS]

Sons of the first humans quarreled, one killing the other, and succeeding generations did not behave much better. God got fed up with humankind and sent a great flood that wiped out everyone and everything—except one righteous man, Noah, his family, and representatives of every species of animal. [GENESIS]

Much later, Yhwh promised to make a great nation from two descendants of Noah, Sarah and Abraham, and said their tribe would inhabit the land of Canaan, have many descendants, and maintain a close and favored relationship with God. Although Sarah had been barren, God granted her and Abraham a son, Isaac. [GENESIS]

Later, God enabled Isaac's barren wife Rebekah to bear two sons: twins named Esau and Jacob. When grown, Jacob tricked his father into giving him the blessing that should have gone to the elder son,

Esau. Jacob then fled to his mother's family in Mesopotamia. [GEN-ESIS]

There, Jacob married two sisters, Rachel and Leah. All in all, Jacob had twelve sons by his wives and their two slave women. After many years, Jacob took his family westward, where they eventually settled in the hill country of southern Canaan. There he dedicated an altar and made everyone renounce gods other than El. God renamed him Israel. [GENESIS]

Jacob favored his son Joseph, to whom he gave a colorful cloak. This made Joseph's brothers jealous and they sold him to slave traders. Joseph ended up in Egypt and eventually traded upon his ability to interpret dreams to become a powerful man at the Egyptian court. During a famine in Canaan, Joseph's brothers sought refuge in Egypt, where they were protected by their brother. [GENESIS]

Time passed. From each of Jacob's sons arose a new tribe, twelve in all, each named for its forefather. Fearing these fruitful Israelites, the Egyptians pressed them into slavery and the pharaoh ordered all Hebrew boy babies killed at birth. An infant named Moses miraculously survived, however, because his mother put him in a basket and set him adrift in the Nile, where he was discovered and adopted by a daughter of the pharaoh.

After many years, Yhwh called upon Moses to lead his people out of slavery with the help of his brother Aaron. When the pharaoh refused to free the Israelites, Yhwh beset the Egyptians with ten gruesome plagues. [EXODUS]

Overcome, the pharaoh released the Israelites, who set out for "the land flowing with milk and honey" promised to them by Yhwh. When the pharaoh changed his mind, the Egyptian army pursued the ex-slaves all the way to the Red Sea. God held back the waters so the Israelites could pass through to safety, then brought the water crashing down on the Egyptians. [EXODUS]

For nearly a year, the Israelites camped in the wilderness near a mountain (sometimes called Sinai, other times Horeb) where God, through Moses, gave the people numerous rules to live by. God also instructed them to build a portable shrine, called the Tabernacle or Tent of Meeting, to shelter the Ark of the Covenant, a box that held a written version of ten of the most important commandments. [EXODUS]

Although Yhwh traveled with the Israelites in the wilderness, making sure they had enough to eat and drink, the people frequently complained and fought amongst themselves. Yhwh finally decreed that they would spend forty years in the desert and only the next generation would go on to the land promised to them. Even Moses died before they arrived, leaving a military commander named Joshua in charge. [LEVITICUS, NUMBERS, DEUTERONOMY]

Eventually, the Israelites crossed the Jordan River into Canaan, where their ancestors had started out so many years before. Beginning with Jericho, they conquered the towns of Canaan. Then Joshua divided the seized land among the twelve tribes. These tribes, led by warrior chieftains, coexisted in a loose confederation guided by elders known as "judges." [JOSHUA]

Despite God's commands not to mix with the locals, the Israelites intermarried with them and began to worship gods such as Baal and Asherah. A pattern developed: Everyone "did what was right in their own eyes" and ignored Yhwh, bad things happened, then a righteous chieftain or judge loyal to Yhwh appeared and rescued the people, who then returned to Yhwh—for a while. [JUDGES]

Samuel, a judge and prophet handpicked by Yhwh, eventually took charge, but as he aged the people demanded a king so that they might "be like all the other nations." Against his better judgment but at Yhwh's bidding, Samuel anointed a warrior named Saul to rule. When Saul neglected Yhwh's commands, Yhwh directed Samuel secretly to anoint David, a young shepherd of Judah's tribe, as successor to Saul. David was a "man after God's own heart," and to him Yhwh promised eternal loyalty. [1 & 2 SAMUEL, 1 & 2 CHRONICLES]

David was thirty years old when he assumed the throne; he reigned for forty years. He was a skillful general who expanded the boundaries of the tribal lands—now unified into a kingdom called Israel—and established his capital at Jerusalem in the southern highlands. When David was elderly and about to die, he named his son Solomon as his successor although Solomon was not next in line. [1 & 2 SAMUEL, 1 KINGS, 1 & 2 CHRONICLES]

Solomon was not a warrior like his father but an empire-builder known for his great wisdom. He built a temple to house the Ark of the Covenant and forced other nations to pay tribute to Israel. [1 KINGS, 2 CHRONICLES]

Solomon's son and successor lacked his father's wisdom. The people revolted, and the king fled to Jerusalem, where he reigned over the tribal lands of Judah and Benjamin. The ten northern tribes crowned their own king. The northern kingdom was called Israel and the southern kingdom, Judah. [1 KINGS, 2 CHRONICLES]

Centuries of discord followed within the two kingdoms, and they made war against each other as well. While David's lineage continued unbroken in Judah, Israel's monarchs and their dynasties came and went. Again and again, the monarchs and people of both kingdoms "did what was displeasing to" God by building shrines in the hills to worship alien gods. Periodically, a monarch of one of the kingdoms would remove the foreign idols and restore worship of Yhwh alone—but this devotion never lasted very long. [1 KINGS, 2 CHRONICLES]

Approximately two hundred years after Solomon's kingdom split apart, the king of Assyria marched against Israel and captured its capital, Samaria. The conquering monarch forced the Israelites— the ten tribes of the north—to resettle in Assyria, where they were lost to history. [2 KINGS, 2 CHRONICLES]

This left just the small kingdom of Judah in the south. Eventually, a king named Josiah came to power and cleaned up Judah's religious practices. Even so, the Babylonians, who had taken over the Assyrian empire, occupied parts of Judah. Josiah was killed, and within a short time the Babylonian king captured Jerusalem and the royal family, then took Judah's officials, warriors, and ten thousand other captives into exile in Babylon, placing a puppet king on the throne. Ten years later, his troops returned to put down a revolt, leveling the temple, the palace, and the walls of Jerusalem. [2 KINGS, 2 CHRONICLES]

The Judahites passed two generations in exile. Then Persia conquered Babylonia, and the Persian king, Cyrus, allowed the Israelites to return to Judah. The returnees rebuilt and dedicated the temple. A priest named Ezra established the law of Moses as the law of Judea, aided by Nehemiah, a governor appointed by the king. Although ruled by Persia, the Judeans were home once again. [2 CHRONICLES, EZRA, NEHEMIAH]

Truth v. Fact

What a powerful story! A Deity who guides, protects, and, yes, disciplines the people to whom S/he has given so much. Greatness foretold, greatness lost and then regained against all odds—could Hollywood do better? Echoes of an intimate love story pervade this tale: the love of Yhwh for the chosen people.

But is any of this true? Did things really happen the way the Bible says they did?

If by "true" we mean, "Are these stories factual?" then the answer is, for the most part, no. Consider *these* facts:

- The oldest biblical manuscripts date from the first century BCE—many, many centuries after the events described in them.
- No evidence exists for figures such as Abraham, Sarah, or their descendants. The sites in modern Israel venerated as their graves are considered by archaeologists to be "traditional"—in other words, unverified.
- Biblical chronology places Abraham and Sarah in the Middle Bronze Age (2100–1500 BCE), yet their stories are full of anachronisms—such as camels and Philistines—that date to much later periods.
- Egyptian annals do not record the presence of a large group of foreign slaves or their flight to freedom.
- Although an enormous group of Israelites reportedly spent forty years in the wilderness (presumably somewhere in the Sinai Peninsula) before crossing the Jordan into Canaan, archaeologists have been unable to uncover any evidence of their sojourn, despite numerous attempts to do so.
- The earliest source, other than the Bible, to mention Israel is an Egyptian victory monument from 1207 BCE that celebrates the defeat of "Israel" along with a trio of Canaanite cities. Although this tells us that a geopolitical entity known as Israel was in Canaan at the time, it doesn't tell us where it was or what it was.
- Excavated remains of cities said to have been destroyed by Israelite armies indicate that the cities either were not occupied

at the time of the "conquest" or were not destroyed when the Bible says they were.

- The only trace of King David discovered thus far is a fragment of a ninth-century BCE Aramaic inscription that contains the phrases "king of Israel" and "House of David."

- No written records exist from any of Israel or Judah's monarchs. We must rely on inscriptions and annals from Egyptian, Assyrian, Moabite, and other sources to confirm the Bible's history of the monarchy. The earliest is an Assyrian monument that refers to a ninth-century BCE king of Israel.

- Archaeologists have uncovered key biblical cities and found defensive walls, public squares, and buildings large enough to be palaces. But do these cities testify to the wealth and power of David and Solomon?[1] Some date them to a later era, saying the southern highlands were such a backwater it's unlikely Jerusalem could have been the capital of a great nation in the tenth century BCE.[2]

- Evidence of a mighty Israelite kingdom does exist—massive building projects and Assyrian inscriptions testify to its prowess— but it was centered in the north and a century after David and Solomon supposedly reigned in the south.

So, no, we cannot say that the Bible is factual. But if by "true" we mean, "These stories tell us how people understood themselves in relation to the Sacred," then we can say, "Yes, they are true." Biblical characters display all of the strengths and weaknesses humans are known for, from generosity and cleverness to ambition, greed, and pride. We can enter into their stories and learn along with them because the circumstances feel familiar. Their relationships with the Deity also ring true in both their struggles and their intimacies.

Yet the Bible would not have the power to hold us the way it does if we thought it was "merely" truthful—a well-composed fiction—and not also factual to some degree. We moderns want our eternal truths to be based on verifiable facts, even if they merely serve as a framework for the imagination. Fortunately, we have those facts. Archaeologists have uncovered sufficient traces of biblical events to warrant the claim that though it may not be history in the modern sense, the Bible is at least "historical."

History and the Art of Persuasion

There is more than a bit of irony in our search for facts. Modern readers are likely to question the authenticity of biblical stories for the very qualities that defined it as history for its ancient writers. Take, for example, the Bible's verbatim speeches. Whereas we might wonder about the conversations between Moses and God as recorded in the Bible because we doubt anyone was there taking notes, the Bible's original audience knew better than to take them literally: Historians in antiquity routinely composed speeches for their characters that represented what a person of their stature *ought* to have said. Embellishing an event with dialogue or significant details was understood as a *rhetorical* aid, a tool of persuasion.

Until the modern era, all history was written not so much to represent the past accurately as to persuade readers of the author's view of it.

Today's historians strive to place verifiable facts within their context and interpret them in a reasonably unbiased manner. But biblical "historians" were less interested in the facts of human history than in God's sacred intent. The Bible's authors took the legends handed down through the generations—including those desert tales told under the starlit skies—and infused them with their own understandings of God and what God wanted of their people. They were influenced by the politics and culture of the society in which they were embedded, including its ideas about women.

Who were these authors? We don't know for sure, but the attempt to identify them and their circumstances has the flavor of a well-crafted whodunit. The majority of scholars believe four major documents were braided together to make the first five books of the Bible and the books of Joshua, Judges, Samuel, and Kings. (The prophetic books and works such as Ruth, Job, and Proverbs each have their own provenance.) These documents probably were compiled during or after the Babylonian exile—which lasted from 587 to 539 BCE—but at the latest by 520 BCE. (The final documents presupposed that the Jerusalem temple has been rebuilt, and it was dedicated in that year.)

You may be surprised to learn that the four documents—or *sources,* as scholars call them—had distinct points of view and often competing versions of events. Given their disparate notions of the Deity and the destiny of Israel's tribes, it really is a marvel that they all found their way into one collection.

In one way, alas, the documents tend to be uniform: Their accounts focus on men and undoubtedly originated with men—and not just any men, either, but society's literate elite. While women may have contributed something to the mix, it passed through so many hands on its way to us that much of the original was bleached out.

The differences among the four sources account for many of the fits and starts in the Bible, which are so glaring in places that Jewish and Christian sages noticed them in antiquity and questioned the tradition that Moses actually wrote "the five books of Moses." It wasn't until the modern period, however, that scholars developed comprehensive hypotheses about the "who, when, where, what, and why" of these different sources.

Knowing more about how the Bible was composed and compiled will make it much easier for you to undo its complications. It's like becoming familiar with your news sources, whether from television, radio, or the Internet: You learn to recognize their biases and know what to filter out.

As a prelude to unraveling this mystery, read the story of Noah and the flood from Genesis on pages 21–24. Better than anything I could say, it will introduce you to two of the Torah's four primary sources and illustrate the collision of beliefs that occurred when these documents were edited together. Then we'll unpack the passage to learn what's behind it.

NOAH AND THE FLOOD (GEN. 6:5–8:22)

[Genesis 6] 5 The LORD saw that the wickedness of humankind was great in the earth, and that every inclination of the thoughts of their hearts was only evil continually. 6 And the LORD was sorry that he had made humankind on the earth, and it grieved him to his heart. 7 So the LORD said, "I will blot out from the earth the human beings I have created—people together with animals, and creeping things, and birds of the air, for I am sorry that I have made them." 8 But Noah found favor in the sight of the LORD.

9 These are the descendants of Noah. Noah was a righteous man, blameless in his generation; Noah walked with God. 10 And Noah had three sons, Shem, Ham, and Japheth.

11 Now the earth was corrupt in God's sight, and the earth was filled with violence. 12 And God saw that the earth was corrupt; for all flesh had corrupted its ways upon the earth. 13 And God said to Noah, "I have determined to make an end of all flesh, for the earth is filled with violence because of them; now I am going to destroy them along with the earth. 14 Make yourself an ark of cypress wood; make rooms in the ark, and cover it inside and out with pitch. 15 This is how you are to make it: the length of the ark three hundred cubits, its width fifty cubits, and its height thirty cubits. 16 Make a roof for the ark, and finish it to a cubit above; and put the door of the ark in its side; make it with lower, second, and third decks. 17 For my part, I am going to bring a flood of waters on the earth, to destroy from under heaven all flesh in which is the breath of life; everything that is on the earth shall die. 18 But I will establish my covenant with you; and you shall come into the ark, you, your sons, your wife, and your sons' wives with you. 19 And of every living thing, of all flesh, you shall bring two of every kind into the ark, to keep them alive with you; they shall be male and female. 20 Of the birds according to their kinds, and of the animals according to their kinds, of every creeping thing of the ground according to its kind, two of every kind shall come in to you, to keep them alive. 21 Also take with you every

kind of food that is eaten, and store it up; and it shall serve as food for you and for them." 22 Noah did this; he did all that God commanded him.

[Genesis 7] 1 Then the LORD said to Noah, "Go into the ark, you and all your household, for I have seen that you alone are righteous before me in this generation. 2 Take with you seven pairs of all clean animals, the male and its mate; and a pair of the animals that are not clean, the male and its mate; 3 and seven pairs of the birds of the air also, male and female, to keep their kind alive on the face of all the earth. 4 For in seven days I will send rain on the earth for forty days and forty nights; and every living thing that I have made I will blot out from the face of the ground." 5 And Noah did all that the LORD had commanded him.

6 Noah was six hundred years old when the flood of waters came on the earth. 7 And Noah with his sons and his wife and his sons' wives went into the ark to escape the waters of the flood. 8 Of clean animals, and of animals that are not clean, and of birds, and of everything that creeps on the ground, 9 two and two, male and female, went into the ark with Noah, as God had commanded Noah. 10 And after seven days the waters of the flood came on the earth.

11 In the six hundredth year of Noah's life, in the second month, on the seventeenth day of the month, on that day all the fountains of the great deep burst forth, and the windows of the heavens were opened. 12 The rain fell on the earth forty days and forty nights. 13 On the very same day Noah with his sons, Shem and Ham and Japheth, and Noah's wife and the three wives of his sons entered the ark, 14 they and every wild animal of every kind, and all domestic animals of every kind, and every creeping thing that creeps on the earth, and every bird of every kind—every bird, every winged creature. 15 They went into the ark with Noah, two and two of all flesh in which there was the breath of life. 16 And those that entered, male and female of all flesh, went in as God had commanded him; and the LORD shut him in.

17 The flood continued forty days on the earth; and the waters increased, and bore up the ark, and it rose high above the earth. 18 The waters swelled and increased greatly on the earth; and the ark floated on the face of the waters. 19 The waters swelled so mightily on the earth that all the high moun-

tains under the whole heaven were covered; 20 the waters swelled above the mountains, covering them fifteen cubits deep. 21 And all flesh died that moved on the earth, birds, domestic animals, wild animals, all swarming creatures that swarm on the earth, and all human beings; 22 everything on dry land in whose nostrils was the breath of life died. 23 He blotted out every living thing that was on the face of the ground, human beings and animals and creeping things and birds of the air; they were blotted out from the earth. Only Noah was left, and those that were with him in the ark. 24 And the waters swelled on the earth for one hundred fifty days.

[Genesis 8] 1 But God remembered Noah and all the wild animals and all the domestic animals that were with him in the ark. And God made a wind blow over the earth, and the waters subsided; 2 the fountains of the deep and the windows of the heavens were closed, the rain from the heavens was restrained, 3 and the waters gradually receded from the earth. At the end of one hundred fifty days the waters had abated; 4 and in the seventh month, on the seventeenth day of the month, the ark came to rest on the mountains of Ararat. 5 The waters continued to abate until the tenth month; in the tenth month, on the first day of the month, the tops of the mountains appeared.

6 At the end of forty days Noah opened the window of the ark that he had made 7 and sent out the raven; and it went to and fro until the waters were dried up from the earth. 8 Then he sent out the dove from him, to see if the waters had subsided from the face of the ground; 9 but the dove found no place to set its foot, and it returned to him to the ark, for the waters were still on the face of the whole earth. So he put out his hand and took it and brought it into the ark with him. 10 He waited another seven days, and again he sent out the dove from the ark; 11 and the dove came back to him in the evening, and there in its beak was a freshly plucked olive leaf; so Noah knew that the waters had subsided from the earth. 12 Then he waited another seven days, and sent out the dove; and it did not return to him any more.

13 In the six hundred first year, in the first month, on the first day of the month, the waters were dried up from the earth; and Noah removed the covering of the ark, and looked, and saw that the face of the ground was drying. 14 In the second month, on the twenty-seventh day of the month, the earth was

dry. 15 Then God said to Noah, 16 "Go out of the ark, you and your wife, and your sons and your sons' wives with you. 17 Bring out with you every living thing that is with you of all flesh—birds and animals and every creeping thing that creeps on the earth—so that they may abound on the earth, and be fruitful and multiply on the earth." 18 So Noah went out with his sons and his wife and his sons' wives. 19 And every animal, every creeping thing, and every bird, everything that moves on the earth, went out of the ark by families.

20 Then Noah built an altar to the LORD, and took of every clean animal and of every clean bird, and offered burnt offerings on the altar. 21 And when the LORD smelled the pleasing odor, the LORD said in his heart, "I will never again curse the ground because of humankind, for the inclination of the human heart is evil from youth; nor will I ever again destroy every living creature as I have done.

> 22   As long as the earth endures,
>   seedtime and harvest, cold and heat,
>   summer and winter, day and night,
>   shall not cease."

Who Wrote the Bible?

Time for a quiz.

1. How many of each animal did Noah take with him on the ark?
   a. *one pair of every animal*
   b. *seven pairs of every clean animal and one pair of every unclean animal*
2. How many days was the flood on the earth?
   a. *150 days*
   b. *40 days and nights*
3. What bird does Noah dispatch to determine if there is dry land?
   a. *a raven*
   b. *a dove*

If you couldn't make up your mind whether the answer to these questions was "a" or "b," that's okay—because the correct answer to all of the questions is "a *and* b." Genesis 6:5–8:22 was woven together using two distinct versions of the flood story from two sources widely separated by time and point of view.

In the first five books of the Bible (known collectively as the Pentateuch, from the Greek word for "five"), the name Yhwh was used almost exclusively by a storyteller who showed partiality for sites and characters associated with the southern kingdom of Judah. These stories depict the early years of Abraham and Sarah's tribe and feature a particularly close association with the Deity.

More than the name Yhwh characterizes stories from this source, whom scholars, logically enough, call the Yahwist. To begin with, the Deity sometimes is depicted with very human characteristics and behaviors. In the Yahwist's account of creation featuring Adam and Eve in Eden, for example, the first couple "heard the sound of the LORD God walking in the garden at the time of the evening breeze" (Gen. 3:8). In our flood story, Yhwh smelled Noah's sacrifice and was pleased (Gen. 8:21).

Yhwh also shows strong feelings that come out during conversations or in behavior. In the Yahwist part of the flood story, Yhwh "was sorry that he had made humankind on the earth, and it grieved him to his heart"—so Yhwh wiped the slate clean (Gen. 6:6). Yet at other times, this Deity seems to go out back for a smoke, leaving humans to work out their own destinies.

The humans portrayed by the Yahwist also are strong and bold as well as flawed, and as complex as their Deity. They use any means necessary to get what they want. Jacob, who became the patriarch of the twelve tribes of Israel, engaged in an elaborate charade to trick his father into giving him, rather than his older brother Esau, the paternal blessing. His mother, Rebekah, was no better: She goaded him into it and provided the means to do it.

Many believe that the Yahwist spun these stories in Judah sometime between 950 and 850 BCE after the ten northern tribes went their own way. As Judah came into its own, the theory goes, it needed a co-herent story describing its origins. As evidence, scholars point to the ways in which the Yahwist's stories depict a strong bond between Yhwh and the founding families that showcases divine favor for Judah's monarchy.

A biblical scholar named Richard Elliot Friedman, however, dates the Yahwist's stories to a later period in Judah's history. Friedman correlated historic events with Yahwist stories and surmised that they could have been written only *after* Judah lost certain territories in 848 BCE but *before* Assyrians destroyed the northern kingdom in 722 BCE.[3] Friedman's contention is supported by the Israeli archaeologist Israel Finklestein, who believes that Judah was a late bloomer compared with the northern kingdom of Israel, and that the Yahwist's comprehensive history could not have been written as early as many scholars say it was.[4]

Scholars like to refer to the Bible's various sources by the shorthand of a single initial. In the Yahwist's case, you might think this would be Y. Theories about the origins of the Bible, however, were produced by nineteenth-century German scholars, and German uses a *J* for the sound of *Y*. The Yahwist therefore is known as J. Strange as that is for English speakers, it at least helps us remember that the Yahwist wrote in Judah.

The Priestly Writers

Now, back to Noah and his ark. The alternative version of the flood story that was wound around and through the Yahwist's likely was composed by Israelite priests. Although this source, referred to as the Priestly source, or P for short, calls the Deity "Elohim," this is not P's defining characteristic. Rather, the priests are known for the vast collection of laws and regulations that make up much of the Pentateuch. They also wrote stories associated with those laws.

You may wonder why these Priestly writers concerned themselves with an ancient folktale like Noah and the flood. Well, several features of the Yahwist version probably gave the priests palpitations. For example, the Yahwist says, "Then Noah built an altar to the Lord, and took of every clean animal and of every clean bird, and offered burnt offerings on the altar" (Gen. 8:20). The Priestly version of Israel's sacred history claims that sacrifice was inaugurated millennia after Noah, when Aaron became the Israelites' first High Priest during their years in the wilderness. Priestly regulations are quite emphatic: No one makes sacrifices except a priest.

These competing accounts regarding sacrifice explain the different numbers of animals herded onto the ark. The Yahwist needed additional clean animals so Noah could sacrifice several without wiping out the species, whereas the Priestly writers saw no need for more than a pair of animals since no one—not even Noah—would be sacrificing anything.

The priests were responsible, too, for the exacting specifications about how many cubits the ark should be and how many stories it should have. They seemed to like that sort of mind-numbing detail.

In the continuation of the Priestly flood story in Genesis 9:1–17, God prohibits murder and establishes guidelines for what foods humans can eat—very priestly sorts of stipulations. Finally, and most importantly, Elohim establishes a covenant with Noah (Gen. 6:18, 9:8). This is consistent with the Priestly writings throughout the Torah: Complying with their regulations maintained the covenant between God and the people of Israel.

For a long time, scholars assumed that the Priestly document was written during and after the Exile—from 550 to 400 BCE, more or less. Presumably it was an attempt by the priestly caste to preserve what was distinctive about Israel's religion and prevent it from disappearing when an independent Israel no longer existed.

Richard Elliott Friedman, though, has proposed that P was written *before* the Exile as part of a power grab by a cabal of priests.[5] He believes that after the capital of the northern kingdom fell to the Assyrians in 721 BCE, priests and Levites were among those who escaped to

Judah, where they challenged the prestige and influence of the Jerusalem priesthood.

The king at the time, Hezekiah, threw his weight behind the Jerusalem priesthood, who traced their lineage back to Aaron. To assert themselves in their turf war with the refugee priests and Levites, the Aaronites centralized religious practices at the Jerusalem temple, bringing it under their exclusive control and freezing out the northern priests.

Friedman and others surmise that P was penned as a polemical counterpoint to the northern version of events, which exalted Moses, extolling him as a prophet with direct access to God. P's version of the flood is just one of more than twenty-five retellings of older stories from a very different perspective. Additionally, P declared Aaron was Moses' elder brother and put him right beside Moses at critical junctures, as if squeezing Aaron into every available photo op.

So, you can take your pick: the Priestly writings date from either the Exile and after—550 to 400 BCE—or the reign of Hezekiah, 715 to 686 BCE. Personally, I favor the latter: Competing camps of priests sounds very believable and explains oddities in the text.

Annals from the North

Long before the Priestly writers set pen to parchment, and perhaps at the same time as the Yahwist, another storyteller spun tales of the Israelite tribes. In his version of events, the Deity is called Elohim (a name later adopted by the priests), so this writer is called the Elohist.

(*Elohim* is the masculine, plural Hebrew word for God—and why it is plural rather than singular, no one has ever explained satisfactorily.)

Just as the Yahwist focused on sites and characters in Judah, the Elohist featured stories of the patriarchs and matriarchs in the northern area later known as Israel. Unlike Yhwh, who sometimes appears to be physically present, the Elohist Deity is more inclined to speak through dreams or to send messengers. Yet Elohim's influence is more pronounced: Human destiny often is explained as "God's will."

The Elohist also idealizes humans and justifies their morally ambivalent acts. For example, when Abraham had a child by his wife's maidservant, Hagar, out of jealousy Sarah banished Hagar and her son to certain death in the desert. As in the flood story, there are two versions of these events; but, unlike Noah's tale, they were not twisted together. In the Yahwist version (found in Genesis 16), when Sarah complained to Abraham about Hagar, he passed the buck: "Your slave-girl is in your power; do to her as you please." It was not Abraham's finest moment.

But when the Elohist wrote his version of events—recorded in Genesis 21 —he reported, "The matter was very distressing to Abraham on account of his son. But God said to Abraham, 'Do not be distressed because of the boy and because of your slave woman; whatever Sarah says to you, do as she tells you.'" The Elohist depicted Abraham with an active moral conscience, and God as actually in charge.

The Elohist usually is dated from 850 to 750 BCE (Prof. Friedman believes these writings cannot be more precisely dated than sometime between 950 BCE and Assyria's destruction of the northern kingdom in 721 BCE).

Scholars refer to Elohist writings as E, which may not help you remember they were written in the northern kingdom of Israel unless you know that Israel is metaphorically referred to as Ephriam, after one of its major tribes.

J, E, and P: This leaves one last piece to fit into the puzzle.

J + E = JE

When northerners fled from Assyrian incursions in the second half of the eighth century BCE, they took the Elohist (E) stories south, orally or written down. Eventually these were interwoven with the Yahwist (J) traditions to produce a composite known as JE. It's all speculation, of course; no one has ever seen such a document, but the shape of later additions to Israel's sacred history suggests that scribes worked with a consolidation of Yahwist and Elohist traditions and not two distinct texts.

So, before the Priests wrote their version of events, a written "history" of the Israelites existed that included the traditions of both the northern and southern tribes. Apparently this compilation was well known and accepted despite its complex and sometimes contradictory rendering of both humans and the Divine. (On the other hand, since complexity and contradictions are part of the human condition, perhaps these qualities simply made JE's version of events more true of life.)

The Deuteronomist and His History

The Book of Kings tells the following story. Sometime after 640 BCE, King Josiah of Judah ordered the refurbishing of the Jerusalem temple. Lo and behold, artisans working on the project discovered a long-forgotten scroll. Josiah sent these writings, titled the "Book of the Law," to a prophetess named Huldah to be authenticated. When Huldah certified the scroll as genuine, Josiah completely reformed the religious practices of Judah according to its precepts.

While inspiring, this tale probably is apocryphal. The material "found" in the temple most likely originated in a circle of Levitical priests in the north (it favors the religious sites of that kingdom) and was taken south to Judah. During Josiah's reign, someone reworked this material into the "Book of the Law." Because it later became the core of the fifth volume of the Pentateuch—Deuteronomy, chapters 12 to 26—this writer is known as the Deuteronomist, or D.

But that's not the end of the story. Someone later used the "Book of the Law" along with official court records to fashion a full-blown history of Israel and Judah that extended from Moses to Josiah. The Book of Deuteronomy—presented as Moses' last words to the Israelites—is the foundation stone for this history, which continues right on through the books of Joshua, Judges, Samuel, and Kings.

Even more remarkable, there was a first edition of this history and then a second one. The Deuteronomistic Historian (DH), as this author is called, penned the first version during Josiah's reign. Not only did this historian give Josiah more ink than any king other than David, he presented Josiah as the culmination of history, like a bookend to Moses in Deuteronomy and with equal status.

Real events intervened in this glorious history, however: Josiah met an untimely death on the battlefield and the Judeans got shipped off to Babylonia. The Deuteronomistic Historian had to account for these new circumstances, and he did so with a radical, new theology.

Whereas the Yahwist, Elohist, and priests depicted the Deity's making good on promises to Abraham and Sarah's tribe simply out of love for them, the Deuteronomistic Historian now said that God said that Israel would belong to David's descendants only if they were worthy of it. And how was this worthiness to be measured? By how well the Israelites kept the laws of Moses, the basis of their covenant with God.

It was a simple matter to explain the disaster that befell the Israelites—their defeat and exile—by documenting the myriad ways in which monarchs from Solomon to Josiah's father failed to hold up their end of the bargain with God. Given their flagrant disobedience, the dissolution of Israel and Judah became inevitable—at least according to the Deuteronomistic Historian.

These profoundly different notions about the basis of our relationship with the Divine—is it love? or is it obedience?—have continued to clash for millennia, right up to our present day, and accounts for the extremely different views of God found across the religious spectrum.

The Final Draft

Following the Exile, somebody wove together the four major sources, adding miscellaneous bits and pieces along the way. Scholars call this somebody the "Redactor"—R, for short—which is just a fancy word for "editor."

Mr. R may have been a priest. Every major section of the Bible begins with Priestly writings, and they help to structure the overall work.

Additionally, when the Redactor added material, it was written in the style of those Aaronite priests with their issues front and center.

Even so, this editor was careful to include every document bequeathed to him, despite their differences. He had to. By his time, they all would have been well known and held in high esteem. If something had been left out, other scribes would have objected. Still, it's pretty funny when you think about it. P was concerned about giving his version of events to counter JE's, the Deuteronomistic Historian wrote from his perspective—and then everything was edited together into one work. Perhaps Mr. R understood that disparate religious views can stand side by side without any of them being diminished.

Be that as it may, the Redactor did us a favor by incorporating it all. The history of the Bible's composition is there for everyone to see like the layers of sedimentary rock exposed on a cliff wall (except when it is more like a conglomerate with small bits all jumbled together with discrete bits sticking out). Fortunately, Richard Elliott Friedman has made it easy to distinguish the multiple documents by publishing a translation of the first five books of the Bible with different typefaces and colored inks to indicate the sources. It is called *The Bible with Sources Revealed*.

The chart on the next page summarizes the best thinking on the sources behind the Pentateuch, Joshua, Judges, and the books of Samuel and Kings.

Although Mr. R included stories from Judah *and* Israel, from Aaronite *and* Mosaic priests, and mixed folktales with historical events, he couldn't make up for the most glaring lack in his source materials: women's traditions! The next chapter takes up this quandary and talks about how to evaluate historical materials that mention women.

Table 2.1: Sources of the Pentateuch and Former Prophets

Source	Date (BCE)	Region	Characteristics
J— Yahwist	950–850 *or* 848–722	South/ Judah	Uses Yhwh for God, who is represented anthropomorphically. Features early ancestors (whose flaws show) and their intimate relationship with Yhwh (who is given to strong emotions).
E— Elohist	850–750 *or* sometime before 721	North/ Israel	Uses Elohim for God, who is very involved with humans but less immanent than Yhwh. Humans are idealized and their inner worlds and motivations probed.
D— Deuteronomist	640–621	South/ Judah	Written by priests (or the priests and Jeremiah). Teaches that obedience brings blessings. Leads to major religious reforms by Josiah. Revised into Deuteronomistic History.
P— Priestly	550–400 *or* 715–686	South/ Judah	Priests' manual and Torah regulations. Elevates Aaron over Moses. Either an attempt to hold together Israelite religion during the Exile or an alternative to an earlier version of events, JE.

3

PUTTING WOMEN
BACK INTO SACRED
HISTORY

While camped in the shadow of Mount Sinai, Moses called together the "people of Israel" and instructed them to prepare for
what would be the signal event of their forty years in the desert: receiving the laws of Yhwh. After telling them to wash their clothes and
to not approach the mountain from which God would speak, Moses
added, "Prepare for the third day; do not go near a woman" (Ex. 19:15).

"At the very moment when Israel stands trembling waiting for
God's presence to descend upon the mountain, Moses addresses the
community only as men," writes the Jewish scholar Judith Plaskow.
"Women are invisible."[1]

Plaskow calls upon women to reenvision the biblical tradition, "to
stand again at Sinai." By this she means we must assert that *women
were there*—at Sinai and all other junctures of sacred history. To "stand
again" means to claim our place in the collective memory. The task is
enormous, since in most instances biblical writers neglected women or
included them only when their presence was required for the active
participants in history: men.

Being ignored is bad enough, but the Bible also fabricates women's lives to serve theological ends, distorts women's actual contributions to Israel's history, and bad-mouths women who don't toe the party line. No mention of a woman in the Bible can be taken at face value, but negative depictions of women especially should ring alarm bells. Nothing in the Bible is exclusively religious, so we need to be alert to the sexual politics—and just plain politics—in its representations of women.

Not that this is always easy to do. Even knowing about the all-too-human and competing authors of the Bible, it feels natural to listen to these authoritative voices. We're bucking two thousand years of tradition, after all. One alternative is to dig into historical circumstances and explore women's lives as women actually lived them. We also can reinterpret stories and present a different perspective on events as narrated. Last but not least, we can reconstruct the history of women in Israel, inserting them into the silence by using our imaginations and creative talents.

Let's explore all three options.

Excavating Historical Women

On occasion, the official history opens doorways into actual worlds, but we have to excavate to find the remains. Take the story of the Queen of Sheba that is told in 1 Kings 10. Storytellers and artists from the Ethiopian highlands to Hollywood have made much of her visit to Solomon, usually by imagining a passionate love interest between a beautiful queen and a virile king. But the Bible simply tells us that the queen arrived bearing gold, spices, and precious stones, to check out the famous ruler and his legendary wealth and wisdom. She then returned to Sheba, minus her commodities.

The narrator tells his story to bear witness to Solomon's glory, and the Sheban queen is merely a foil for the narrator's ultimate purpose. "Blessed be the LORD your God, who has delighted in you and set you on the throne of Israel!" declares the queen (1Kgs. 10:9), emphasizing the

Deuteronomistic Historian's view that Yhwh alone was the source of the king's bounty.

As history, the story doesn't fly. Sheba never existed and Solomon's court, if it did, left no records. Yet 1 Kings 10 contains enough clues to allow us to follow the mythic queen back to an actual homeland. By digging deeper—with a Bible dictionary or encyclopedia, magazine articles, and museum collections—we lose the great queen, who likely never existed anyway, but gain an appreciation of the dynamic international economy of a flourishing, seventh-century-BCE Judah.

Whoever penned this story probably was thinking of Saba, an ancient kingdom in the southwest corner of the Arabian peninsula (the Yemen of today) that controlled access from the Gulf of Aden to the Red Sea. Saba was the source of the frankincense and myrrh traded via camel caravans throughout the Near East and Mediterranean in the first millennium BCE.

Yes, they mined and crafted gold, as the biblical story suggests, but also produced bronze and carved the local alabasterlike stone into objects used at home and traded along with their signature incense and spices. The Sabaeans were so wealthy and influential that their language was the lingua franca of the southern Arabian peninsula for nearly fifteen hundred years.

This knowledge sheds new light on 1 Kings 10. The story does not document a meeting between the royalty of ancient kingdoms ca. 950 BCE, when Solomon supposedly lived. It does suggest, however, that when the Deuteronomistic Historian was writing, ca. 640 BCE, trade flourished between southern Arabia and Judah. DH took events of his own day and used them as the basis of a story about a previous time. (These anachronisms turn up more than you would imagine.)

The inaccuracy matters little, though, because DH wasn't writing a history of trade; rather, the pious authors wanted to promote the Yahwist tradition and buttress their claim that monotheism was established in Israel by the very earliest years of the monarchy—and that even foreign queens acknowledged Yhwh's greatness.

Reinterpreting the Historical Record

Although the biblical historians were kind to the Queen of Sheba, stories that feature women who exercise power often are less generous. A good example of bad press is the story of Athaliah found in 2 Kings 11. Athaliah was a member of Israel's royal family—a daughter of the infamous Jezebel—who had been married off to the king of Judah. After Jezebel's husband died, her son ruled in his place until murdered by a usurper, whereupon Athaliah seized the throne. (This would have been around 842 BCE.)

Athaliah's first act was to slaughter all male children of Judean royal descent. Unbeknownst to her, however, one child, an infant, was hidden away. After six years, a Yahwist priest brought forth the child, and the royal bodyguards turned on their queen, murdering her and pledging allegiance to the new child-king.

At least that's the official story, which paints Athaliah as a bloodthirsty, power-grabbing she-monster.

Now, imagine this:

You hear the sound of hoofs pounding in the courtyard, the shouts and wails, and even before you are told, you know he is dead. Your son, the king, the babe you nursed yourself because you had lost so many. The chubby toddler your handmaids chased through the women's quarters, every one of them in love with his dark curls and extravagant rosy lips.

A door from the women's quarters opens and closes. No time for reminiscences. You have to act quickly or you will forfeit your life. You and he had discussed this possibility, consulted counselors, extracted promises.

"My lady Athaliah, the king . . ."

"Yes, Milcah, I know." You turn to face the woman whose wrinkled face is wet with tears. "But who? How?"

"He was visiting with Israel's king when a troop of men arrived, led by Jehu . . ."

"That viper!"

". . . who has declared himself the new king of Israel!" Milcah begins to wail. "Oh my boy, my baby boy!"

You seize the woman by the shoulders. "Shush, Milcah, and listen to me. Summon the commander of the army and the king's vizier. There's no time to lose."

But the heavy tread outside the chamber door tells you Milcah needn't bother. For a second, you do not breathe. A knock comes, and you inhale deeply. Good. If a rebellion were in progress, there would be no such niceties.

Milcah slides back the latch on the chamber's cedar door. A broad-chested man armed with a sword enters, followed by a shorter man in robes. The latter limps slightly yet manages to move with commanding grace. Your son chose his advisers well.

The soldier speaks first. "We await your orders, Queen Mother."

"It will be as the king commanded," you say, watching his face closely. He merely nods, bows, turns, and strides out. No hesitation. For the moment, at least, it seems as if everything will go according to plan.

You turn to the other man to confirm the next steps. "Who will remain loyal to the king, Obadiah, and me?"

"The army, for certain—the commander will see to that—and most of the king's counselors. With Jehu on the throne of Israel, our opposition will press for war against the north, but the loyalists will resist that for now. I'll watch to see who questions the . . . the elimination of other possibilities. As for the priests, well, . . ."

"Yes," you say, "they have hated me since the day I arrived from the north."

"Without the army, they are nothing. I will arrange for their announcement of your queenship."

"You are as helpful as my son said you would be, Obadiah."

"I always believed our alliance with Israel was for the best. As he was the best," the man says, his voice now low, eyes glistening. "I will see that his mother is honored." Obadiah bows and withdraws.

The plan is in motion. There remains just one thing to see to. Turning, you say, "Milcah, do you know what the commander is about to do?" Only a few had been privy to the king's intentions. Milcah was your mother's handmaid and has served you forever, but will she countenance this terrible yet necessary deed?

"It is the children, isn't it, my lady?" asks the elderly woman, her face a blank.

"Yes, Milcah, the children."

"For Jezebel's daughter, I would kill them myself."

That night, servants are still on their knees scrubbing blood from palace floors when the high priest of Yahweh announces to the assembled courtiers that the Queen Mother, Athaliah, daughter of Ahab and Jezebel, is now sovereign of the kingdom of Judah, her coronation to be held after a suitable period of mourning for her son, King Ahaziah. If the priest and his minions feel any regret about such an announcement, the torch light glinting from the iron swords of the soldiers lining the walls of the throne room dissuades them from saying so.

From the dais, you look out over the assembly and wonder who are yours and who are theirs and when they will begin to undermine your rule.

You do not know that they have already begun: In a far-off room, a young woman suckles a princeling as a river of tears streams down her face in memory of the one sent to be slaughtered in his place. The bereaved mother looks down at the long lashes now closing in sleep and beseeches God Almighty that the grief she feels will someday be visited tenfold upon that sorceress Athaliah. Then the woman leans back and sighs deeply, certain that Yahweh will prevail.

Athaliah may still seem bloodthirsty and power-grabbing to you, but it is important to understand her motives before we condemn her lack of charity toward the Judean royals, says Claudia V. Camp, writing in *The Women's Bible Commentary*.[2] Athaliah's father, the king of Israel, most likely married her into the Judean court to bolster his alliance with the southern kingdom. With her mother, husband, and son dead and a usurper on Israel's throne, Athaliah lacked the authority she needed to rule and had nowhere to turn. She was an outsider and dependent upon supporters of the alliance forged by her husband and maintained by her son. Had she permitted her son's children to live, opponents would have rallied around one of them immediately and staged a coup.

In any case, killing political rivals was a gruesome fact of court life. That's how her own son, King Ahaziah of Judah, was killed. Although not the assassin's intended target—he just happened to be in the wrong place at the wrong time—Ahaziah, too, was murdered (2 Kgs. 9). The usurper then sought out and killed seventy princes of Israel to seal the deal.

Athaliah was further handicapped by her descent from Jezebel, whom biblical prophets called a "harlot." We still think of a "jezebel" as a sexual miscreant, but her real crime—for the Deuteronomistic Historian anyway—was being a devotee of the deities Baal and Asherah, a natural affiliation given that she had been a Phoenician princess before marrying into Israel's royal family. Nowhere does DH say Athaliah was guilty of the same "heresy"; it was enough that she was her mother's daughter.

According to Camp, there was yet another covert enemy in Athaliah's tale. The narrator notes that among those rejoicing at the belated crowning of the child-king were "all the people of the land" (2 Kgs. 11:14). These were not the peasants who actually worked the land but a network of clan leaders, the kingdom's power brokers. When Athaliah arrived on the scene and saw them with the new monarch, she "tore her clothes and cried, 'Treason! Treason!!'" immediately recognizing that without their backing, she could not rule. Camp speculates that these turncoats were Judean nationalists opposed to the "foreign" queen's north-south alliance. For six years, they had bided their time, then saw their opportunity and took it.

In delegitimizing Athaliah, DH demonstrated his bias for Judah, the Davidic dynasty, the religion of the priests, and male rulers. Were Athaliah a man, the Bible's historians might have determined that her actions bore the hallmark of a bold, decisive leader. Instead, she was designated as an example of what would happen to women who acted outside their assigned roles.

Standing Again

To reinterpret Athaliah's actions, I took the official record and examined it from a different perspective, imagining what might have motivated a widowed queen mother more than twenty-five hundred years ago. But what if there are no records? What are we to do in the face of silence? How exactly do we "stand again at Sinai"?

One remedy is to use our creativity and imagination—the third option we have for weaving ourselves into the fabric of biblical history.[3]

Can we really do this—make up something where nothing exists? In fact, Jewish tradition gives us a perfect tool for this work: midrash, a literary form developed by early rabbis. When contemporary circumstances required specificity the Bible lacked, the rabbis would start with a biblical story and then, using its characters or context, spin a new tale that addressed the question at hand. Modern women of many religious persuasions have used the form to create everything from short parables to book-length works.

Here is one example of what biblical scholar Elisabeth Schüssler Fiorenza calls a "narrative amplification" of an existing story: "Miriam's Song" by Julia Stein, taken from her book *Shulamith,* a collection of poems about biblical and modern Jewish women. Stein supplies a missing viewpoint by assuming the voice of Miriam to describe the ten plagues that preceded the Israelites' release from bondage in Egypt.

Miriam's Song

I swept the house clean through nine plagues,
swept when Moses turned the river into blood,

swatted at frogs all day in the Egyptians' kitchen,
chased frogs in the bedrooms, whacked at them

on the beds, jumped after frogs in the kitchen. Next
I cleaned off lice from the heads of the Egyptians.

When my brother sent flies, the Egyptians had me
stand over their meals and beds swatting at flies.

After the Lord killed their cows, we laughed
even as we smelled that horrible stench.

Then I spent hours wrapping up the boils
all over the Egyptians' skin rejoicing.

The Egyptians made us women go into the fields,
round up their cattle, drive them into barns,

lock the doors against the pounding hail.
The day the locusts devoured the plants

I swept my house and swept three more days that
the Egyptians sat in darkness, for only we had light.

Before the tenth plague I swept once more,
then roasted lamb and cut up bitter herbs we ate

remembering four hundred years of slavery
that terrible night the Angel of Death screeched

and screamed as he flew over our houses
on his bloody way to kill the Egyptians' sons.

We were leaving so I baked my bread unleavened,
packed clay crockery, black pots onto a rickety cart.

I wanted to smash the pyramids.
We'd built them well. They'd last. A pity.

At the Red Sea, after we climbed onto the land and
saw Pharaoh lead his chariots into a gap

riding between two huge cliffs of water when
mountains of water crashed down on them,

I called the women who came with cymbals and drums,
"Come dance now for we are flying into freedom."

Words aren't the only medium available to shape a new history for ourselves; we can use music, our bodies, paint, cloth, clay, or any other means at our disposal. But *how* we create this alternate history is less important than *what* we put in it. In our history-making, Schüssler Fiorenza urges us to reject the violence and alienation that pass for business as usual and to go beyond the limited roles assigned by biblical scribes. Based on those moments in our lives when we have stood up for ourselves and defended others, we can posit women as dynamic actors in the biblical story. If biblical historians could promote their version of events, so, too, can we.

The Name Game

The Bible's long lists of names—in genealogies, royal pedigrees, and census lists—have earned for it a reputation of being *bor*-ing. Yet all this name-dropping provides additional clues about women in the biblical era.

Genealogies

The Hebrew Bible's two dozen genealogies perform multiple rhetorical tasks for biblical historians.[4] In Genesis, genealogies actually form the framework for the narrative. God had promised Sarah and Abraham "descendants without number," yet three generations of women initially were barren. The genealogies that bookend each generation's stories tell us that Yhwh provides the means to fulfill promises.[5]

The biblical genealogies are an anomaly in Near Eastern literature. It suggests that kinship relations were building blocks of Israelite society and probably guided social obligations, inheritance rights, and marriage choices, and determined who was "up" and who was "down" in extended family networks.

Within these networks, biblical women acted as intermediaries (through marriages that linked groups of men) and generally were limited to domestic roles as wives and mothers. Yet, as we will see, the matriarchs of the Bible "exercise great power over husbands, father-in-law, and father in situations involving the family, children, and sexuality."[6] Often women had to use this power covertly or resort to trickery, but it was power nonetheless.

Biblical genealogies are, of course, *patrilineal*: they trace descent through the father. Even so, stories in Genesis suggest that a mother's lineage was important and that not just any woman could inherit Yhwh's blessing. For example,

- God pointedly reminded Abraham that Sarah, too, was blessed and that "she shall give rise to nations" (Gen. 17:16), promises that paralleled God's commitments to Abraham.
- In deference to Abraham's wishes, his son Isaac married a woman from his own tribe rather than a local Canaanite (Gen. 24).
- When Isaac's son Jacob needed a wife, he went to his mother's clan in Mesopotamia to locate a suitable mate. Jacob ended up marrying two of his first cousins on his mother's side (Gen. 29).

Royal Pedigrees

Occasionally the inclusion of women's names point to historical possibilities. Take, for example, the royal lineages listed in 1 and 2 Kings. Fifteen out of eighteen record names of the monarch's mother, as in this example: "Amon was twenty-two years old when he began to reign; he reigned two years in Jerusalem. His mother's name was Meshullemeth daughter of Haruz of Jotbah" (2 Kgs. 21:19).

This formulaic inclusion of mothers' names testifies to the power of queen mothers, maintains Claudia V. Camp in *The Women's Bible Commentary*. She points out that when King David's widow Bathsheba appeared before her son, King Solomon, he rose, bowed, and seated her at his right hand (1Kgs. 2:19). Camp speculates that queen mothers may have served as the king's stand-in and counselor, as well as representing the needs of the people to the king.[7]

How could a mere woman have acquired this degree of political authority? Because the queen mother most likely was viewed as the human representative of the mother goddess Asherah, says Susan Ackerman of Dartmouth College.[8] (For a very long time, the Canaanite goddess Asherah was worshipped as the divine partner of Yhwh. Chapters 13 and 14 tell all about it.) The prevailing belief at the time was that Yhwh and kings of the southern kingdom of Judah were father and son, metaphorically speaking (Ps. 2, 89). Asherah, as Yhwh's consort, was therefore the king's surrogate mother, and the actual queen mother became Asherah's stand-in.

The Deuteronomistic Historian presents one queen mother's devotion to Asherah, negatively of course, in the story of Ma'acah, who served both her son and grandson at the Judean court, until the latter removed her in anger. Her offense? "She had made an abominable image for Asherah" (1Kgs. 15:13). Ackerman believes Ma'acah erected this image—a wooden pole, perhaps, to represent the tree closely associated with Asherah—in the Jerusalem temple itself. The royal palace and temple were adjacent and the temple was a sort of royal chapel for the monarchy.[9]

Census Taking

Like other authorities in the ancient Near East, Israelite leaders periodically sought to ascertain who could be called upon to pay taxes or bear arms, so they would take a census. Few passages demonstrate so clearly as census rolls who really counted in ancient Israel—literally, for only men and (male) clan leaders were named.

With a few interesting exceptions.

Among a list of Israelites returning to Judah from exile in Babylonia are descendants of Solomon's servants, including "Hassophereth" (Ezra 2:55). Tamara Cohn Eskenazi reads the Hebrew—*hassoperet*—literally, as "the female scribe," not as a proper name as the NRSV and other versions do. She suggests it refers to a group, possibly a guild, that traces its descent from a female scribe.[10]

Also listed among the returnees are priests' descendants, including "Barzillai (who had married one of the daughters of Barzillai the Gileadite, and was called by their name)" (Ezra 2:61). Whether Barzillai relinquished his family name for the inheritance that went along with joining his wife's clan or merely for the glory of the association, we don't know, but the explanation suggests that such things happened.

Similarly, Nehemiah records the names of the Judeans who showed up to rebuild the walls of Jerusalem. Among the workers, "Shallum son of Hallohesh, ruler of half the district of Jerusalem, made repairs, he and his daughters" (Neh. 3:12, JPS).

Speaking of women's status after the Exile, Eskenazi says these appearances of women's names "do not establish gender balance, but they nevertheless reflect women's presence in symbolic and practical ways."[11]

WOMEN WITH POWER IN THE ANCIENT WORLD

It's more than wishful thinking to claim higher status for certain biblical women. There were historical precedents.

At the time of Mesopotamia's first empire (2371–2200 BCE), the king appointed his daughter, En-heduanna, to a powerful post as high priestess of the municipal deities of Ur and Uruk, two southern cities. For generations, scribes copied her eloquent hymns to Inanna, goddess of love and war. Other royal women also developed influence during this period, although usually through their brothers or fathers. Even nonroyal women were able to own businesses and conduct transactions in their own name.

In the kingdom of Babylonia, which stretched from modern Baghdad south to Basra, ca. 2017–1793 BCE, women had many of the same property rights as men. A few women were educated, and some even became scribes.

Perhaps for this reason, a curious custom regarding inheritance evolved. Wealthy families would consecrate daughters to the celibate service of a deity so that they would not produce heirs. (The more heirs, the smaller the piece of the inheritance pie.) These women were called *naditus,* which perhaps meant "fallow." Although in some cities they lived apart in cloisterlike buildings, *naditus* actively managed their lands and wealth, made real estate deals, and were the source of many loans. Ironically, some *naditus* gamed the system and passed on their inheritance to younger women, usually other *naditus.* Court documents reveal that when males in the donor families challenged these transactions, the men lost because the *naditus* were too powerful.[12]

How to Read Sacred History

You'll find a list of passages featuring women in "historical" writings at the end of this chapter. The roster includes prostitutes and concubines, queens and commoners—all of them utterly fascinating. If you'd like to do some exploring on your own, asking these questions of an excerpt can help you find your way.

Where are the women? If a woman is depicted, is she named or unnamed? What is her role? Does she act or is she merely a foil for the male protagonist? What is her relationship to the males who also are included? If no women are mentioned, do you assume their presence? Why or why not? What role do you imagine that they play? Envision women in the roles of the male protagonists. How does that change the dynamic?

Who wrote your passage: J, E, P, or DH? Notes in your study Bible, *The Bible with Sources Revealed,* or an introductory textbook to the Hebrew Bible can help you determine the source. Consider this writer's special interests and worldview.

What time period is depicted and when was the passage written? Differentiate the setting *in* the passage from the setting *of* its writer.

Where was it written? The northern and southern kingdoms produced distinctive perspectives on their common history.

Why was this passage written or included? What is it trying to persuade you to believe or do? What does it argue for or against? You may never have a definitive answer to these questions, but ruminating on them will help you develop your rhetorical skills.

REWRITING SACRED HISTORY

If you have qualms about reworking the Bible's sacred history to account for women, be assured that biblical scribes themselves rewrote that history as well. The books of Nehemiah, Psalms, and Sirach (plus the Acts of the Apostles in the New Testament) all contain versions of Israel's history, and each presents a different take on the original. If you'd like to play rhetorical detective, compare two or more of the following passages:

- Neh. 9:6–37
- Ps. 78
- Sir. 44–49

As you'll find, each version was geared for its particular setting and audience. Psalm 78 and Sirach recounted their history in poetry; Nehemiah's was in the form of a speech by Ezra. The latter castigated the ancestors because they "acted presumptuously and stiffened their necks and did not obey [God's] commandments" (Neh. 9:16). Sirach, on the other hand, preferred acclaim: "Now let us sing the praises of famous men, our ancestors in their generations" (Sir. 44:1).

Each author highlighted different events and ascribed different meaning to these events, which led to varying messages in their stories.

Nor are these the only examples of revisionist history in the Bible. Later scribes reworked various laws, giving them a slant that matched their theological orientation. (Compare, for example, the statute pertaining to Hebrew slaves that is found in both Ex. 21:2–11 and Deu. 15:12–18.)

The supreme revision, however, is 1 and 2 Chronicles. Writing after the Exile, its author, nicknamed the Chronicler, drew upon Samuel and Kings, and an assortment of other biblical and nonbiblical sources to retell the "history" of the united kingdom of Israel and the House of David. Regrettably, he did not add to the storehouse of stories about women and, in fact, he deleted those appearing elsewhere that "threaten the Chronicler's portrait of David as Israel's foremost hero."[13]

All the more reason to compile our own versions of sacred history.

A More Likely History of Israel

The Bible depicts the ancient world as if it orbited around a tiny kingdom on the eastern edge of the Mediterranean—the tract of land known at various times in antiquity as Canaan, Israel, Judah, Judea, Palestine, and Syria Palaestina.

Nothing could be further from reality. There *were* great civilizations in the ancient near East—Egypt and Babylonia, for instance—but Israel was not among them. Fifty-five miles at its widest and approximately 140 miles in length, it had no major deposits of ore or precious stones, nor was it the site of notable advances in the sciences, mathematics, or technology.

What is more, most of the biblical customs that seem exotic or novel to us were hardly unique to the Israelites. Israel was the beneficiary of thousands of years of human cultural development, including writing, pottery, metalworking, brewing, agriculture, and animal husbandry. Even certain ideas about its Deity, as chapters 13 and 14 will show, were hand-me-downs. And yet, its one claim to fame—monotheism—has proved to be as enduring as all those other cultural innovations.

Table 3.1: Timeline of Biblical History

History According to the Bible	Date BCE	History According to Archaeologists
Patriarchs and matriarchs lead nomadic lives in Fertile Crescent, eventually settle in Egypt.	1850–1700	Canaan is comprised of numerous little kingdoms with walled towns at their center, mostly populated by peasants. Relations among towns are not necessarily cordial.
	1700	Rudimentary alphabet is developed in Canaan.
	1550–1200	>Egypt rules Canaan. The population grows poorer, towns decline. Peasants revert to nomadic life as herders, sell themselves into servitude, or become brigands. >Assyria develops as militaristic state organized around army and warfare.
	1400	Anatolian metalworkers learn how to smelt iron ore. A new generation of weaponry results; wars are fought to acquire the new technology.
Moses leads Hebrew slaves out of Egypt; delivers laws authored by Yhwh. Israelites travel for 40 years in the wilderness.	1250	No evidence of Moses or migrating Israelites.
Led by Joshua, Israelite tribes cross the Jordan and conquer Canaanite cities. Land is divided among 11 tribes. Judges govern.	1200–1000	Canaan revives: 300 new villages, small and unwalled; 75,000 inhabitants by 1000, mostly in hills and valleys of northern highlands. Its culture is continuous with earlier settlers. Thought to be "Proto-Israelites." No evidence of conquest.

(continued)

History According to the Bible	Date BCE	History According to Archaeologists
		>1207: Egyptian pharaoh boasts of defeating "Israel." >1196: Philistines occupy coast of Canaan after defeat by Egypt.
The people demand a king. At Yhwh's behest, Samuel anoints Saul, who later falls out of favor with God.	1025–1005	No evidence of Samuel or Saul.
Samuel anoints David, Saul's adjutant, as next king. Civil war erupts but David wins. David chooses Jerusalem as capital.	1005–965	No contemporary evidence of David.
Solomon succeeds David with help of cabal. Heir apparent assassinated. Solomon builds Jerusalem temple ca. 950.	968–928	Major walled cities are occupied at this time; may be evidence of Solomon's kingdom.
Ten northern tribes revolt against Solomon's heir and form separate kingdom, Israel, with capital at Samaria. Davidic dynasty continues to rule territory of Judah from Jerusalem.	922	950–850: Yahwist collects stories of southern tribes. (Alternate date: 848–722)
Prophets Elijah and Elisha are active in northern kingdom.	800s 811–722	884–842: Omride dynasty rules northern kingdom. Large-scale building projects in Samaria and other cities. Regional military power. Elohist collecting stories in northern kingdom. Assyria dominates Israel economically and politically. The population soars to 350,000. International trade in olive oil and wine.
Assyria captures northern capital and forcibly removes large segment of of Israel's population.	722	Israel and Egypt collude against Assyria; Israel stops paying tribute. Assyria retaliates.

(continued)

Table 3.1 (continued)

History According to the Bible	Date BCE	History According to Archaeologists
Hezekiah rules Judah. Centralizes sacrifice at Jerusalem temple.	727–698	Renaissance in Judah: increased wealth and literacy. Jerusalem expands to Jerusalem temple. 150 acres; population: 15,000. The total population of Judah reaches 120,000. Priestly writers at work (?). >Hezekiah joins Egyptian coalition against Assyrians. Assyria lays waste to Judah in 701; Jerusalem barely survives siege.
Hezekiah's successor allows pagan cults to flourish once again. Blamed for ultimate downfall of Judah.	698–642	Monarchy institutes policy of appeasement with Assryia. Economy flourishes under centralized planning and distribution. Judah joins Arabian caravan trade. Dense settlements around Jerusalem and to south and east.
Josiah promulgates regulations from "Book of the Law." Deposes idolatrous priests. Assassinated by Egyptians.	640–609	Core of Deuteronomy written. Revised into Deuteronomistic History after Josiah's untimely death. >New Babylonian superpower challenges Assyria.
Babylonian king Nebuchadnezzar sacks Jerusalem, takes royal family and 10,000 captives to Babylon. Appoints puppet king.	598/597	Priesthood and ruling elite sent to Babylonia. >Judah forms alliance with Egypt.
Babylonians capture Jerusalem and destroy temple, city walls, palace.	587	Babylonian army destroys numerous settlements and much of Jerusalem. Number of exiles estimated at 2,000–20,000. 75% of population remains. Large colony of exiles in Egypt.

(continued)

History According to the Bible	Date BCE	History According to Archaeologists
Cyrus, king of Persia, permits Judeans to return.	538	Beginning around 550, Persians encroach upon Babylonia; capture Babylon in 539. Cyrus permits Judeans to leave; many remain in Persia. A few thousand exiles drift back each year: 45,000 by 520; additional 50,000 by 458.
Second temple completed in Jerusalem	520	Priestly writers at work (?).
Ezra reestablishes Yhwh's laws in reconstruction Judah. Nehemiah oversees of Jerusalem's wall.	458–432 332 250	Biblical documents combined and edited around this time. Alexander the Great defeats Persia in eastern Mediterranean. Dies in 323. Greeks establish kingdoms in Egypt and Syria-Palestine. Oppressive conditions for peasants. Hellenism challenges traditional Jewish culture. Biblical documents begin to be translated into Greek.
Maccabees lead revolt against Greek rulers who suppressed Jewish religious practice.	164–142 142–163 63	Descendants of Maccabees known as Hasmoneans rule over Judah as independent kingdom. Rulers soon adopt oppressive practices of Greek overlords. Judea becomes Roman colony.

To help you put the Bible's sacred history into perspective, the table on pages 50–53 pairs highlights of the Bible's sacred history with events in the more likely history of Israel as revealed by archaeology.

Tutorial on Sacred History:
The Femme Fatale in Judges 16

The story of Samson and Delilah is a good place to practice reading biblical histories. It recounts how the strongman Samson became enamored of a woman named Delilah, although he did not marry her. Bought off by Samson's political enemies, the Philistines, Delilah wheedled out of Samson the secret of his strength: his uncut hair. Delilah then cut her lover's hair, enabling the Philistines to take Samson captive. But when Samson's hair grew back, his strength returned and he pulled down the pillars supporting their temple, killing himself and many Philistines.

After reading Judges 16:4–31, think about whom the storyteller wants you to sympathize with. What is the intended reaction to Delilah? What are we actually told about Delilah? Can you think of reasons why she might have collaborated with the Philistines? How do you think Philistines might have told her story?

If you read more of Samson's story in Judges 13–16, you will learn that he was a ruffian and brigand. And although he was supposedly a Nazarite—consecrated to Yhwh—he did everything he wasn't supposed to do, except cut his hair. How does this complicate the story of his affair with Delilah?

In our day, the sexual dalliances of prominent men—politicians and sports stars, in particular—often generate sympathy for the men and blame for the women involved. What is it about men with power that is reflected in these current events as well as Samson's story?

WHERE ARE THE WOMEN IN THE
BIBLE'S SACRED HISTORY?

Josh. 2:1–21, 6:22–23*	Rahab the prostitute aids Israelite spies in Jericho.
Josh. 17:3–6	The daughters of Zelophehad petition to inherit land.
Judg. 4:1–16	Deborah the prophetess initiates warfare against a Canaanite king.
Judg. 4:17–23	Jael assassinates a Canaanite general.
Judg. 11:34–40*	Jephthah's daughter becomes a burnt offering.
Judg. 16:4–21	Samson falls for Delilah; the Philistines buy her services.
Judg. 19:1–30	A Levite's concubine is ill-used.
Judg. 21:1–14	The Israelites make war to obtain wives.
Judg. 21:15–25	Israelite men abduct women at Shiloh for wives.
1 Sam. 1:1–28*	Hannah asks Yhwh for a son.
1 Sam. 18:20–29	Saul promises his daughter Michal to David.
1 Sam. 25:2–42*	Abigail, a clever wife, rescues her boorish husband from disgrace.
2 Sam. 11:1–27	David falls for Bathsheba and murders her husband.
2 Sam. 13:1–22	Absalom, David's son, rapes his half sister Tamar.
2 Sam 20:15b–22	A wise woman negotiates and saves her city.
1 Kgs. 1:1–4	Abishag attends David in his old age.
1 Kgs. 1:11–21, 28–31	Bathsheba negotiates on behalf of her son.
1 Kgs. 3:16–28	Two prostitutes argue over a baby.
1 Kgs. 14:1–18	Jeroboam's wife seeks an oracle from the prophet Ahijah.
1 Kgs. 17:7–16, 17–24*	Elijah helps a widow, then revives her son.
1 Kgs. 21:1–29*	Jezebel lies to help her husband obtain a vineyard.
2 Kgs. 4:1–7	Elisha aids a widow with a bottomless jug of oil.
2 Kgs. 4:8–27	A woman of Shunem befriends Elisha and he rewards her.
2 Kgs. 9:30–37	Jezebel is assassinated by a usurper.
2 Kgs. 11:1–21	Athaliah reigns for seven years.

4

STORIES:
TELLING TALES BEHIND
GOD'S BACK

Born in Chicago, I was only a toddler when my family moved to the East Coast where I grew up. Yet when I returned to the Chicago area many years later for graduate school, I felt a surprising intimacy with the city. How could this be?

It must have been the stories.

My father, a Chicago native, had put me to bed many nights with stories of his childhood in the northern suburbs. My mother, meanwhile, had filled my ears with tales of the family's years on the south side where we lived when I was born, and my brother and sister added their own memories. Lake Michigan, the Loop, the Art Institute of Chicago, and the Brookfield Zoo: I had no conscious memory of having been to these places, but the treasure trove of stories fostered familiarity.

Such is the power of stories to shape our sense of who we are, where we come from, and where we are going.

The narratives spun by ancient Israelites served similar functions: The stories that ended up in the Bible explained their past, told them how they ought to live, and sought to help succeeding generations establish a relationship with the Divine. These same stories can nourish readers today, when read with understanding.

This chapter and the next explore the ways biblical storytellers fashioned worlds out of words. Along the way, we'll pay special attention to how women were represented and misrepresented. Once you catch on to *how* storytellers shaped their stories, *what* they were trying to get across becomes easier to recognize. And you'll be prepared to stand back and consider a story's true intent.

Wives, Mothers, and Daughters

First, some bad news: Women in the Bible are defined by their roles as wives, mothers, and daughters. Only prostitutes are unattached to men. Single women live in their father's house and eventually marry. Their fathers, uncles, or brothers decide their fate. Older single women are universally widows. All women are mothers, or hope to be.

Powerful women are limited by their gender and roles—or are recast as "bad girls." Even the exceptional "good" woman gets whittled down to size so she won't stand taller than a man.

This web of relationships and restrictions may reflect the social realities of the time, but the biblical scribes writing these tales were more concerned with theology than biography or sociology. For information about real women's lives in ancient Israel, read chapter 12.

Let's begin our exploration of biblical narrative by meeting the women of the Bible most worth getting to know. Along the way, I'll point out (in italics) the various ways that biblical storytellers undercut their female characters or pushed them to the background.

Eve, Mother of All the Living

No one gets more bad press than the First Woman, who is accused of getting herself and her partner kicked out of paradise and starting humankind on a downward spiral (Gen. 2:4–3:24).

Here's another way of looking at Eve: She was not so much deceived

by the crafty serpent as she was persuaded by him through a sophisti-
cated theological exchange during which Eve elaborated on God's
commands, thus becoming the First Theologian. Using the brains God
gave her, she sized up the situation and decided she would benefit by
knowing the difference between good and evil—and so ate the forbidden fruit.

By contrast, the man said nothing. "His presence is passive and
bland. . . . He does not theologize; he does not contemplate; . . . Instead, his one act is belly-oriented," observes Phyllis Trible, in *God and
the Rhetoric of Sexuality*.[1] When confronted by Yhwh about what they
had done (*they,* not just the woman), the man played *the blame game*:
"'The woman whom you gave to be with me, she gave me the fruit from
the tree, and I ate'" (Gen. 3:12). He blamed Eve and even pointed the
finger at God for giving him a helpmate!

The Matriarchs: Sarah, Rebekah, Rachel, and Leah

The wives of the Bible's great patriarchs—Abraham, Isaac, and Jacob—
were no shrinking violets. Sarai (later called Sarah) accompanied her
husband Abram (renamed Abraham) from their home in southern
Mesopotamia all the way across the Fertile Crescent to Canaan, on to
Egypt, and back to Canaan again. She was so beautiful that she stole
the hearts of both an Egyptian pharaoh and a Canaanite king.

Sarah lived to a ripe old age and, amazingly, still had the where-
withal to give birth to Isaac, the heir promised by Yhwh, who continued the dynasty that became Israel. (Although we have no evidence
that Sarai/Sarah actually existed, I am sure that countless women lived
out her qualities of courage and endurance—not to mention beauty.)

Despite her valor, the Bible ultimately depicted Sarah as a shrew
who mistreated and then banished her maid, Hagar, along with the son
Hagar had conceived with Abraham (Gen. 16, 21). Biblical storytellers,
you see, *never permitted wives to overshadow their husbands in piety,
morals, or attention to the Deity*. Abraham had to take top billing, and

even though he acted like a jerk when he passed Sarah off as his sister to the pharaoh and Canaanite king, he is meant to be fondly remembered as a founding father.

In general, *the Bible does not depict wives as interesting in and of themselves*. "The wife-figure serves either as a prized object, the acquisition of which signals the husband's political success or his special relationship with Yhwh."[2] When Abraham sent a servant to Mesopotamia to obtain a wife for his son Isaac, for instance, the servant prayed to Yhwh for assistance in locating the right woman that he might "know that you have shown steadfast love to my master" (Gen. 24:14). Immediately, the servant encountered Rebekah, who was soon betrothed to Abraham's son in absentia. Rebekah was "very fair to look upon" and, with a generous and industrious spirit, welcomed the unknown servant and watered his camels; but to the storyteller, she was a mere token of Yhwh's love for Abraham.

That wasn't the end of Rebekah, however. Married to Isaac and pregnant with twins who warred in her womb, she sought guidance from Yhwh. The prophecy she received contradicted tradition: The older twin would serve the younger. When the twins were grown, Rebekah helped the younger son, Jacob, fulfill his divine destiny by encouraging him to steal the paternal blessing from his older brother. Yet the storyteller made Rebekah appear to be *motivated by self-interest*: he said she helped Jacob because she liked the younger son better than the elder (Gen. 25:28).

The Bible tells us that Jacob worked for seven years to earn the hand of the "graceful and beautiful" Rachel—only to be tricked by his father-in-law into marrying her older sister Leah, whom Jacob did not love (Gen. 29). Jacob finally wed his beloved Rachel after working for an additional seven years. The storyteller then exploited the *competition between the women* by making much of the fact that Leah was fertile and produced many sons, but Rachel could not. No doubt this rivalry was modeled on actual stresses and strains in polygamous households, but it overshadows the more important point: that the two sisters, together with two of their maids, produced the sons who became the progenitors of "the twelve tribes of Israel."

Fortunately for us, Rachel and Leah's tale of wombs and woe received a long overdue rewrite in *The Red Tent*. This novel by Anita Diamant tells the story of Jacob's women from their point of view and represents the range of possibilities—friend, companion, helper, nursemaid, and, yes, occasionally competitor—in women's relationships. It is a wonderful corrective to the received tradition. Happily, we can go and do likewise, reinterpreting women in the biblical tradition and reconstructing their stories.

Good Wives

Abigail, wife of a boor named Nabal, is the Bible's prototypical good wife (1 Sam. 25). "Clever and beautiful," she saved her husband's life by acting decisively after he rebuffed appeals for food and supplies from the powerful warlord David. Recognizing the danger, and without consulting Nabal, Abigail ordered up donkey-loads of foodstuffs and intercepted the famous warrior on his way to kill her husband and his men. Throwing herself at David's feet, Abigail apologized and acknowledged that her husband was a fool. Later apprised of his close call, Nabal had a stroke and died.

When David learned of Nabal's death, he invited Abigail to become another of his wives. And how did our plucky heroine respond? She bowed, told him she was unworthy of his attentions, and rode off into the sunset with him. And that's the last we hear of Abigail.

Granted, a woman as enterprising as Abigail was not likely to turn down a general, but the story illustrates the dictum that *Biblical women acted autonomously or out of moral concern only when it would not compromise their husbands' standing.* Abigail's husband, Nabal, didn't count in this equation; from the first, the storyteller described him as "surly and mean." Once Abigail became David's wife, however, her days of independent action were over.

The Bible tells us quite a bit about how the patriarchs arranged marriages for their sons. *But when wives took conjugal relations into their own hands, things never worked out quite right.* Tamar married one of Jacob's grandsons only to have him die without children (Gen. 38). Under law, Tamar was entitled to marry her brother-in-law, which she did, but that husband also died. (The Bible makes clear that God, not Tamar, was responsible for the men's deaths.) Her father-in-law then refused to give her his last remaining son.

Like Abigail, Tamar was ingenious. She also was not above guile: She disguised herself as a prostitute and solicited her father-in-law. Bingo! She became pregnant with a son, although her father-in-law nearly had her killed before he realized the child was his.

The story does not really celebrate Tamar's triumph, however. Even while demonstrating the unfairness of patriarchal social practices, Tamar is more of an antiheroine, her unorthodox methods reinforcing the accepted wisdom that women always need adult supervision.

Daughters

Girls are better off reading Judy Blume than relying on the Bible for guidance, because *biblical daughters are the property of fathers, uncles, or brothers, and are used to cement their male relatives' relationships with other men—or with God.* Take the tale of Jephthah's daughter in Judges 11, for example. When Jephthah was hired by tribal elders to lead the fight against their enemy, he vowed that if he prevailed, he would make a burnt offering to Yhwh.

After Jephthah carried the day, he returned home, and his daughter ran out to greet him. Too bad for her, because Jephthah had told God that he would sacrifice "whoever comes out of the doors of my house to meet me" (Judg. 11:31).

Genesis tells us that God intervened to prevent Abraham from sacrificing Isaac. No one intervened on behalf of Jephthah's daughter, although her father granted her the two months she requested to wander the mountains with her companions. Then she went home to be sacrificed.

If this young woman is supposed to be the model of a dutiful daughter, then young women everywhere are in trouble. She is self-denying to the point of death, even justifying her father's behavior by accepting his logic: He made a vow to Yhwh and it must be kept. To add insult to injury, the narrator focuses on Jephthah, forgoing details about the daughter's inner world—even her name!—or actual fate, which is not described.

Two stories of unsanctioned sexual encounters offer another glimpse into biblical views of daughters. In Genesis 34, we are told that Jacob's daughter Dinah "went out to visit the women of the region" and returned "defiled" by the son of a local potentate, who later offered to marry her. (It's not clear if she was raped or seduced.) In another tale, King David's daughter Tamar was raped by her half brother (2 Sam. 13). In both instances, brothers of the girls assumed the right to avenge their sisters' violation and to do so with cunning and ferocity, suggesting that *the real victims of a sexual assault are the males of the family and their honor.*

There is no way to repair such "texts of terror"[3] except to follow Anita Diamant's model and reconfigure them. *The Red Tent* is narrated by Dinah, and while it doesn't avoid sadness and loss, Dinah is depicted as admirably resilient and, at the end, healed.

The Few, the Brave

Mercifully, there are exceptions to the conventional plots involving women. The Book of Ruth features two spirited, independent women: the widows Naomi and her daughter-in-law Ruth. Adrift without male protectors, Ruth pledged herself to Naomi: "Where you go, I will go; where you lodge, I will lodge; your people shall be my people, and your God my God" (Ruth 1:16).

The shrewd older woman subsequently guided Ruth through the delicate dance of acquiring a benefactor and husband, a task Ruth threw herself into with gusto—and success. Although a redactor hijacked the story at the end and turned it into a genealogical treatise—Ruth's son, we are told, became the grandfather of the great King David—he could not obliterate the courage of these two heroines.

The Book of Ruth is exceptional not for what God did but for God's absence. Naomi and Ruth relied on each other and their wits; God was a no-show.

In the Apocryphal book of Judith, on the other hand, the pious heroine concocted her bold plan to defeat the Assyrian army besieging her town only after praying to Yhwh. Nonetheless, at the critical juncture it was just her and her handmaid with a sword in the tent of the Assyrian general, but they pulled off the assassination that ended the siege.

A few of my favorite bold women make only cameo appearances in the Hebrew Bible. There was the wise woman who lived in a town called Endor; she was a necromancer who consulted with ghosts (1 Sam. 28:3–25). At King Saul's request, she materialized the long-dead prophet Samuel so the king could seek his counsel. When Saul collapsed after the ghostly encounter, the woman assumed the role of wife and nurse-maid and revived him with a meal she herself cooked.

As for the Bible's "bad girls," you have to at least admire their cheek. The unnamed, malevolent counterpart of the "good wife" Abigail, for example, was married to an Egyptian courtier named Potiphar. Potiphar employed Jacob's son Joseph as overseer (Gen. 39). Potiphar's wife, we are told, repeatedly attempted to seduce the "handsome and good-looking" young man, but he virtuously refused her entreaties out of loyalty to his employer. To spite him, Potiphar's wife told her husband that Joseph had raped her, and Joseph landed in jail. (We don't know what happened to her, but Joseph managed to come out okay.)

A list at the end of the chapter points you to more tales of inventive biblical women. If you take the time to journey into their stories, you will probably notice that they're generally cast in a limited number of scenarios. For that, you can blame the "type scene."

Déjà-vu All Over Again:
Recurring "Type Scenes"

A type-scene is a fixed plotline that recurs camouflaged with a different cast of characters and change of scenery. Scholars speculate that ancient audiences expected a fixed inventory of such scenes to appear in every hero's tale. Artistry lay in how well the storyteller managed this set of predetermined motifs.[4] Audiences apparently wanted novelty—but only within certain limits.

The Bible's women generally show up in stories that have them:

1. Struggling to become pregnant and produce an heir
2. Fighting with another woman for a sexual partner
3. Seducing an unwary male in order to become pregnant
4. Becoming engaged
5. Dodging the affections of a man who is not her husband

As you can see, the conflict driving all of these plots centers around genealogy and gynecology: The male line was threatened by complications pertaining to the fertility or sexuality of a woman, and something had to be done. (No type-scenes were built around daughters, perhaps because unmarried girls did not offer the same dramatic possibilities as barren women who threatened to end the family name.) Clearly, this list does not exhaust the possibilities for women's lives—except in the minds of the storytellers!

Esther Fuchs, author of *Sexual Politics in the Biblical Narrative,* calls these scenarios the Annunciation, Contest, Temptation, Betrothal, and Adultery type-scenes.[5] The following digest of type-scenes in the Hebrew Bible will help you quickly grasp the gist of each story and note differences that indicate subtle shifts in emphasis.

— A N N U N C I A T I O N —

CAST:

a barren wife, an heirless husband, and the Deity

CONFLICT:

the woman is unable to produce the desired heirs

RESOLUTION:

Yhwh restores fertility to the woman, and a son is born

At least six annunciation scenes appear in the Bible. One of the more compelling involves Hannah, first wife of the pious Elkanah (1 Sam. 1). Hannah's barrenness made no difference to Elkanah: "Am I not more to you than ten sons?" he pleaded. Elkanah's second wife, however, tormented Hannah unmercifully for her lack of progeny.

Finally, during one of the family's annual pilgrimages to Yhwh's shrine, Hannah prayed to God for a son, promising to dedicate the child to Yhwh should God grant her request. Observing her anguished, mumbled pleading, the temple priest came forward and chastised poor Hannah for being drunk!

"No, my lord," she told him, "I am a woman deeply troubled," whereupon she poured out her sorrow over her lack of a son. The priest then assured Hannah that God would grant her petition.

Hannah did indeed become pregnant and gave birth to a son. When the child was weaned, she left him at the shrine the priest to raise. The boy was Samuel, and, favored by God, he became a great prophet, judge, and kingmaker. What's more, Hannah bore three more sons and two daughters for Elkanah.

Another annunciation scene (2 Kgs. 4) involves a wealthy woman in the town of Shunem whose elderly husband had not been able to bless her with a child. Because she had been generous to the prophet Elisha, he and his apprentice decided to reward her with a pregnancy, which took her by surprise: "No, my lord, O man of God; do not deceive your servant," she pleads.

Fast-forward several years. The promised son had been born, then fell ill and died. So the woman hunted down Elisha and demanded that he return with her to revive the boy. When the prophet hesitated, the Shunnamite did what a mother's got to do: stir up the guilt. "Did I ask my lord for a son?" she prodded. "Did I not say, 'Do not mislead me?'" The prophet got off his duff and brought the child back to life.

Besides barren wombs, the common thread among annunciation stories is the key role played by the Deity. A priest, angel, or Yhwh may communicate with the women, but God alone received credit for being the one who opened wombs. Why certain women were barren and others fertile remained mysterious. Piety seemed to have nothing to do with it: Sarah laughed at the Divine suggestion that she would bear a child, but that bit of irreverence did not change her destiny. Bearing children might have been a social necessity, but it remained outside the control of the ones most in need of bearing them—women.

Other annunciation scenes include Sarah's anxiety about an heir, which drove her to borrow Hagar's womb (Gen. 16, 21); Rachel's frustrating barrenness (Gen. 29–38); Rebekah's problems conceiving her twins (Gen. 25); the story of Samson's mother (Judg. 13).

— CONTEST —

CAST:

one husband, two wives (one favored, the other secondary)

CONFLICT:

the favored wife is barren, the other is not; the second
torments the first for her lack of fertility

RESOLUTION:

God reverses the barren one's fortunes and she
delivers a son

Husbands in these scenes were portrayed as bewildered outsiders who took no responsibility for the situation, despite having married both women and subjected them to the built-in aggravations of polygyny. A narrator depicted an "envious" Rachel, for example, pleading with Jacob: "Give me children, or I shall die." Despite having worked for fourteen years to earn her hand, Jacob evinced little sympathy. "Can I take the place of God, who has denied you fruit of the womb?" he replied (Gen. 30, JPS).

Unhooked from their larger social context, type-scenes of this variety play out as catfights that imply women are irrational creatures. Rachel, for example, bartered with Jacob's other wife (and her sister) Leah for some mandrakes—a supposed aphrodisiac—by offering Leah a night with Jacob. Leah took her opportunity and conceived a sixth son for her husband. (Oddly, this exchange suggests that males were commodities to be bartered for. When Leah announced, "You are to sleep with me, for I have hired you with my son's mandrakes," Jacob did as he was told.)

The perceived discontent of barren wives is again illustrated by Rachel and Leah's rivalry. At long last, when "God heeded her and opened her womb," Rachel named her son Joseph, because "God has taken away [*asaph*] my disgrace."

Several Annunciation scenes double as Contests between rival wives: the stories of Sarai/Sarah and her handmaid Hagar in both their versions—the Yahwist's (Gen. 16) and the Elohist's (Gen. 21)—as well as Hannah's tale (1 Sam. 1) and the traditions concerning Leah and Rachel.

— TEMPTATION —

LEAD PLAYER:

a fertile woman

CONFLICT:

no husband to produce a child

RESOLUTION:

woman seduces unwary male and produces offspring

In Temptation scenes, the women are on their own; no husbands are around to take advantage of their fertility. Storytellers generally depicted such women using morally dubious means to conceive, which apparently was what audiences expected of unsupervised females.

The nameless daughters of Lot, for instance, fled with their father from God's destruction of Sodom (Gen. 19). Living in a cave and fearing perpetual childlessness because "there is not a man on earth to come in to us after the manner of all the world," they got their father drunk and had sex with him. The young women achieved their objective and gave birth to sons.

The aforementioned story of Tamar and her father-in-law (Gen. 38) is another Temptation plot.

In the Book of Ruth, the eponymous heroine aggressively pursued her patron, Boaz. Granted, her mother-in-law, Naomi, called the shots, but it was Ruth who lay down at night beside a drunken Boaz during the barley harvest and, as instructed, uncovered his "feet" (a common euphemism for a man's genitals, as the notes in your study Bible should tell you). When Boaz awoke during the night and found himself with Ruth in this compromised position, negotiations ensued that ultimately resulted in their marriage.

Biblical narrators have nary a judgmental word to say about all this plotting and seduction. Women presumably could ignore the rules that governed female sexuality when the continuity of a male line was at stake. Indeed, the Bible celebrated such resourcefulness by including their stories.

Yet, a certain ambivalence hovered about these women, their actions, and their progeny. To elicit snickers, apparently all a storyteller had to do was introduce someone as a Moabite or an Ammorite, the tribes founded by the offspring of Lot's incestuous daughters.

A woman could be bold, it seems, but she wouldn't necessarily be celebrated for it.

— BETROTHAL —

LEAD PLAYER:

a single man

CONFLICT:

single Israelite male seeks single Israelite female

(only virgins need apply)

RESOLUTION:

man travels and discovers virgin by a well (suggestive of female fertility); marriage follows

When it comes to virgins—Lot's daughters excepted—sexual initiative was frowned upon. The men take the lead in betrothal scenes, which unfold according to the rules of patriarchal marriage. Abraham sent a servant to search for Isaac's mate (Gen. 24); Jacob found Rachel for himself (Gen. 29); and Moses first saw his future wife watering flocks (Ex. 2). In each case, the girl's father decided the match; the young woman had nothing to say about it.

— ADULTERY —

CAST:

one wife, one husband, another man, and the Deity

CONFLICT:

two men desire one woman,
threatening the patriarchal marriage

RESOLUTION:

reunification of woman with appropriate mate

All of the Bible's Adultery scenes involve married women and "other" men. If a married man made whoopie with a single, unbetrothed woman, it wasn't considered adultery under Israelite law. It might be rape, seduction, or prostitution, but because a man controlled his own sexuality, it was not adultery.

Bedding down with someone else's wife, however, was a no-no. That infringed on another man's exclusive claim to "his" woman's sexuality and progeny. Since the Bible's adultery stories were about married women and "other" men, "the 'real' victim in the adultery type-scene was the husband."[6] His rights were being violated.

For reasons that are not always clear, the husband in these stories passed his wife off as his sister, making her vulnerable to the advances of another man, usually a king. Two of these scenes involve Sarai/Sarah and Abram/Abraham. The first is a Yahwist tale set during their journey to Egypt to escape famine in Canaan. Abram worried that the Egyptians would kill him to seize his beautiful wife (Gen. 12). "Say that you are my sister," he pleaded with Sarai/Sarah, "so that it may go well with me because of you, and that my life may be spared on your account."

Sarai/Sarah acquiesced with this strange request, and Abram/Abraham lived. But the Egyptians coveted his wife, and "the woman was taken into Pharaoh's palace." This leaves open the question of just how far Sarai/Sarah was taken: into the pharaoh's bed, perhaps?

Yhwh intervened, however, afflicting the pharaoh's household with plagues—previews of coming attractions as it turned out—and the Egyptians sent the couple on their way. Then the whole scene played out again in an Elohist story about a Philistine king named Abimelech (Gen. 20). When the king confronted Abraham about his dissembling, the patriarch rationalized it by claiming that Sarah really was a half sister: his father's daughter but not his mother's. Nothing in the Bible supports this claim and, as one rabbinical commentator noted, even if Sarah were a half sister, more importantly, she was his wife![7]

Abraham's bumbling lies revealed his ethical lapses; in contrast, the pagan king was a model of moral probity. "You have done to me things that ought not to be done," he scolded Israel's great patriarch. The story displays the Elohist's characteristic concern for law and ethics.[8]

The Yahwist also told a story about the Philistine Abimelech, but had Abraham's son Isaac passing his wife, Rebekah, off as his sister (Gen. 26). The king discovered the actual situation on his own when he "looked out of a window and saw him fondling his wife Rebekah." The storyteller may have intended us to laugh at Isaac getting caught in flagrante delicto with his own wife: "Yitzhaq" (Isaac) and "fondling" ("metzaheq") in Hebrew produce a pun based on their similar sounds.[9]

The wives in these scenes don't get to say anything about being loaned to a monarch, nor is the man ever sanctioned for his behavior. Adultery-type scenes most likely were written as arguments against actual adultery—at least on the part of women—because the wives always end up back with their husbands. *Polygyny*—one man with many wives—may serve patriarchal interests, but *polyandry*—one woman with many husbands—threatens them.

One other variation of the Adultery-type scene is worth mentioning: King David's liaison with the beautiful Bathsheba, wife of one of David's generals (2 Sam. 11–12). It is a tale charged with sex, sexism, and intrigue. David spied Bathsheba bathing, sent for her, and satisfied his lust. We never hear from Bathsheba regarding her wishes, only that she conceived as a result of their tryst.

The story remains more than a little morally ambiguous. Unlike the other adultery tales, the woman was not returned to her rightful owner. The king eliminated Bathsheba's husband by sending him into battle to be killed. Although David eventually was chastised severely by his prophet-in-residence, and the child of his infidelity died as punishment, Bathsheba and David's next son, Solomon, succeeded David on the throne. The ultimate outcome suggests that David actually was the "rightful" husband. At the very least, it appears that Israel's monarchs had privileges that pagan kings did not.

Now that you know something about what storytellers said about women, it is time to look more closely at how they spun their tales. In the next chapter, we'll examine the four elements that support a story: narrator, characters, plot, and time and space.

WHERE ARE THE WOMEN IN BIBLICAL NARRATIVE?

the Book of Ruth	Two widows struggle to survive.
the Book of Esther	A beautiful Jewess becomes queen of Persia and saves her people.
Judith 8–16	A beautiful, chaste, and pious widow saves her city from the Assyrians.
Susanna (addition to Daniel)	A beautiful, chaste, and pious virgin is falsely accused of fornication.

Genesis	
2:4–3:24	Adam and Eve strike out on their own.
6:1–5	The "sons of God" mate with human women.
12:10–20	In Egypt, Abraham passes Sarah off as his sister.
16:1–15	Sarah sends her servant Hagar to Abraham to conceive an heir.
18:1–15	Messengers from God tell Abraham that Sarah will conceive.
19:1–11	To protect his guests, Lot offers his daughters to a mob in Sodom.
19:30–38	Lot's daughters become pregnant by their father.
20:1–18*	In Gerar, Abraham passes Sarah off as his sister.
21:1–21	Sarah banishes Hagar to the desert with Ishmael.
24:1–67	Abraham sends a servant to his brother-in-law Laban to find a wife for Isaac. Rebekah meets him at a well.
25:21–27	Previously barren, Rebekah conceives and bears twins: Jacob and Esau.
26:1–11	In Gerar, Isaac passes Rebekah off as his sister.
27:1–46*	With Rebekah's help, Jacob tricks Isaac and cheats his older brother out of the blessing meant for the eldest.
29:1–20	Jacob flees to his uncle Laban. He meets Rachel at a well.

29:21–30	Laban tricks Jacob into marrying his older daughter, Leah.
29:31–35	Leah bears Jacob four sons. Rachel is barren.
30:1–24	Leah bears more sons; Rachel bears Joseph. Their maidservants Bilhah and Zilpah bear sons for Jacob. Leah bears Dinah.
31:19–35	Rachel steals her father's household gods.
34*	Simeon and Levi avenge their sister Dinah's seduction by tricking her seducer.
38*	Tamar tricks her father-in-law to conceive a son.
39	Potiphar's wife tricks Joseph, and he lands in jail.

Exodus

1:15–22	Two midwives trick the pharaoh and save Israelite boy babies.
2:1–10*	Moses' mother and the pharaoh's daughter trick the pharaoh and save Moses.
2:15–22	Moses flees to Midian and marries Zipporah, whom he meets at a well.
4:24–26	Zipporah saves Moses' life.

Numbers

12:1–16*	Miriam and Aaron challenge Moses.
25:1–9	Moabite women lure Israelites for sex and sacrifices.
27:1–11; 36:1–12	The daughters of Zelophehad ask to inherit in their father's name.

5

HOW TO READ

A STORY IN THE BIBLE

When I was eight years old, my literary heroine was the plucky sleuth Nancy Drew. I loved how she would jump into her speedy roadster with her chums, Bess and George, and immerse herself in the latest mystery. Nothing was too daunting for our Nancy.

Eliciting meaning from the Bible is a lot like Nancy's detective work. We search for clues and interrogate witnesses—the narrator and characters in our stories—to solve the mystery of what the storyteller is trying to tell us. Then we can ask the question closest to our hearts, "What does this mean to me?"

Like any gumshoe, we will have to dig for answers, but the sleuthing itself can be its own reward. Over the years, I have found that the process of unraveling the secrets of a story makes me feel like one of the "profilers" in television crime shows: I feel as if I get inside the mind of the storyteller and the world of the Bible. Along the way, my inquiry challenges and changes me—the very reasons I read the Bible in the first place.

Reading biblical narratives would seem to be easy enough. We all tell stories, and we've heard them from the time we were born. Perhaps you wonder: Where's the mystery in reading stories in the Bible?

While it's true that biblical stories are made up of the same four elements that drive all narratives—a narrator, characters, plot, and time and space—stories in the Bible are extremely compressed. They lack the details—descriptions of characters and settings, lengthy dialogue, access to the characters' inner world—that fill out contemporary short stories or novels. You need to make the most of what's there in order to get beyond the surface of "who did what?" Using "What Do You See?" in appendix 1 and the pointers here will help you unlock the meaning of these stories.

To practice our investigative methods, we will use the tale of two feisty midwives from Exodus 1. We'll read through it once and see what we come up with. Then we'll apply some of Nancy's techniques. I think you'll be surprised at how much information we can wring from a story—knowledge that we can then use to make meaning for ourselves.

The Mystery of the Hebrew Midwives

The setting is Egypt, where the Israelites have lived for generations. The time is some years before the Exodus. The storyteller has just explained that the king and the Egyptians "dread the Israelites" because there are so many of them and they are so powerful. To prevent them from increasing their numbers still further and joining forces with Egypt's enemies, the king appoints taskmasters "to oppress them with forced labor." The Israelites keep on having babies, however. So the king gets a bright idea.

15 The king of Egypt said to the Hebrew midwives, one of whom was named Shiphrah and the other Puah, 16 "When you act as midwives to the Hebrew women, and see them on the birthstool, if it is a boy, kill him; but if it is a girl, she shall live." 17 But the midwives feared

God; they did not do as the king of Egypt commanded them, but they let the boys live. 18 So the king of Egypt summoned the midwives and said to them, "Why have you done this, and allowed the boys to live?" 19 The midwives said to Pharaoh, "Because the Hebrew women are not like the Egyptian women; for they are vigorous and give birth before the midwife comes to them." 20 So God dealt well with the midwives; and the people multiplied and became very strong. 21 And because the midwives feared God, he gave them families. 22 Then Pharaoh commanded all his people, "Every boy that is born to the Hebrews you shall throw into the Nile, but you shall let every girl live."

Pretty straightforward, right? Two Hebrew midwives fear God more than they fear the king of Egypt. They refuse to kill boy babies, and then they lie about it. God rewards them, but the pharaoh has the final word. We have two heroines, but things still look bad for the Israelites.

Now let's dig into the story. First, we'll make a list of the questions that surfaced as we read. These are the ones that occurred to me:

- Women are rarely named in the Bible but the narrator records the midwives' names. Why?
- What is this "fear of God" that enables the midwives to stand up to the most powerful man in Egypt?
- The midwives lie to the pharaoh about how Israelite women give birth. In what situations is it okay to lie?
- Why are we told three times that God rewarded the midwives?
- Does the pharaoh really have the last word on the matter?

You may have other questions.

Let's start by interrogating the narrator, a figure whom we usually ignore but who invisibly pulls strings to shape the story. In this case, he puts us on the side of the Israelites—but how and why? And what does the narrator's preference tell us about God's preferences?

The Voice of the Story

The narrator is the *voice* of a story. The narrator is not identical with the storyteller, although the narrator may reflect the author's opinions. The narrator is a *persona*, a personality fabricated in order to tell a story. Even if the narrator's presence is so subtle that we cannot detect it, we learn only as much about the characters or plot as the narrator lets us know. The Bible has many—and diverse—narrative voices because it was compiled from many sources.

Our assignment is to learn how the narrator is influencing what we read. The first thing to determine: what's his perspective, the perch from which he observes events? Technically, this is known as the narrative *point of view* and is abbreviated POV. A change in the point of view can result in a radically different story.

You can get a clearer picture of the narrator's POV by asking a couple of questions:

- What does the narrator know?
- What range of action does the narrator show us?

The Exodus narrator knows everything and goes everywhere. He has access to the Egyptian court, the inner lives of the midwives, and God. That makes him *omniscient* (privy to a character's thoughts as well as actions) and *omnipresent* (present everywhere).

The range of action, however, changes from one statement to the next. If the narrator were using a camera instead of words, one minute we'd see a close-up of the king speaking with the midwives, and the next minute a wide-angle shot of the countryside, with a series of cuts showing babies being born in different households. The close-ups supply intimacy; the wide-angle shots provide context.

We need to ask one other question of the narrator: What's his social status? That's because "biblical texts take sides in ideological debates, which usually center around issues of power," observes Renita J. Weems of Vanderbilt University.[1] Most of the men who wrote the Bible were among society's elite—the scribes, priests, and sages—yet some of them spoke on behalf of the dispossessed. There is a push-and-pull in the Bible between an elite POV and a prophetic call for justice. We'll be able to determine on which side of the divide our narrator falls if we pay attention to how the story's content is used within the larger narrative.

In this case, the pharaoh, representing the power of the state, flexes his muscle, yet two midwives—mere women—manage to thwart him, at least initially. The way the narrator tells the story shows that he strongly supports the midwives. Why is the narrator rooting for the underdog? What's his motive?

We need to investigate further to build our case.

Characters

Characters in biblical narratives are witnesses who provide insight into the storyteller's purpose. As biblical detectives, our job is to get them to spill the beans about why they're doing what they're doing. There won't be much to go on: Biblical narrators rarely use adjectives and adverbs and then only to move the plot along or explain an action. We have to glean what we can from characters' statements and behavior.

The characters in our Exodus story include the king of Egypt and two midwives (who speak and act as one), plus Yhwh, who is not much of a presence. As in most biblical narratives, social roles—king, midwife, deity—determine how the characters function in the plot.

Because of the difficult-to-decipher Hebrew in this passage, it is unclear if the midwives are Israelites or Egyptians who serve Israelites. Yet, although women in the Bible often go unnamed or are designated as "the daughter/wife/mother of so-and-so," the narrator tells us the midwives were called Shiphrah and Puah. This indicates the women's actions were noteworthy because, in the Bible, it's not what people believed that was important, but how they acted.

Lights, camera, action. The Exodus story informs us that the midwives "did not do as the king of Egypt commanded them, but they let the boys live" (1:17). Why? Biblical tales usually are short on explaining motivation, but the narrator tells us twice that the midwives acted as they did because they "feared" God, that is, they placed divine law above the pharaoh's. They thought and acted in moral terms.

The king also was afraid—not of God, but of the Israelites, because he thought only in political terms. The fearful king ordered the midwives to kill all Israelite boy babies. Then, taken in by the midwives' deception, he ordered his people to do what the midwives didn't. Neither plan worked out; why not?

Part of the answer lies in the king's command to kill only *boy* babies. To the pharaoh, males are the featured players and females an afterthought, even though, in practical terms, killing girls would be more likely to reduce the birth rate. With this blind spot, he miscalculated the resourcefulness of the midwives, and, later, the courage of Moses' mother and sister, who first hid Moses then set him adrift on the Nile, and even the sympathies of his own daughter, who found Moses and took him in. Fearing Israelite men, the king was undone by "mere" women. Don't you love the irony?

Thinking more broadly, the pharaoh's irrational fear of the Israelites prompted him to make decisions that were both cruel to the Israelites and ultimately disastrous for the Egyptians. Clearly, fear does not produce good social policy.

We still need to consider the actions of one more character: the Deity. The narrator tells us that because the midwives feared God, the Deity "dealt well" with them. Goodness may be its own reward, but these divine gifts are consistent with the promises made throughout the Pentateuch.

Speech, Speech! Like decisive action, speech reveals a great deal about a character. In Exodus, the narrator craftily uses speech to indicate social class. The king did not ask the midwives if they would cooperate; he *ordered* them to kill all the boy babies, speaking in the imperative as most biblical royals do. The lack of response from the midwives tells us they are social inferiors: Narrators rarely record answers from lower-status individuals to higher-ups.

When the king called the midwives a second time, demanding to know why things had not gone according to plan, the narrator displayed the midwives' chutzpah both through what they said and what they left unsaid. First, they replied with a bald-faced lie: "Because the Hebrew women are not like the Egyptian women." Then they left out the "I am your humble servant" language that should accompany exchanges between a king and commoner.

Renita J. Weems celebrates the midwives' speech for its audacity. The king does not catch on to the midwives' lie because he honestly believes Israelites and Egyptians are different species. He does not even grasp the insult implied by the midwives' excuse that "[the Hebrew women] are vigorous and give birth before the midwife comes to them," which insinuated that Egyptian women were pampered poodles and needed much assistance.[2]

By lying, the midwives averted genocide. Weems, who is African American, observes that lying "is the conventional weapon of the powerless, especially women" in the Hebrew Bible.[3] When you lack privilege, she says, you cannot allow those who have it to define what is "truth"; you must shape the truth according to what serves your community. The midwives responded to the king with *their* truth, and this proved essential to the Israelites' survival.

The tricky part, of course, is that lying is easy. How are we to discern when the cause is just? In this case, the midwives left us a clue: They favored the underdog Israelites over the Egyptian power elite. The narrator is suggesting that we, too, are to side with the oppressed.

Privilege and oppression are not fixed qualities, however; they must be evaluated within changing circumstances. In subsequent generations, Yhwh's prophets would excoriate wealthy Israelites for failing to assist their less privileged brethren.

INTERROGATING CHARACTERS

What to look for:

- List all the characters. Note if they are named.
- Copy down the verbs associated with each character.
- What adjectives or adverbs are associated with each character?
- Look for clues about a character's temperament; moods; and unspoken thoughts.
- Is there anything left unsaid that reflects on a character's inclinations?
- Ordinary actions usually are left out. Are any mentioned, and if so, what do they reveal about the character?
- How do the characters shape the truth, either by what they say, restate, or leave unsaid?

Things to think about:

- Do you resonate with any character? In what ways does he or she speak to you or for you?
- Have you ever been in similar circumstances? How do the characters' behaviors reflect your own?
- Is there anything about a character's speech or actions that disturbs you? Why?
- If you were to emulate a character's conduct, what would you do?

We have two more story elements to explore: plot, and time and space. Let's see what light they shed on our investigation.

Plot

"If the characters are the soul of the narrative, the plot is the body," observes Shimon Bar-Efrat, author of *Narrative Art in the Bible*.[4] A plot organizes individual actions to create a meaningful chain of events. A narrator structures the plot to grab our interest, arouse our emotions, and endow events with meaning. Conflict—how it is initiated, conducted, and resolved (or not)—drives all plots. The conflict in our story centers on the pharaoh and the midwives within the context of the ongoing conflict between the Egyptians and Israelites.

The smallest unit of a plot is a single incident, such as the king's giving the midwives an order and their disobeying it. Through an accumulation of incidents, the narrator builds an episode much like the midwives-pharaoh story. Incidents usually occur chronologically; *why* events follow as they do—their causes—is less obvious.

Looking closely, I spy one causal link in verse 18 of our story: "So the king of Egypt summoned the midwives . . ." The word "so" at the beginning of the sentence refers to a prior action—the midwives' disobedience—to explain why the king acts as he does. There are no such references to explain why the king wanted all of those children killed. We have to deduce that from the king's fear of the Israelites and his desire to "deal shrewdly with them" (v. 10). In the next incident, the midwives pull the wool over the pharaoh's eyes, using *false* causality: "Because the Hebrew women are not like the Egyptian women."

In addition to "so," "and" often links actions: "*So* God dealt well with the midwives; *and* the people multiplied and increased greatly" (v. 20). In other words, the midwives lied to Pharaoh *and so* certain things happened. Finally, "Then Pharaoh charged all his people. . . ." (v. 22). "Then" denotes a time subsequent to the previous actions but also marks his words as a response to his inability to gain the midwives' cooperation.

These elements fit into the categories of "Cause and Effect" and "Connecting Words" in the table "What Do You See?" found in appendix 1.

Although nearly microscopic, these features are important because they explain motives. There is a significant difference between Pharaoh's national-security interests and the fear of God that motivates the midwives. Identifying motives helps us make choices about whom to emulate.

Stages of a plot. Usually a plot moves from initial discord through a chain of events to a crisis or climax that serves as its turning point. Resolution follows and, from there, a quick march to the conclusion of the story. If done well, we get an emotional charge as the tension that has built up over the course of the conflict eases.

In Exodus 1, the conflict is immediate and basic: The king wants Israelite baby boys killed, but the midwives resist his command. The king's second interview with the midwives brings things to a head. The midwives lie effectively, crisis is averted, and God wraps things up by rewarding the women.

But wait! The pharaoh speaks yet again, renewing the conflict: "Then Pharaoh commanded all his people, 'Every boy that is born to the Hebrews you shall throw into the Nile, but you shall let every girl live.'" Where does this episode end and why does that matter?

It matters because knowing where our story ends will help us pinpoint its dramatic center, the climatic turning point. Recognizing the story's turning point reveals its intent. Without understanding the intent, we'll be like the Hebrew slaves trying to make bricks without straw: The meaning won't hold together.

At first reading, the structure of a plot may not be obvious. Using pen and paper, I played around with the elements of the story, outlining them in different ways. Finally, I realized the narrator had structured his tale with the key element in the middle surrounded by concentric rings of material. Here's what I saw:

A^1 Pharaoh speaks.
B^1 Women act.
C   Pharaoh speaks, women respond.
B^2 God acts.
A^2 Pharaoh speaks.

The king spoke three times but never acted. The women acted (result: the boy babies lived), and God acted (result: the midwives are rewarded with families of their own). Like a diamond in a brooch, Shiphrah and Puah's response to the king is accentuated. If I had been otherwise unable to glean the storyteller's motive, detecting this structure would tell me what I needed to know.

Note that although the king literally had the first and last word, in a delicious bit of dramatic irony he did not have the metaphorical "last word," because the midwives have made a fool of the most powerful man in Egypt. Even his final command will not bear fruit. We must wait until the next scene to know this for certain, but already we've seen the futility of the king's bluster. In fact, this story wonderfully foreshadows the failure of the entire Egyptian effort to contain the Israelites.

Time and Space

Telling Time. Time is so deep in the background of a story that readers rarely notice it. Yet as Ms. Drew certainly knew, pinning down the sequence of time is critical to solving a mystery. Within a story, it gives us a clear indication of what the narrator thought was important—and what we are challenged to think about.

Although it may not seem like it, most of the Bible moves at breakneck speed. Biblical narrators push us toward climactic events, eschewing the interpretations, explanations, or other asides that halt time in contemporary stories.

When did the pharaoh order the midwives to appear and how long did their audience last? We don't know. Nor do we know how long it was before the pharaoh called the midwives back to him again. Or when God gave them families. We have to let go of any desire for specificity and focus on the things the narrator deems important: the king's commands and, sandwiched between them, the midwives' pivotal lie.

Yet when it serves his purpose, the narrator could be quite precise, as in the next chapter of Exodus where he stated exactly how long a Levite woman hid the baby who would become Moses: three months (Ex. 2:2). In that instance, the narrator wanted readers to think about what it would take to keep an infant under wraps—literally and figuratively—for three months. Imagine the tension in the household, and the mother's fearful determination. Knowing the exact duration of seclusion suggests that the baby's survival was extraordinary.

TRACKING TIME

To help you determine what is important to the narrator, observe the following:

- How is time stretched or compacted?
- What is the duration of time?
- How is the sequence of events ordered?

Making Space. The internal space of biblical stories is huge: the entire Fertile Crescent from Mesopotamia to Egypt. Do not expect much detail about places in the Bible, however, unless it advances the plot. In Exodus 1, for example, we learn nothing about the pharaoh's palace, nor do we know where the midwives lived. Because description stops narrative time, narrators in the Bible use it sparingly. This lack can be frustrating if you are visually oriented, but it also enables you to give your imagination free rein!

When characters move from one place to another, narrators supply the origin and destination, but only rarely the points in-between. Unfortunately, the significance of most place names is lost to modern readers. By consulting a Bible atlas (appendix 2 tells you about such reference works), you can gain a sense of the terrain.

Examining the Evidence

Let's review the evidence we've gathered through our investigation.

We interviewed a narrator who was rooting for the underdog. We uncovered a king who thought solely in political terms and believed in rigid categories of who's "in" and who's "out," even though this way of thinking did not benefit him or others. We met two midwives who "feared God" and lied to protect Hebrew boy babies, outwitting the pharaoh in the process. Our narrator structured the plot so that the midwives' lie is dead center in the story. To keep the focus on Pharaoh's encounters with the midwives, the narrator revealed little about time or place.

From the evidence, I think we can deduce that the story champions bold action on behalf of underdogs, even if it entails lying. It also suggests that ethical concerns trump political ones. The theme of the weak triumphing over the powerful runs through the entire Bible. It is a comforting message—unless you're a member of society's elite.

I might have arrived at the same conclusions without all the detective work, but I don't think I would have learned the lessons in the same way. The thirty to sixty minutes spent investigating put me into the story as a one-glance reading could not. It was as if I stepped into the story and wrapped it around me like a shawl. Moving through my day, it hovered in the back of my mind and influenced how I saw the world and made decisions.

To my mind, this is what constitutes a "biblical worldview": not a set of beliefs or a predetermined list of right and wrong, but the ability to have a dynamic encounter with the Bible and bring its messages to bear in our lives. Nancy Drew herself could not offer us more.

QUESTIONING A STORY

Here is a review of questions to ask of a biblical story.

The Narrator

> *What does the narrator know?*
> *To what extent is the narrator present?*
> *What range of action does the narrator show us?*
> *To what degree is the narrator objective—or not?*
> *In what ways are the narrator's voice gendered?*

What is the social status of the narrator?

What does the narrator want readers to believe or think?

Characters

How does the narrator describe the characters?

What does the narrator say about the characters' inner dispositions?

Does speech reveal anything about the characters?

What do the characters' actions say about them?

Plot

What background information—exposition—does the storyteller provide?

What incidents make up the episode?

What causal links does the narrator create? (Look for "so," "and," "then.")

What is the turning point of the episode?

How is the conflict resolved?

What does a diagram of the scene show you?

Time and Space

When does the story take place?

What is the duration of time in the story?

How is time stretched or compacted?

What is the emotional pace of the story?

How is the sequence of events ordered?

What strategies does the storyteller use to put us in more than one place within the story?

THERE IS NOTHING NEW UNDER THE SUN

To other residents of the ancient Near East, certain biblical stories must have sounded quite familiar. That's because Israelite storytellers drew upon a repository of plots, themes, and characters held in common with other cultures in the region.

Consider this excerpt from the official biography of Sargon (ca. 2371–2316

BCE), whose empire stretched from Mesopotamia to western Iran and northern Syria.

> Call me Sargon.... Because my mother did not want anyone in the city of Asupiranu to know that she had given birth to a child, she left me on the bank of the Euphrates river in a basket woven from rushes and waterproofed with tar. The river carried my basket down to a canal, where Akki, the royal gardener, lifted me out of the water and reared me as his own. He trained me to care for the gardens of the great king. With the help of Ishtar, divine patron of love and war, I became king of the black-headed people and have ruled 55 years.[5]

Moses' childhood starts to look a little less fantastic.

Several centuries after Sargon, a Babylonian poet (ca. 1700 BCE) wrote down a traditional tale about a fellow named Atrahasis. The story said the gods became annoyed because they couldn't sleep; there were too many humans and they were "as noisy as a bellowing bull."[6] To clear the decks, certain gods sent a great flood.

But there was one man, Atrahasis, "Whose ear was open [to] his god Enki./He would speak with his god/and his god would speak with him."[7] Enki told Atrahasis to build a boat. "Reject possessions, and save living things."[8] Atrahasis did as he was told, gathered his family and various animals onto the boat, then sealed the door with pitch. They survived the flood, and Atrahasis made a burnt offering to the gods.

In the version we know, the one man who had God's ear was Noah, and he, too, offered sacrifices in thanksgiving.

Tutorial: The Wily Ways of Moabite Women (Nu. 25:1–5)

As the Israelites slowly made their way toward "the promised land," Moses must have thought more than once that herding cats would have been a better career choice. The Israelites whined about the food, made and worshiped a golden calf, declared they would have been better off in Egypt where at least there were cucumbers to eat, and generally acted like sulky adolescents. And then, like adolescents, they discovered s-e-x, not a problem in itself except that they chose partners whom Moses deemed culturally inappropriate: Moabites!

Numbers 25 recounts this Israelite sex scandal with a composite of stories from two traditions: the Yahwist and the Priestly writings. The first segment (v. 1–5), by the Yahwist, offers a nice little case on which to practice your detective skills.

> 1 While Israel was staying at Shittim, the people began to have sexual relations with the women of Moab. 2 These invited the people to the sacrifices of their gods, and the people ate and bowed down to their gods. 3 Thus Israel yoked itself to the Baal of Peor, and the LORD's anger was kindled against Israel. 4 The LORD said to Moses, "Take all the chiefs of the people, and impale them in the sun before the LORD, in order that the fierce anger of the LORD may turn away from Israel." 5 And Moses said to the judges of Israel, "Each of you shall kill any of your people who have yoked themselves to the Baal of Peor." (Nu. 25:1–5)

Here are a few points of information that may help your investigation.

- Shittim (literally, "the acacias") apparently lay east of the Jordan River on the plains of Moab, and was the last stop before the Israelites launched their campaign to subdue Canaan.
- The Hebrew in verse 1 is more literally translated as "the people profaned themselves by whoring with the Moabite women" (JPS).
- Peor was a mountain in Moab and site of a shrine to the local manifestation of Baal, storm god, divine warrior, and one of Canaan's primary deities.

- In describing emotions, the Yahwist gets physical. When Yhwh is said to be angry or incensed, the Hebrew actually reads, "God's nose got hot."
- Executing the offending Israelites was intended not just to punish them but also to appease Yhwh, who was provoked because they had defied a central tenet: do not worship any other deity.

What did you observe and what questions do you have?

Using "Questioning a Story," on pages 86–87, what do you discover about the narrator, characters, plot, and setting?

I couldn't help noticing that once again, "the people" meant Israelite men only and that Moabite women got the blame for introducing the men to Baal worship. It's the "blame the women" strategy again, and it is used whenever *apostasy* (abandoning the exclusive worship of Yhwh) crops up. The underlying assumption seems to be that sexual desire blinds men to their duties to God and family. The Bible is mute on the subject of foreign males tempting Israelite females to denounce Yhwh, however. What do you make of that?

Additionally, I was startled by the "fierce anger"—that hot nose!—of Yhwh, who wanted *all* of the chiefs not just killed, but impaled and put on display "in the sun" as a lesson for all to see!

Do you have as much difficulty with this depiction of God as I do? And why is Yhwh so jealous of other deities? It makes Israel's Deity seem petty.

I suspect that J launched his intense polemic against Baal of Peor because the exclusive worship of Yhwh was not well established at the time this story was formulated. If slaughter was the only remedy for apostasy, whoever devised this story was really worried about competing cults. (We'll hear more about the rivalry between partisans of Yhwh and partisans of Baal in "God, Gods, and Goddesses," chapter 13.)

Then there's the matter of God's "hot nose." Although at times I think I'd like an avenging angel to swoop down and smite my enemies,

I don't really want anyone harmed. And I definitely don't want God that angry at ME! No, righteous anger is just too destructive.

One could conclude that Numbers 25 authorizes you to destroy anyone who does not believe as you do. Do you think that's a plausible or reasonable interpretation? What might mitigate that conclusion?

How do you feel about God's anger? Is righteous indignation a factor in your life? What do you see as its pitfalls and possibilities?

6

BIBLICAL LAW CODES:
WHO LET THE LAWYERS IN?

> If a man seduces a virgin for whom the bride-price has not
> been paid, and lies with her, he must make her his wife by pay-
> ment of a bride-price.
>
> — EX. 22:15 (JPS)

> Slaughter the bull before the LORD, at the entrance of the
> Tent of Meeting, and take some of the bull's blood and put it
> on the horns of the altar with your finger.
>
> — EX. 29:11—12 (JPS)

> But if you will not obey the LORD your God . . . The LORD will
> afflict you with the boils of Egypt, with ulcers, scurvy, and itch
> of which you cannot be healed.
>
> — DEU. 28:15, 27

Spend any amount of time with the Bible and, at some point, you
will stumble into the seemingly random assortment of commandments, prohibitions, instructions, threats, and imprecations that
sprinkle its pages.

In fact, fully one-third of the Pentateuch, including the entire book
of Leviticus, comprise legal documents: laws codes (seven in all),

treaties, loyalty oaths, and census taking. More show up in the books of Joshua, Ezra, and Nehemiah.

If you wonder why we should bother reading these admittedly mind-numbing materials, here is a little known secret: The legal documents in the Bible illuminate the world of their authors better than almost any other biblical writings. They tell us in a direct and immediate way what mattered most to these people, how their community was to be organized, who they believed God to be, and—most important for us—how women were regarded. Grasp the essentials of the biblical legal system, and you're a long way toward understanding what the Bible is all about.

In this chapter and the next, we will determine how the Bible's legalisms touched women's lives by surveying the laws that regulated such intimate functions as sexuality, childbirth, and menstruation. Because many of these laws are rooted in a peculiar understanding of "holiness," I'll start by explaining why Israelite priests spent so much time worrying about whether their people were "clean."

Along the way, we'll keep asking what these legal arrangements mean to us today, other than being curious archaic customs.

As you read about the Bible's legal materials, keep in mind that we're trying to understand how the ancient Israelites viewed them, not how they are used today.

Nothing Special

More than 3,700 years ago, when the Babylonians inscribed their laws onto an eight-foot obelisk, at the top they carved a portrait of their sun god, Shamash, handing the laws over to their king. Ancient Near Eastern societies believed that fundamental principles—ideas about justice and fairness, for example—were gifts from their gods. So, odd though it may seem to us, legal documents are not out of place in religious writings of this period.

The Bible depicts Yhwh dictating regulations to Moses (and

sometimes Aaron), who then proclaimed them to the Israelites. This supposedly took place as the Israelites wandered in the wilderness on their way from Egypt to Canaan.

In actuality, Priestly writers penned the bulk of the Bible's laws. Others came from the combined Yahwist-Elohist (JE) document or Deuteronomy, which means they date from the eighth century BCE and later. By inserting all of the legal materials into the story of Moses in the wilderness, the Bible's final editors presented them as the divinely or-dained bedrock of Israelite society.

Although numerous prophets asserted that the Israelites were not like the other nations, in fact, Israel and other Near Eastern societies had countless regulations in common. Although the rituals prescribed in the Bible were specific to the Israelites, numerous laws pertaining to re-lationships between community members had parallels among the laws of the Hittites, Assyrians, and Neo-Babylonians who preceded them. It turns out that Israel's social values were identical to its neighbors' about matters such as personal property, land transactions, marriage, inheri-tance, and incest.

The forms of these laws, too, were fairly uniform across the ancient Near East. Most were stated as *case law.* That is, the law introduced a situation—"If a certain person does such-and-such"—and followed with the legal consequence of that unlawful behavior: "then *this* will happen." Here is an example of case law from Exodus 21:

> When individuals quarrel and one strikes the other with a stone or fist so that the injured party, though not dead, is confined to bed, but recovers and walks around with the help of a staff, then the assailant shall be free of liability, except to pay for the loss of time, and to arrange for full recovery.

Laws also were stated as simple imperatives in the negative: "All the things that swarm upon the earth are an abomination; they shall not be eaten" (Lev. 11:41).

An eye for an eye. Just as the content and form of biblical laws are similar to those of other ancient societies, so, too, is one of the Bible's foundational legal principles: "An eye for an eye." This *law of retribution* extracted a penalty from the guilty party commensurate with the injury. It was used by regimes throughout the region in an attempt to establish state-sponsored justice as an alternative to family or tribal members seeking revenge.

Suffice it to say, women were not among the cadre of priests and scribes who wrote the law codes or enforced them. That did not prevent these men from promulgating laws that affected women, including regulations concerning sexual relations, marriage, childbirth—even menstruation. As we explore the legal world of ancient Israel we will keep asking: Did women have standing in this courtroom? Were their voices heard? For the most part, the answer is no, but there are exceptions and we'll look at those, too.

Purity and Pollution

Both the breadth and randomness of the Bible's many laws are mind-boggling. This is especially true of regulations pertaining to what the Bible calls "ritual purity," which shaped everyone's lives but notably affected women. Why are grasshoppers okay to eat but not snails (Lev. 11:20–23, 41–42), both of which have a place in the cuisines of many cultures? What is so wrong about weaving together wool and linen or planting more than one crop in a field (Deu. 22:9, 11)? Why can't a priest go where there are dead bodies (Lev. 21:11), even for the funeral of his mother or father? And why are women "unclean" during menstruation (Lev. 15:19–24)? Clothing, diet, agriculture, reproductive health, and myriad other aspects of everyday life: Was there nothing too obscure to regulate?

Modern minds try to find rational reasons for such regulations. Perhaps they were simply premodern ideas about hygiene and healthy living. Or, at the other extreme, we imagine that ancient Israelites codified haphazard irrational prejudices. Maybe they just thought eating snails was icky and therefore banned it.

But it is not that simple—or complex. Looking at patterns of observances and prohibitions, rather than individual statutes, reveals an entire moral system.

For starters, when you see the words "unclean" and its opposite, "clean," which are used by most Bible translators, substitute in your mind the words "impure"and "pure"; they better express what is meant. Then consider that the Israelites' quest for "purity" was not about banishing dirt. Nor were the priests making absolute moral judgments, as if "pure=good" and "impure=bad."

At their heart, the regulations concerning purity have to do with attaining *holiness*—and what exactly that means can be difficult to grasp. Most of us associate holiness with someone like Mother Teresa who dedicated her life to doing good. "Not me!" we think. "I could never be like that," or, "Who would *want* to be like that?"

But that's not what the priests intended. "Holy" is a translation of the Hebrew word *kadosh*, which more properly means "dedicated, set aside, whole, complete." Within the context of ancient Israelite religion, being "holy" meant that you were a part of Yhwh's posse and acting according to Divine dictates.

While "doing the right thing" was one aspect of holiness, it did not mean being a Goody Two-shoes. The Israelite system of sacrifices assumed that humans routinely screwed up and needed ways to restore harmony with God and their community. To be holy simply meant participating in the system and when one became impure, restoring purity through the prescribed rituals.

The ancient Israelites were hardly alone in scrupulously defining purity and impurity. *Pollution taboos*, as they are called by anthropologists, are a common feature of preindustrial cultures. The anthropologist Mary Douglas said that at their core, rituals of purity and impurity are an attempt to "make unity of experience"—part of the collective attempt at meaning making that all cultures engage in.[1]

In a homogeneous society where everyone knows and agrees upon the ground rules, such strictures make it possible for people to live together successfully. Of course, behavior that is taboo—that is, forbidden because it is dangerous to community harmony—in one culture may be acceptable in another. However arbitrary the rules seem to outsiders, within the system they form a coherent whole.

As you read the Priestly materials in Exodus, Leviticus, and Numbers—a list at the end of chapter 7 tells you where to find these materials—be on the lookout for answers to these questions:

* With what issues did the priests concern themselves?
* Can you imagine why, in an ancient, Iron Age culture, these matters might have been of interest?
* What kinds of remedies were assigned to establish purity?
* Are there significant differences between taboos for men and women?

Women Under Biblical Law

One could read the Bible's law codes and conclude that a woman was merely property to be disposed of at the whim of the males to whom she was related, whether father, brother, or husband. Yet Israelite women were parties to the covenant that bound Israel to Yahweh and had more rights and privileges than slaves in most situations. Guarded, restricted, and often excluded, yes, but women were not chattel.

In fact, no absolute statement can be made about the legal status of Israelite women.

* Some regulations treated women and men equally. To give just one example, women and men suffering from "scale disease"— apparently a skin disorder—went through the same quarantine and used the same procedures to reestablish purity (Lev. 13).
* Other laws, however, distinguished between women and men of the same category. Male slaves were to be liberated after six

years of service; female slaves were not (Ex. 21). If a female slave were released, she would take valuable property—her children and her sexuality—with her, thwarting the purpose of her purchase.

- Certain laws benefited women even though they were not specifically named. For example, farmers were enjoined from reaping to the edges of their fields or stripping bare their vineyards so that "the poor and the alien" could gather food from what was left (Lev. 19:9–10). This proviso improved the lot of luckless widows and indigent, abandoned wives.

- Entire categories of regulations, such as those regarding menstruation and childbirth, pertained solely to women, although the laws did not necessarily disadvantage them. (It's hard to know the practical effect of these regulations, or even the extent to which they were followed.)

- Women felt the sting of inequality most in laws pertaining to the religious cult (women could not be priests or temple functionaries), inheritance (no rights unless there were no sons), and anything to do with their sexuality.

A woman's legal standing was not determined by gender alone, however; family role also played a part. Wives were subordinate to their husbands, but both parents had authority over children: Offspring who cursed or struck either parent could be put to death (Ex. 21:15, 17). Social standing and economic condition also determined a woman's status under law. If a woman were married, her options changed depending upon whether she was the free wife of a free man, the slave wife of a free man, or the slave wife of a bondsman.[2]

Before we look at specific laws pertaining to women, however, we need to examine their underlying premise: the code of honor and shame.

Honor and Shame

shame *n.* A painful emotion caused by a strong sense of guilt, embarrassment, unworthiness, or disgrace.

honor *n.* 1. Esteem; respect. 2. Reputation; good name.

Most cultures define what is and what is not honorable behavior, and expect constituents to live according to these standards. Shame is considered the proper response to improper behavior by a family member. The loss of honor has to be redressed by action or speech.[3]

Gender plays an important role in the honor-shame balance. Whereas women must avoid shameful acts, men typically act to restore honor. This was especially true among the Israelites when it came to unmarried, unbetrothed females. Israelites highly valued chastity in young women, although anthropologists debate the reasons why. (If you think about it, virginity in a prospective bride is overrated, since a premarriage pregnancy demonstrates fecundity. And, cultures can assign paternity irrespective of biological input.)

Be that as it may, in an honor-shame system that esteems virginity, the males in a family are obligated to guard the chastity of their young women. The men's ability to protect that virginity testifies to the honor of the family and establishes their masculinity. A defiled woman "unmans the men."[4] It tells the community that the males in the family are unable to control "their" women and brings shame on the family. The men must then take action to restore their lost honor.

Generally, biblical laws reserved vengeance, a family's simplest means of redressing shame, for the community's elders. But biblical laws did not challenge the basic assumption that a girl was under the authority of her father (or uncle or brother) and had no right of her own to consent to sex.

The proverbial double standard ruled biblical sexual standards. A married woman who had sex with someone other than her husband, or an unmarried woman who had sex with *anyone*, risked being stoned to death. Yet, men, married or not, could consort with a prostitute without meeting the same fate. Such relations fell outside the definition of adultery. (Chapter 12 takes a closer look at "the world's oldest profession," the despised but indispensable feature of any society that restricts the availability of its "honorable women.")

Ironically, the Bible's recognition of women as legal persons distinct from their husbands spelled trouble for women who transgressed the sex codes.[5] Other Near Eastern societies allowed the husband of an adulterous woman to decide her fate. For better or worse, an Israelite woman was liable for her own behavior and punished according to an impersonal set of statutes.

Marriage and Seduction

Forget the white dress, ring bearer, and big cake: Marriage in the ancient world was simply a legal contract arranged between men on behalf of their respective families. An exchange of goods sealed the relationship. The groom compensated the bride's father for the loss of his daughter's labor by paying a "bride price." The bride entered her new family with a dowry, gifts provided by her father. These arrangements were so commonplace that the Bible does not bother to legislate them—except for two laws that pertain to the seduction of unmarried girls who were betrothed to their seducers.

The first statute was designed to clip the wings of Israelite Casanovas who might attempt to lower a girl's bride price by deflowering her. (Using their logic, she would be worth less because she was no longer a virgin.) Under this law, a seducer had to pay the girl's father the full bride price—and the father had the option of taking the money and refusing to let his daughter marry her seducer (Ex. 22:16–17).

While the payment repaired the damage to the father's honor and deterred men who ignored the right of other men to control "their" women, the law did not benefit the girl. If the seduction was mutual—an attempt at elopement—the father could thwart the couple by refusing to let them marry. On the other hand, if the seduction actually was rape, the father could force the girl to marry her rapist.

A law in Deuteronomy, on the other hand, stipulates that a seducer had to pay the girl's father a high bride price (fifty shekels), marry the girl, and never divorce her (Deu. 22:28–29). Like the other statute, it prevented men from being free and easy with another man's woman, but used a bigger club than the forfeiture of a bride price: marriage for life, no matter how miserable it made you.

There's more to this statute than it seems on the surface. The Hebrew verb used to describe the seduction is ambiguous; it could refer to rape or sexual activity in which the girl collaborates. Maybe it was deliberately vague to protect a girl's honor: Girls weren't supposed to let themselves be seduced, but if she was raped—well, she had an excuse. The drawback of this sort of connivance, besides the high cost, was that these Romeos and Juliets had better be certain of their desires: There was no going back—ever!

Unhappy grooms and slandered brides. Another law in Deuteronomy dealt with grooms who accused their new brides of not being virgins (Deu. 22:13–21). This was a serious accusation, since an unmarried nonvirgin would be put to death. And if not dealt with in a way that satisfied everyone, the rumors that resulted from such slander could wreck a family's honor.

This craftily constructed law made it unlikely that the death penalty would ever be invoked, however. Once charges were made, the woman's parents had the opportunity to prove her virginity by bringing to the town elders the bloody sheets from the marriage bed. If the sheets had been in the safekeeping of the groom's family, the bride might have had reason to worry, but they were kept by her parents, who could easily fabricate the necessary evidence.

A bridegroom who complained without cause got his comeuppance: He was publicly flogged, had to pay one hundred shekels to the bride's father, and could never divorce his wife. *That* would have deterred a man from trying out the goods, then changing his mind.[6]

Newlyweds. Another law protected new brides from losing their bridegrooms to the army during the first year of marriage (Deu. 24:5). The deferment was justified by saying it permitted the man "to give happiness to the woman he has married." This sounds very sweet, but more likely the provision was designed to avoid the problems associated with young widows by ensuring the man had time to father an heir.

Rape. The harsh Deuteronomic laws for rape pertained only to virgins who were promised to another man, since seduction laws covered the rape of a betrothed virgin by her fiancé. According to Deuteronomy 22:23–27, a girl raped in the country incurred no guilt, but one raped in the city was stoned along with her attacker. The lawmakers apparently believed that in the country there would be no one to hear the girl's cries, whereas a girl in the city could not be raped because when she screamed for help, someone would hear her and intervene.

The latter case hardly fits with what we know about women's responses to rape. There are many reasons why a woman might not scream or be heard if she did. You have to wonder how many Israelite women covered up their shame lest they be unjustly executed.

Rape as a consequence of war was a whole other matter. In such situations, women had no recourse. The laws governing holy war (Deu. 20:1–20) permitted Israelite soldiers to take women, children, livestock, and anything else as booty once they had dispatched the enemy's males. Only trees bearing food were proscribed. (Didn't anyone see the irony of sparing trees while countenancing rape and pillage?)

This wasn't the end of the matter, however. Lawmakers had to figure out how to incorporate female war booty into Israelite society. So, they wrote a statute stipulating that while ordinary captives might be sold for profit, a beautiful woman (their qualifier, not mine) whom a soldier desired to make his wife underwent a monthlong waiting period (Deu. 21:10–14). This supposedly allowed her to lament her lost family but more likely guaranteed that the captive was not pregnant with another man's child. The law also said that if the soldier decided he no longer wanted the captive, he had to divorce her rather than sell her into slavery because he had "defiled" her.

The divorced woman's "freedom" was fraught with peril, however. Turned out of her captor's house, she was woman without a context, a foreigner without resources or a family network.

Levirate Marriage

Chapter 4 recounted the story of Tamar, the widow who pursued her father-in-law for sex, hoping to become impregnated with the son she never had the opportunity to conceive with her husband (Gen. 38). Tamar's legal right to that son derived from the regulations for "levirate" marriage: the responsibility of a man to marry his dead brother's widow (Deu. 25:5–10). (*Levir* is Latin for "husband's brother"; the Hebrew word is *yavam*.) The law created a legal fiction: The first son engendered by the deceased husband's brother bore the name of the deceased and inherited family property in his name.

These regulations contradict the laws against incest (Lev. 18:16; 20:21), which prohibit relationships between brothers- and sisters-in-law. Apparently the property interests of the clan outweighed other scruples: If a widow married "a stranger," the land inherited by her sons would be controlled by her new husband and clan holdings would be diminished.

The levirate law provided for a man to refuse such a union if it undermined the inheritance of his own offspring. Refusal had its downside, however. Under terms of the law, the spurned sister-in-law could shame the man publicly in the presence of the town elders by pulling off his sandal, spitting in his face, and cursing him. That ritual left her free to remarry whomever she pleased.

Rules like the ones establishing levirate marriage suggest that although a woman married into a family, she remained an outsider who threatened its integrity.

Menstruation

All things considered, the purity regulations surrounding menstruation were rather mild. For seven days a woman was considered impure, but contact with her resulted only in an impurity that dissipated, after washing, by evening (Lev. 15:19–24).

But Ellen Frankel, writing in *The Five Books of Miriam,* objects that the priests took something normal and made it categorically abnormal. Whereas other conditions requiring quarantine and purification are episodic, voluntary or abnormal, menstruation is "ongoing, predictable, and a sign of bodily health."[7]

The priests, you see, were unnerved by anomalies, and menstruation is an anomaly: Women bleed but are healthy. Bleeding suggests infirmity, yet menstruation demonstrates fertility and the capacity to give birth. Additionally, although Leviticus stipulates that menstrual impurity communicates itself to objects and other people, a man who has ejaculated does not make others impure, except the woman with whom he has had sex (Lev. 15:16–18).

Women might not enter the impure state associated with menstruation all that often—most Israelite women died young and, while alive, ordinarily would have been pregnant, giving birth, or nursing, whereas unmarried girls still living with their parents did not participate in the purity rituals—but even so, the regulations are a good example of a commonplace female experience that became suspect when subject to control by men.

And, they leave us with questions. Who cooked and cared for children during the seven days of ritual impurity associated with menstruation? Could women move about in public during this time or did they fear contaminating others? Did menstruating Israelites experience their seven days as a respite from the familiar workload and an opportunity to bond with other women in their extended families as depicted in *The Red Tent?* Were the prohibitions even observed? We can't know for sure.

THE WAY OF WOMEN

A story concerning Rachel, Jacob's wife, offers a tantalizing tale of how one woman used her menses to thwart male privilege (Gen. 31:17–35). The Elohist, writing several hundred years before the priests promulgated their regulations, depicted Jacob as fleeing from his cruel father-in-law, Laban, along with Rachel and Leah, his concubines, children, and livestock. Unbeknownst to Jacob, Rachel had stolen her father's "household gods" (presumably statues of pagan deities) and hidden them among their goods.

When Laban caught up with Jacob, he rampaged through the camp, searching for his idols. At last, he arrived at Rachel's tent. Would she be found out? The consequences would be serious because Jacob had sworn to kill the person caught with Laban's gods.

No need to worry. Crafty Rachel had hidden the idols in a camel's cushion, then sat upon the cushion. As Laban searched her tent, she begged his pardon for not rising, explaining "for the way of women is upon me."

Rachel's claim provided her with an unassailable alibi. For once, biology trumped male prerogative: Laban's claim on his property and Jacob's right as head of household to pronounce a death sentence.

That which usually ensnared women in protocols and restrictions made this one triumphant.

Giving Birth

Since priests believed that changes in a person's physical condition resulted in impurity, it was logical that under biblical law women were impure following childbirth. Yet even scholars scratch their heads over the statutes in Leviticus 12 that specified boy babies and girl babies engendered different spans of impurity for the mother.

If the baby were a boy, a woman was highly impure for seven days after parturition and capable of contaminating sacred objects even from afar. For the next thirty-three days, she was in a lesser state of impurity and could resume sexual relations with her husband. For girl babies, however, the time periods were doubled: The mother was highly impure for fourteen days and could communicate impurity by direct contact for sixty-six days.

No one has a good explanation of why there should be a distinction. Perhaps we should chalk it up to yet another example of male religious functionaries exhibiting their awe-inspiring bewilderment regarding female biology.

At least the specific numbers used in these calculations—seven and thirty-three, and fourteen and sixty-six—are not as random as they might seem. Add each set of numbers together and you get a multiple of four or forty: $7 + 33 = 40$; $14 + 66 = 80$. Four and forty are numbers—like three, seven, and twelve—that represented wholeness and completeness to the Israelites, and consequently appear throughout the Hebrew Bible.

Widows and Inheritance Laws

Although Israelite women had few legal rights, the Bible demonstrates a consistent level of concern for widows, along with the fatherless and strangers ("resident aliens"). Yhwh was identified as a God "who executes justice for the orphan and the widow" (Deu. 10:18).

Kinsfolk constituted a person's social safety net in ancient Israel, so women who had no family—especially no male protectors—were economically vulnerable. This fact of life drives the Book of Ruth: Lacking husbands or sons, Ruth and her mother-in-law, Naomi, struggle to survive.

A number of laws attempted to mitigate the uncertainties of widowhood. Israelites were enjoined from taking a widow's garment as security for a loan (Deu. 24:17), for example, and admonished not to harvest fields and vines completely so that "the alien, the orphan, and the widow" could glean for food (Deu. 24:19–20).

We shouldn't give the Bible too many compassion credits, however. "If women had equal access to property and privilege, then the law would not have to worry about widows," observes Tikva Frymer-Kensky.[8]

The fundamental problem was that women did not inherit land or goods when their fathers died; everything went to their brothers, with a double portion to the firstborn. Inheritance laws were based on the assumption that women married and moved into their husband's extended household, so they did not need their own land. And since families depended upon grazing and farmlands as well as water rights remaining under their control, they did not want daughters taking land rights with them when they left.

The exception. But what of fathers who had only daughters and no sons? What happened to the land then?

The Priestly writers took up this problem in Numbers 27, depicting Moses listening to the appeal of the daughters of a fellow named Zelophehad, who asked for a portion of their deceased father's land just as their uncles were getting. "Why should the name of our father be taken away from his clan because he had no son?" they argue. Their request was so extraordinary that Moses had to consult Yhwh about it. Fortunately for the girls, the Deity assented to their request.

But there was a catch: The women simply held the land for the next generation. They did not own it outright. When the daughters married, their father's land and name would go to his grandsons.

The sonless patriarch proviso created unintended consequences. If the daughters who inherited land married outside of their tribe, a portion of their father's land went with them. So the priests amended their ruling.

In Numbers 36, they depicted Zelophehad's brothers appealing to Moses once more. Moses clarified his intent by specifying that Zelophehad's daughters could marry "whom they think best"—as long as the groom belonged to a clan of their father's tribe.

Although these rulings were placed within the context of land allotments made to the tribes before the Israelites entered Canaan, such a distribution probably never took place and we don't know if Zelophehad or his daughters ever existed. The rule making actually reflected a period much later when diverse parties, including non-Israelites, vied for the same pieces of real estate. Still, in honor of this one exception to patriarchal law, let us celebrate the names of the women who supposedly dared to ask for more: Mahlal, Tirzah, Hoglah, Milcah, and Noah.

The Worth of a Woman

A deeply dispiriting proviso in Leviticus 27 sums up biblical attitudes toward the female sex. Petitioners who consecrated themselves or their child to Yhwh were to pay to the temple a sum worth a year of labor. Priests converted the value of this labor into shekels (the local currency) according to age and sex, so that the family would know how much money they owed the temple. Here's how women stacked up to men in the priests' estimation:

Age	Male	Female
1 month to 5 years	5 shekels	3 shekels
2 to 20 years	20 shekels	10 shekels
20 to 60 years	50 shekels	30 shekels
above 60 years	15 shekels	10 shekels

One could argue that in an agrarian society, a man's labor in the fields provided the most value to the community and that men, being generally bigger and stronger, could work harder and longer, so their labor was worth more than a woman's. But that rationale undervalues the special labor that women undertake, then as now. Women could do many of the things men did, but no man could do what most women did—give birth and assure the future of the tribe.

If truth be told, Israelite priests actually were more progressive than are our high priests of labor today. U.S. economists include in the Gross Domestic Product *none* of the household labor that sustains tens of millions of families, although the GDP is supposed to be the market value of all the goods and services produced in a year. Hard to imagine, but in more than twenty-five hundred years, the value of women's work has verifiably diminished.

7

BLOOD, FIRE,

AND PROMISES: FURTHER

LEGAL AFFAIRS

Open the Book of Leviticus and you will be met by blood and fire: The first seven chapters are a veritable priest's handbook for animal sacrifice, the "offering by fire of pleasing odor to the LORD."

Imagine this scene in the courtyard of the Jerusalem temple where these sacrifices took place:

Petitioners streamed up the staircase pulling oxen, sheep, and goats, or carrying live pigeons and baskets of ground grain. Sensing that the end was near, the creatures roared and bleated, emptying their bowels in terror. A priest's knife silenced their cries. As the life's blood poured out, workers caught it in basins; later, it would be dashed against the altar in a sanctifying ritual. With sharp knives, functionaries decapitated, butchered, and skinned the carcasses. As priests laid fatty pieces on the coals, the air turned thick with smoke and the stench of charred flesh. Chanted litanies rose along with the fumes. The tumult overwhelmed the senses.

This is holiness?

To the modern, Western observer, no. But around the world, animal sacrifice was—is—a common component of worship and healing. We could simply skip over this aspect of the Israelite religion and dismiss it as of no account to us now. But we would lose something significant, if for no other reason than that these rites were performed for five hundred years or more.

The priests who penned the protocols for animal sacrifice placed them alongside stories of the wilderness journey from Egypt to Canaan, making them appear to date to the time of Moses and Aaron. Yet these writings most likely originated in Judah during the last centuries before the Exile in the sixth century BCE. It is difficult to know how precisely they describe actual practices, although we know sacrifice of some sort occurred at the Jerusalem temple from its rebuilding in 517 BCE until its destruction by the Romans in 70 CE.

Does God actually require bloodletting to establish a relationship? The Israelites thought so. Sacrifice was prescribed in order to purify or give thanks, and to atone for breaches of God's commandments. Why? Many anthropologists have attempted to answer this question; one named Nancy Jay did so in a way that took gender into account. It's worth considering her ideas to help us make sense of a major aspect of ancient Israelite religion and its impact on women.

Blood Sacrifice

Jay looked at a wide range of cultures that offered sacrifices to their deities—including the Aztec, Hawaiians Ashanti, Nuer, and Israelite—and concluded that although the details of the sacrificial cults might differ radically, they all shared two characteristics: Sacrifices were performed only by men, and they were rituals that both integrated and excluded. By that, she meant sacrifices gather together and distinguish members of the participating tribe (or clan or group) and exclude others. Sacrifice thus plays a part in forging group identity.

But exactly whose identity is being established when only men can sacrifice? Who is included and who is excluded?

Jay argued that sacrificial rituals are used to bond one generation of men to the next, thereby establishing continuity. Before DNA testing, paternity was not a sure thing; men lacked the clear biological link to the next generation that all mothers possess naturally. All but left out of the reproductive cycle once they had deposited their sperm, men required a means to anchor themselves to their male offspring and the sense of immortality that progeny provide. Sacrifice is thus "a remedy for having been born of women."[1]

Understand this, and animal sacrifice becomes intelligible: It mimics the bleeding that occurs when women give birth. Through making sacrifice, men attempt to acquire—albeit symbolically—an authority equivalent to the birthgiver.

Yet the differences are profound. When men sacrifice, they do not spill their own blood and bring forth a new life. Rather, they spill another creature's blood and take its life. They kill as a counterweight to women's giving birth to new life. I am probably not the only one who finds this symbolic symmetry—death-dealing in place of life-giving—profoundly disturbing.

Looking specifically at the Israelite sacrificial system, we find more gender disparity. Although Israelite women could give animals and grains to the priests for sacrifice and sometimes enjoy the meat that was returned, the male priests controlled access to the holiness that resulted from such sacrifices. And unlike men, women were never said to "stand before Yhwh," even when present for a sacrifice. The hereditary priests and Levites might have been birthed by women, but they became the sole means of rebirth—into purity—through the death they inflicted on sacrificial animals. Excluded from biological birth, they monopolized symbolic birth.

Sacrifice did more than grant certain men the equivalent of reproductive rights. Nancy Jay pointed out that sacrificial systems generally restricted who ate what part of a sacrifice, as a means of accentuating the differences among social groups within a larger community.

That was certainly true of the Israelites. At the Jerusalem temple, the ultimate fate of the sacrificed body and the remainder of its blood depended upon the degree of sin and who had committed it. The more serious the sin or the higher the status of its perpetrator, the more convoluted the blood ritual and the larger the portion of flesh consumed by fire. The identity of the individual who ate the remains also varied according to what and who occasioned the sacrifice. Thus sacrifices helped to maintain the pecking order within Israelite society—and women were never at the top.

The Covenant Between Yhwh and Israel:
Divine Promises and Pagan Rituals

Sacrifice may have been used to mend broken relationships with God, but the intimacy between Yhwh and Israel was not founded on blood. It was based on a *covenant* (the Hebrew word is *berit*), in which each side promised the other under oath to do or refrain from doing certain things for their mutual benefit.[2]

The Israelites, for example, promised to love God with all their heart, and soul, and might (Deu. 6:5), and to refrain from making gods of silver or gold to worship alongside Yhwh (Ex. 20:23). Yhwh, in turn, promised Abraham, "I will make you exceedingly fruitful; and I will make nations of you, and kings shall come from you" (Gen. 17:6).

The overarching framework of Exodus, Leviticus, Numbers, and Deuteronomy is a stop-and-go covenant-making process that began at Mount Sinai on the third new moon after the Israelites left Egypt (Ex. 19) and ended forty years later on the plains of Moab, just before the Israelites crossed the Jordan River into Canaan. The Book of Joshua contains details of two ceremonies designed to renew the covenant: the first as the Israelites crossed the Jordan (Josh. 3–4), the second after they "conquered" Canaan (Josh. 24).

Several aspects of the covenant make it of interest to women. Most important: It included every Israelite, male and female. Women might be viewed as peripheral components of the covenant and not addressed directly, as Judith Plaskow reminds us in *Standing Again at Sinai* (see chapter 3); nonetheless, women are assumed to be part of the community.

This communal orientation has special meaning for women. Our modern world acclaims autonomy, independence, personal achievement and success, exalting one's "personal relationship" with God. Women psychologists, on the other hand, have reminded us of our essential connectedness and interdependence, and our participation in a living tapestry of relationships.[3] The biblical covenant offers a communitarian spirit that aligns with women's effort to reweave the broken web of relatedness and affirms, "We are all in this together."

It can be hard to see the beauty of this arrangement, however, because of the language in which the Bible expressed it. While the content of the covenant between Yhwh and Israel was unique, it adopted its structure from contemporary international treaties put in force by the Hittites and Assyrians. At their core, such treaties were an oath taken in the presence of the national deities, who acted as guarantors of the terms of the treaty, and a curse (*imprecation*) that forecast divine wrath for any kingdom that dared go back on its word.

We can reclaim the core of the biblical covenant by examining the ways it borrowed from ancient treaty making. Enigmatic passages of the Bible—including glimpses of a Deity that no one would want to cozy up to—will become understandable. You can then decide what's usable and what's not.

Lords and Vassals

The ancient treaties used as a model for the biblical covenant typically were made between a militarily superior ruler (officially known as the *suzerain* [sōō´ zə rən]) and a lesser political entity, the *vassal*. These were not friendly contracts between equals—more like a master-slave relationship. Violations often unleashed a scorched-earth military campaign.

For the most part, the biblical covenant was far more benign: Israel and Yhwh might be unequal partners, but the agreement was based on a relationship of mutual love and affection. Yet despite its kinder, gentler foundation, the biblical covenant borrowed the threatening language and menacing rituals of pagan pacts.

Terms of the treaty. In the ancient Near Eastern treaties, vassals typically swore they would:

- Regard the suzerain's enemies as their enemies
- Refrain from making other alliances
- Extradite political enemies and refugees
- Report suspected insurgents
- Maintain peace with other vassal states

The first two stipulations were very important to the biblical covenant: The Israelites were not to make "alliances" with other gods, and enemies of Yhwh (just about everyone) were Israel's enemies, which accounted for the numerous "holy wars" described in the Bible.

Ancient Treaties and the Biblical Covenant
Here's a breakdown of the elements that made up ancient treaties along with their biblical parallels.

The preamble. A preamble typically included the names and various titles of the lord and the vassal, his descendants, and his people. Hittite treaties opened with extensive PR on behalf of the lord detailing what the ruler had done for his subjects. This was intended to bolster the lord's authority.

The preamble found in the Bible threw in some eye-popping pyrotechnics: smoke and earthquakes accompanying Yhwh's appearance on Mount Sinai before the assembled Israelites (Ex. 19–20). God's self-description, however, was elegantly simple ("I am the LORD your God") as was the history that Yhwh invoked ("who brought you out of the land of Egypt, out of the house of slavery"). Although the Bible recounts longer summaries of the Israelites' history elsewhere, this was its essence, repeated again and again throughout the wilderness journey.

Divine witnesses. The lord and vassal were not the only parties to the treaty. Gods were invoked, and the vassal had to swear in the presence of those divine witnesses.

Exodus does not mention witnesses to the covenant making, but Deuteronomy shows Moses calling upon "heaven and earth to witness against you today" (Deu. 30:19). These words echoed the supplications to earth and sky deities in Near Eastern treaties.

When the Israelites renewed their covenant with Yhwh in Canaan, Joshua invested the people themselves with the ethical obligation to observe the stipulations and to enforce them among themselves: "You are witnesses against yourselves that you have chosen the LORD, to serve him," he commanded (Josh. 24:22). Yet Joshua also erected a large stone in the sanctuary as "a witness against us; for it has heard all the words of the LORD that he spoke to us" (Josh. 24:27), a curious throwback to the local custom of worshipping stone monoliths as stand-ins for the gods.[4]

Stipulations. Stipulations were a list of what the vassal had to do—or else.

Although the Pentateuch ultimately accumulated more than six hundred statutes and admonitions, immediately following the preamble in Ex. 19–20, a terse summary of the terms of the treaty appeared: eight prohibitions along with two obligations, more commonly known as the Ten Commandments.

(Different religious traditions number the stipulations differently; perhaps there actually are eleven or twelve. Ten is the generally accepted number, however.)

Safekeeping and public reading of the treaty. Hittite treaties dictated that a copy would be kept in a sanctuary under the watchful eye of the witnessing deity and read to the assembled people so they would know its terms.

Because the Priestly writers portrayed the covenant as being enacted when the Israelites were in the wilderness, there was no temple in which to deposit a copy of the treaty. Instead, Exodus 24–25 relates that Yhwh inscribed the Ten Commandments upon stone tablets and then instructed Moses to build a box (the Ark of the Covenant) in which to store them along with a portable shrine (the Tent of Meeting, also called the Tabernacle) in which to place the box.

Exodus 24 also depicts Moses reading the terms of the covenant to the Israelites: a miscellaneous collection of laws now called the Book of the Covenant (Ex. 20:18–23:33). To conclude, Moses sprinkled sacrificial blood on the assembled people.

Blessings and curses. "Blessings" described the good fortune accrued by well-behaved vassals; "curses" gave a glimpse of the future faced by the disobedient.

By the time the militaristic Assyrian empire dominated the ancient Near East, the blessings and curses in treaties had been pared down to curses alone, or at least they became the central feature. Deuteronomy 28, written when Judah was a vassal to the Assyrians, mirrors this trend. It has fourteen verses of blessings for observing God's commandments but fifty-four threatening everything from boils to infertility to cannibalism should the Israelites stray.

Remarkably, a copy of an Assyrian treaty from 677 BCE still exists, and comparisons between it and Deuteronomy 28 show Israelite scribes borrowed generously from that very treaty. For example, Deuteronomy 28:23 warns, "The sky over your head shall be bronze, and the earth under you iron," and the Assyrian treaty reads: "May [the gods] make your ground like iron . . . Just as rain does not fall from a bronze sky."[5]

Deuteronomy 28:27 warns against a seemingly haphazard collection of physical ailments. Yet each disease mentioned also was named in the Assyrian treaty, but associated with a particular Assyrian god. The Deuteronomist borrowed the curses and dropped their heavenly association. A comparable list of blessings and curses is appended to the law code found in Leviticus 26, although neither the word "blessing" nor the word "curse" is used.

Ratification ceremony. It wasn't enough merely to agree to a treaty; the parties also participated in a ceremony that spelled out certain provisions through ritual. The sacrifice of an animal, for example, foreshadowed what would happen to those who transgressed the terms of the agreement.

A ceremony of this sort appears in Exodus 24. The people of Israel, gathered at Mount Sinai to hear from Moses what Yhwh had decreed, agreed to the stipulations presented in the Ten Commandments "with one voice," and further agreed that "all that the LORD has spoken we will do" (Ex. 24:3). Moses then built an altar and erected twelve stones to represent the twelve tribes. To bind Israel to the treaty, young men slaughtered oxen and burnt them as an offering, with Moses dousing half the blood of the oxen on the altar.

It's not easy to see how this ceremony relates to the Ten Commandments, however, because a later collection of laws was interposed between them. Events make much more sense if you read the commandments in Exodus 20, then jump to the ratification ceremony in Exodus 24.

The Imperial Deity. That Israelite priests and scribes framed their relationship with Yhwh in terms of a legal obligation made under oath shows us how they viewed their Deity: as a powerful monarch willing to offer protection to Israel but only on condition of absolute obedience, which would be enforced through physical retribution.

Fortunately, the Bible provides resources for understanding God as someone other than sovereign. Yhwh offered care and protection to Adam and Eve by making "garments of skins" for them before they left the garden of Eden (Gen. 3:21). God acted on behalf of the oppressed through the work of two midwives who refused to kill Israelite boy babies (Ex. 1:15–22). A psalmist thanked the Deity because "you knit me together in my mother's womb" (Ps. 139:13). God created the earth out of formless void and "saw that it was good" and blessed humankind, made in God's image (Gen. 1). The Deuteronomist likened God to an eagle that "hovers over its young; as it spreads its wings, takes them up, and bears them aloft on its pinions" (Deu. 32:11). Sophia, a female personification of Divine wisdom, appeared in the streets and called people to take instruction from her (Prov. 8). The prophet Jeremiah described God's yearning for Israel as a mother yearns for her child: "I am deeply moved for him; I will surely have mercy on him" (Jer. 31:20).

Perhaps we would do better remembering the relationship expressed by the covenant, rather than the terms in which it was stated.

Tutorial: The Case of the Jealous Husband, Nu. 5:11–31

Of all the biblical laws dealing with women, the strangest has to be the one that catered to husbands who became jealous of their wives but lacked proof that their wives actually were fooling around. The law seems to have pertained to pregnant women whose husbands weren't sure the baby was theirs. Since adultery was a capital offense, charges of infidelity were serious business. Numbers 5:11–31 detailed what priests were to do when a man became suspicious, justifiably or not, and it entailed a unique trial by ordeal.

The law stipulated that a man with the "spirit of jealousy" was to take his wife to a priest along with an "offering of jealousy" of two quarts of barley flour. Here's what the priest did next:

- Put some holy water in an earthen vessel and added a pinch of the dust from the tabernacle floor
- Brought the woman "before the LORD," disheveled her hair, and placed in her hands the "grain offering of remembrance"

- Said an oath stipulating that if the woman had "gone astray," when she drank the brew God would make her an "execration and an oath" among her people and make "[her] uterus drop, [her] womb discharge." The woman was to reply to the oath, "Amen. Amen," which meant she concurred.
- Wrote down the curses and washed them off in the water that contained the dust
- Burned a small portion of the grain offering on the altar

Then the woman drank the holy water mixture and either miscarried or not. Even if the man's jealousy proved to be baseless, he was "free from iniquity."

What do you think about this recipe for determining guilt? There is nothing else quite like it in the Bible, although other ancient Near Eastern cultures used trials by ordeal. A Babylonian law code specified that a women suspected of adultery was to be thrown into a river for the river deity to decide her guilt or innocence. The Israelite provisions seem mild by comparison.

What might have been the effect of drinking such a potion under the circumstances described? Was it likely to cause a woman to miscarry?

Why do you think it was so important to settle matters of jealousy? In the context of honor and shame, what social functions would such an ordeal fulfill?

What would a woman have to do to protect herself from unwarranted suspicion, since there was no punishment for her husband's false accusations?

What would have been appropriate punishment for false accusation by the man?

If you could compose an ordeal for a man suspected of adultery, what would it be?

WHERE ARE THE WOMEN IN THE BIBLE'S
LEGAL DOCUMENTS?

Exodus

20:8–11	Sabbath regulations
21:2–6, 7–11	rights of Hebrew slaves
21:22–23	injury to a pregnant woman
21:17	dishonor to parents
21:26–32	personal injuries
22:16–17	rape of a virgin
22:21–27	protection of vulnerable populations

Leviticus

12:1–8	childbirth
15:19–24	menstruation
15:25–30	bloody discharge
18:6–23	illicit sexual relationships
20:10–21	adultery and illicit sexual relationships
21:7–9, 13–15	marriage to priests
27:2–7	relative value of labor

Numbers

30:3–16	women's vows

Deuterotomy

5:14	Sabbath regulations
10:17–18	justice for widows, orphans
15:12–18	Hebrew slaves
16:9–11	Festival of Weeks
17:2–7	stoning for worshipping other gods
18:10	sacrifice of daughters forbidden
20:7, 14	women in wartime
21:10–14	as spoils of war

21:15–17	rights of firstborn sons of first wives
22:5	prohibition of cross-dressing
22:13–21	virgins under the suspicion of not being virgins
22:22	adultery
22:23–29	rape
22:30	prohibition against marrying father's wife
23:17–18	prohibitions against "temple prostitutes"
24:1–4	limits on remarriage
24:5	rights of newlyweds in wartime
25:5–10	levirate marriage
25:11–12	punishment for a woman who grabs a man's genitals

Ezra

10:1–44	divorce proceedings against foreign wives

Table 7.1: Legal Documents in the Hebrew Bible[6]

LAW COLLECTIONS		
Source	**Writer**	**Verse**
Book of the Covenant	JE	Ex. 20:22–23:19
Ethical Decalogue	JE	Ex. 20:1–17
Ritual Decalogue	JE	Ex. 34:13–26
Priestly Traditions	P	
Cultic instructions		Ex. 24:15–31:18
Sacrifices		Lev. 1:1–7:38
Priests		Lev. 8:1–10:20
Purity		Lev. 11:1–15:32
Day of Atonement		Lev. 16:1–34
Votive gifts		Lev. 27:1–34
Adultery		Nu. 5:1–6:21
Levites & priests		Nu. 8:5–26; 18:1–32
Miscellaneous		Nu. 15:1–41

(continued)

Table 7.1 (continued)

TREATIES: THE SINAI COVENANT		
Source	**Writer**	**Verse**
Red cow purification		Nu. 19:1–22
Inheritance		Nu 27:1–11; 36:1–12
Calendar of festivals		Nu. 28:1–29:40
Women's vows		Nu. 30:3–16
Holiness Code	H/P	Lev. 17:1–26:46
Deuteronomic Code	D	Deu. 12–26, 28
Curses Collection	Unknown	Deu. 27:14–26
Invitation, preparation	JE	Ex. 19:2b–15
Sacrifice, ceremony	JE	Ex. 24:3–8
Renewal at Moab	JE	Ex. 34:1–12, 27–28
Renewal in Canaan	DH	Josh. 24:1–28

8

POETRY:

LOVE, LAMENT, TRIUMPH,

AND THANKSGIVING

> Oh, give me of the kisses of your mouth,
> For your love is more delightful than wine.
> Your ointments yield a sweet fragrance,
> Your name is like finest oil—
> Therefore do maidens love you.
>
> —THE SONG OF SONGS,
>
> BY SOLOMON (JPS)

Eros-tinged love poems, psalmists beseeching God for aid, prophets calling on the people to repent: A strong poetic current runs through the Hebrew Bible. Ecclesiastes, Job, Lamentations, Proverbs, Psalms, the Song of Songs, and many of the prophetic works were written primarily in poetry; the prose of other books is sprinkled with everything from brief couplets to lengthy celebrations of heroic victories.

In fact, one-third of the Hebrew Bible was written in poetry.

Our general term now for all of these verses is *psalms*, which comes from the Greek word *psalmos*, used to translate *mizmor* long ago when the Hebrew Bible was rendered into Greek. The Bible also refers to *qinah*, which are laments and dirges.

The Psalter appeals to me because it embraces the entire range of human experience, emotions, and desires. In the psalms you will find undiluted grief, joy, forbearance, anger, vindictiveness, thankfulness, and fear. I am still startled on occasion by the raw fury of certain psalms.

But there is much more poetry in the Bible than what we know as psalms and laments. And some of it—such as the Song of Deborah, describing two ferocious woman warriors, and the Song of Songs, which dares to speak openly of women's sexual desire—takes us closer to actual women's lives than we are likely to get anywhere else in the Bible.

Ironically, it is not the Bible's poetry that makes it unique but its prose. Ancient literature was almost all in verse. Prose was used for business transactions or governmental decrees and military records, but not ordinarily for telling the deeds of the ancestors or gods.

We will examine a few of the many uses to which poetry was put in biblical texts, especially poetry that celebrated women and that women used to celebrate others. Finally, you will have the opportunity to discover in detail how a psalm was constructed—and to write your own if you so choose. Our undertaking will be a journey with much beauty to savor.

How to Recognize a Hebrew Poem

Biblical poetry doesn't rhyme and has no meter. Rather, it is distinguished by lofty language that compacts an idea into a few vivid words or phrases. Observe how this petitioner cried out to God:

> My life ebbs away: all my bones are disjointed;
> my heart is like wax, melting within me;
> my vigor dries up like a shard; my tongue cleaves to my palate;
> You commit me to the dust of death. (PS. 22:15–16, JPS)

The lines tend to be short and concise: three or four Hebrew words. And with connecting words omitted, the terse, telegraphic style heightens the impact of what *is* said, thus increasing the emotional intensity. Every word is loaded with meaning, and the unexpected images—"My heart is like wax, melting within me"—linger in the mind.

The poems are meant to be spoken, words and sounds repeated to heighten the effect: "Let me see your face, let me hear your voice; for your voice is sweet, and your face is lovely" (Song of Sol. 2:14).

You'll also notice that the poems' structure gives them power: They're generally written in two-line *versets* that echo, contradict, or comment on each other (scholars call this *parallelism*).

The first verse of Psalm 117 reads:

> Praise the LORD, all nations
> Extol him, all you peoples.

Here, the second line rephrases the first for emphasis. But a second line can also provide contrast, as when the prophet Jeremiah, speaking for Yhwh, says:

> With weeping they shall come
> and with consolations I will lead them back (JER. 31:9).

Here, one verse gives us two very different images of the people of Israel. The first line depicts them as utterly dejected when they were exiled by the Assyrians. The second line declares that they will not only return but will be consoled by God as they do so.

Robert Alter, a professor of comparative literature, has cataloged the different ways Hebrew poets heightened the affect of their verses, moving from general to specific geographic designations (starting with "Judea" and moving to "Jerusalem," for example), or showing in the second line the consequences of an action described in the first ("water over the fields" as the result of "rain").[1]

Rediscovering Psalms

Next to Adam and Eve, the poems known as psalms are probably the most familiar biblical compositions. Bits and pieces of them show up in the liturgies and hymns of Judaism and Christianity—and also on wall calendars, refrigerator magnets, greeting cards, and even in popular songs ("By the Waters of Babylon" by reggae master Bob Marley, for example).

For several summers, I worked in the kitchen of a Vermont girls' camp, where a mural of mountains and forests brightened the tiny room in which dishwashers labored. Up near the ceiling, the artist had added the opening verse of Psalm 121: "I lift up my eyes to the hills from whence does my help come" (RSV). Since many translators read the Hebrew as a question that presumes God as the answer—"From whence does my help come?"—I was never sure whether the artist was taking a position on a scholarly debate or was so besotted by the grandeur of the surrounding Green Mountains that she simply thought mountains themselves were adequate for salvation. Psalms are like that; they lend themselves to multiple interpretations and many settings.

The biblical Psalter contains 150 psalms divided into five books, presumably as a parallel to the five books of the Pentateuch. (The Apocrypha includes an additional psalm, the 151st). Most are not long; they average thirty lines. Credited to King David, ca. 1000 BCE, the psalms actually were written by unnamed bards working in different times and places—but they *are* very old. The priestly instructions included in the Pentateuch do not mention psalms, but most scholars assume they were associated in some way with Israelite religious culture.

Scholars have spent much time cataloging the varieties of psalms, which include songs that

- Lament losses
- Offer praise and thanksgiving

- Celebrate the monarchy of King David
- Exalt Jerusalem as Zion
- Present Wisdom teachings such as those discussed in the next chapter

The psalms' unalloyed emotions are one reason why humans have used the psalms for millennia to express fury at God, demand vengeance, and plead piteously for help. "O God, break the teeth in their mouths; tear out the fangs of the young lions, O LORD," wrote one psalmist, demanding that God punish the evil-doers who have "venom like the venom of a serpent" (Ps. 58). "Happy shall they be who take your little ones and dash them against the rock!" exulted another psalmist, looking forward to the day when Yhwh would repay the Babylonians for dragging the Judeans into exile (Ps. 137).

These raw emotions have allowed psalms to function as a form of therapy for both individuals and communities, says Hebrew Bible scholar Walter Brueggemann. Reading the psalms, especially the laments, helps us articulate the pain and grief for which we have no words, and which we may fear because of its strong emotional power. Psalms even recognize this fear of being overwhelmed by our feelings and experiences.

> Rescue me from sinking in the mire;
> let me be delivered from my enemies and from the deep waters.
> Do not let the flood sweep over me, Or the deep swallow me up,
> or the Pit close its mouth over me. (PS. 69:14–15)

Tragedy disorients us by radically revising our expectations and assumptions, whereas psalms, says Brueggemann, reorient us by "evok[ing] and form[ing] new realities that did not exist" before we sang, said, or read them.[2] They heal because they express confidence that things will change: "from the depths of the earth you will bring me up again," affirmed the poet of Psalm 71. As we become grounded in the new direction, grief dissipates. It is not easy, but it is possible.

For many women, the preponderance of masculine language in most translations hinders them from using psalms in this life-giving way. Fortunately, there are now renditions with more gender-neutral language, such as the collection *Psalms Anew*, edited by Nancy Schreck and Maureen Leach.[3] Here is their reworking of Psalm 54, contrasted with the version in the NRSV.

Psalms Anew	*NRSV*
Save me, O God, by the power of your name, and defend me by your might.	Save me, O God, by your name, and vindicate me by your might.
O God, hear my prayer; listen to my supplication.	Hear my prayer, O God; give ear to the words of my mouth.
The insolent rise to attack me; the ruthless seek my life; they have no regard for God.	For the insolent have risen against me, the ruthless seek my life; they do not set God before them.
But God is my helper, the one who sustains my life.	But surely, God is my helper; the Lord is the upholder of my life.
May their own evil recoil on those who slander me! Silence them by your truth, O God.	He will repay my enemies for their evil. In your faithfulness, put an end to them.
I will offer you a willing sacrifice and praise your name, for it is good.	With a freewill offering I will sacrifice to you; I will give thanks to your name, O LORD, for it is good.

God has rescued me from every trouble,	For he has delivered me from every trouble,
and I have seen the defeat of my enemies.	and my eye has looked in triumph on my enemies.

I resonate with the *Psalms Anew* version because instead of using the third-person masculine pronoun "he," the psalm directly addresses God. This not only avoids the suggestion that God is masculine, it increases the intimacy. (The NRSV translation also addresses God but not as consistently.) Because poetry is notoriously difficult to translate, the psalters in the many versions of the Bible read quite differently. Gender-neutral reworkings of poetry fall within the range of possibility, without stretching to mere paraphrases.

INSPIRATION FROM RESPIRATION

On more than one occasion I've visited Christian monasteries where psalms form the backbone of the community's daily periods of prayer. In one week, these monastics chant the entire psalter, usually *antiphonally*—with group A reading one line and group B the next. The chanting is done in a measured pace, not too fast and not too slow.

It turns out that there is more than devotion involved in this exercise. During a stay at an Anglican convent, a nun explained how reciting the psalms put the community in sync. "We must literally breathe together," she said to explain how she and her sisters managed to start their designated verset together. "We rush into chapel from our work, preoccupied and hearts racing, but before long our breathing slows and coordinates. It's as if we become one giant heart beating together."

Anyone who has meditated knows that watching the breath is an easy way to focus your attention, slow the heart rate, and increase feelings of calm. In the case of those Anglican sisters, breathing together also brought their community together.

The Song of Songs

How did the sensual love poems attributed to Solomon make their way into the Bible? No one quite knows, but a story has been handed down that the great, first-century-CE rabbi Akiba addressed a colloquium debating the suitability of the Song of Songs as scripture and said, "The whole world is not worth the day on which the Song of Songs was given to Israel, for all the Writings are holy, but the Song of Songs is the Holiest of Holies."[4] Akiba apparently swayed the assembly and the Song stayed.

Commentators usually suggest that Akiba lobbied for including the Song because he read it as an allegory of God's love for the people of Israel, innocent of any taint of eroticism. While the good rabbi might indeed have read the Song of Songs as allegory, I think this summary sells the man short. Unless one understands the reference points of an allegory's symbolism, the allegory has no zest. I prefer to think that Rabbi Akiba identified the Song as "the Holiest of Holies" precisely *because* he grasped the sensual delight embedded in the Song. How else would he have known its language as the perfect expression of God's love?

In any case, for hundreds and hundreds of years, these ardent verses with their none-too-subtle double entendres were read as if God were holding forth on the virtues of Israel, or the Christian Church, or the Virgin Mary—*anything* but carnal knowledge.

Thankfully, critics in the eighteenth century began to jettison allegory and to read the Song more straightforwardly. Today, few would dispute the Song's erotic intentions and its close parallels with Egyptian poetry of the same ilk. Rather, the debate focuses on whether the Song is a unified composition with a narrative thread that binds a pair of courting lovers, or a random collection of love lyrics involving various couples.

The Song presents other puzzles as well. When is the speaking voice intended as male and when is it female? Who is holding this dialogue?

Could the references to the "dark, but comely" maiden (1:5, JPS) with her frightening eyes and battle imagery bear any relationship to the cults of the Great Mother goddess that flourished throughout the Mediterranean contemporaneously with the Song?[5] How literally are we to take the maiden's violent encounter with the watchmen in 5:7?[6] These and other questions make the Song a marvelously challenging encounter.

For women, the Song offers nearly oppression-free terrain. The lyrics do not mention God, law, ritual, Israel, genealogies, or history; neither do they represent hierarchy, rule, dominance, or submission.[7] The Song openly celebrates female eroticism and, reversing the dictum of Genesis ("Your desire shall be for your husband" [3:16]), depicts a maiden boldly declaring, "I am my beloved's, and his desire is for me" (7:10).

Not all women commentators are in love with the Bible's book of love. J. Cheryl Exum, marveling at how women tend to lose their critical faculties upon encountering the Song, warns of "Ten Things Every Feminist Should Know About the Song of Songs." These include:

- The danger of mistaking the narrative voices of the Song for those of real women (and men), when they may typify only the poet
- Believing that a woman wrote the lyrics (we just don't know; every verse could be read as if a male or female wrote it)
- Confusing the Song's destabilizing of "conventional biblical gender stereotypes" for gender equality (highly unlikely given the patriarchal culture of the time).[8]

She also notes that the Song reflects varying attitudes toward love, sex, and the body, not just the ideal feminists would like to claim.

Yet even Exum acknowledges that women can say, "Thanks for your text, and I'll decide how to read it"—which is perhaps the definitive approach, not just for the Song but for all of the Bible.[9]

Oh, and how does Solomon figure into things? He doesn't, really.

The book's first verse—"The Song of Songs," meaning the ultimate song, "by [or concerning] Solomon"—was no doubt added long after it was composed.

Even so, Carole R. Fontaine, professor of Hebrew scriptures, says we should at least give a nod in Solomon's direction because without his name attached, women in oppressive religious traditions would not be reading these verses. For them, the Song provides a much needed respite from the Bible's otherwise monolithic male dominance.[10]

The Song of Deborah

Would you be surprised to learn that despite the rampant misogyny in the Bible, one of its oldest poems, found in Judges 5, celebrates two women—and not as mothers but as warriors? Written sometime around 1100 BCE, the "Song of Deborah" tells how this judge and prophetess, with the help of a warlord named Barak, led the Israelite tribes to victory against the armies of Canaan, commanded by a general named Sisera.

The poem then describes how Sisera fled, seeking refuge in the tents of a second woman, Jael, only to be assassinated by his hostess, who drove a tent peg through his skull once he was asleep. (Ouch!) That women were cast as heroes of a victory hymn is even more remarkable considering that the other hymns known from this period honored Egyptian pharaohs.[11]

Perhaps because this poem originated at a time when Hebrew compositions borrowed heavily from their Canaanite neighbors, its depiction of Deborah bears a striking resemblance to Anat, an indigenous warrior goddess, says Bible scholar Susan Ackerman. Deborah does not wear a necklace of skulls and act uncompromisingly bellicose, yet she "does appear Anat-like in her role as a female military champion."[12]

Ackerman maintains that the portrait of Jael, too, was influenced by the Canaanite goddess but in her role as divine lover. When Jael—who played the perfect hostess by providing curds when her guest asked merely for water—slaughtered Sisera with a tent peg, it was a role reversal: Jael became the vanquishing warrior and the general assumed the role of ravaged victim usually assigned to women.

Furthermore, Sisera's death throes were described in words that evoke both birth and the posture of sex.

> He sank, he fell, he lay still at her feet;
> at her feet he sank, he fell;
> where he sank, there he fell dead. (JUDG. 5:27)

What the NRSV daintily translates as "at her feet" could be rendered more precisely as "between her legs."

These gender reversals are not evidence that the poem's author was female, says Susan Niditch, Amherst College professor of religion. Niditch points out that the "Song of Deborah" emerged during a period when the Israelite tribes still struggled to gain traction in a land not yet their own. To be an Israelite, therefore, was to live on the margins. Who better to represent this underdog struggle than women who one-upped their adversaries?[13]

The "Song of Deborah" is even more remarkable when compared to the prose description of the same events that was written much later but inserted before the poem. In Judges 4, Deborah was depicted only as a prophetess and judge. When she learned that the Canaanites were oppressing the Israelites, she did not issue a call to arms but summoned Barak. With her encouragement, Barak agreed to lead the armies—and Deborah dropped from view in the battle narrative that followed.

The older version is far more compelling, even pairing heaven and earth as partners in combat. Deborah commands on the ground, while God—envisioned as divine warrior—"marches" to battle amidst cosmically induced earthquakes and hurricanes.

A third woman included in the poem is missing from the prose version: Sisera's mother, who gazed out the palace window, wondering why her son delayed returning home. We, of course, know what she does not—that he is dead—and momentarily we sympathize with her impending discovery. But then her ladies-in-waiting reassure her, saying, "Are they not finding and dividing the spoil?—A girl or two for every man?" (v. 30). (The original Hebrew does not say "girl" but "womb," thus clarifying the use to which these women-as-war-booty would be put.) Their casual cruelty doubles the irony, since the ladies who speak so blithely about other women will soon become war booty themselves.

The "Song of Deborah" called its heroine "a mother in Israel" to indicate her stature as a leader in peace as well as war. Susan Ackerman argues this title did not refer to literal motherhood but to being a good and effective counselor who used her skills to protect Yhwh's people. Since "protection" sometimes entailed taking up arms, "a mother in Israel" had to step forward as military commandant when necessary.[14]

You can read Judges 4 and 5 and decide for yourself which version of Deborah you prefer. The battlefield Deborah is not nice, but she is noble, which is why I admire her. When I need a boost, I think of the commandment Deborah and imagine I hear her shout, "Awake! Arise!"

"Her Downfall was Appalling":
Lamentations and the Politics of Shame

The Book of Lamentations makes me think of the morning I locked my apartment door and turned away, not knowing if I could ever return. It was a raw March day in 1978 and I was living in south-central Pennsylvania along the Susquehanna River. Earlier in the week, I had awakened to the news that an accident at the nuclear power plant ten miles downstream from my house had released an unknown amount of radiation. Three days had passed and the situation at the plant had gotten worse, not better. Now I was about to throw my suitcase in the car, scoop up my elderly parents, and drive south to Virginia, where my sister would harbor us.

As I put my key in the lock and slid the deadbolt into place, a bleak possibility seized my mind. If the reactor core had melted as some feared, I might never come home to all that I was leaving behind. And nothing I had done led to this moment. It was beyond my control.

Residents of Jerusalem may have felt something akin to my thoughts of loss when the Babylonian army fell like hungry wolves upon their city in 586 BCE. To memorialize those events, poets created a series of laments that convey pure misery: complaints salted with acknowledgment of guilt and desperate pleas for God's help. Although the poetic style of Lamentations is comparable to psalms of lament, the praise characteristically found in psalms was stripped out, leaving unadulterated woe.

Despite—or perhaps because of—the poets' grief over the destruction of Jerusalem, the poems in Lamentations are particularly artful. Yet in contrast to the Song of Songs, where female desires were celebrated, the lamentations offer women more difficult terrain.

Of the book's five compositions, four are alphabetic acrostics in which each verse begins with the next letter of the alphabet. Lamentations also offers a fine example of *personification*—the assignment of human qualities to an inanimate object—in its use of a female image to depict Jerusalem and Judah.[15]

> Alas!
> Lonely sits the city/Once great with people!
> She that was great among nations/Is become like a widow;
> The princess among states/Is become a thrall.
> Bitterly she weeps in the night,/Her cheek wet with tears.
>
> (LAM. 1:1–2, JPS)

Though some might celebrate this feminine presence, we, too, have reason to cry, "Alas!" for the personification reveals the poet's—and his contemporaries'—ambivalent attitude toward women.

Initially, the personified "Daughter Zion," who appears in chapters 1, 2, and 4, is an immensely sympathetic figure. Quickly, however, the sympathy shifts to scorn:

> Jerusalem has greatly sinned,/Therefore she is become a mockery;
> All who admired her despise her,/For they have seen her disgraced;
> And she can only sigh/And shrink back.
> Her uncleanness clings to her skirts;
> She gave no thought to her future;
> She has sunk appallingly, With none to comfort her.
>
> (LAM. 1:8–9, JPS)

The condemnation and vituperation continues. She is called "a filthy thing" and described in verse after verse as utterly crushed and without friends or allies.

Although the poet at times allows "Fair Zion" to speak, her words only reinforce her culpability: "I have been very rebellious," she moans (1:20) amidst calls for Yhwh to do to her enemies what God has done to her. In the most heartrending manner, the poet repeatedly evokes the lost and starving children of Judah—and then makes the startling accusation that "the hands of compassionate women have boiled their own children" (4:10) in the absence of other food. (The same charge also is made in 2:20.)

Sinful and impure, even a cannibal: this depiction of "Fair Zion" is problematic for women readers. When, for example, the poet describes Zion as filthy, he uses the word (*niddah*) designating the ritually impure state associated with menstruation. She also is described as having been seen naked in public, another source of shame.

Overall, the poet sketches "daughter Zion" in terms that bring to mind women abused physically and sexually, and female victims of war, famine, and natural disaster. But the poet also stipulates that Zion is to blame for her condition because of her waywardness, and that Yhwh is the agent of her destruction, punishing her for her transgressions. God is thus framed as an abuser who beats his wife "for her own good" and because "she was asking for it." Zion becomes the abused spouse who blames herself: "If only I hadn't made him angry!"

The male voices in Lamentations only highlight Zion's special culpability for her condition. The voice of Chapter 3, the centerpiece of the five-chapter compilation, begins "I am the man who has seen affliction" and continues in a personal lament bewailing the many ways in which God chastises him. Yet the (male) voice never admits guilt, never says what he did to merit such grievous retribution. When the poet turns to professions and prayers of hope in Chapters 3 and 5, the female persona is missing. Daughter Zion thus is associated solely with degradation and sin.

Nowhere does the poet say that the actual women of Judah are any more sinful than the country's male inhabitants. But the gendered language of Lamentations suggests the mixed feelings the poet harbored toward women. They are victims to be pitied and protected, but they also are shameless creatures associated with deceit and degradation. If you read these eloquent poems without being aware of the way in which certain qualities adhere to certain genders, it is all too easy to assign these characteristics to real women—and to God.

But women are not inherently impure. God is not an abuser. And men are not blameless. Proceed in Lamentations with caution.

Women's Voices?

Two additional biblical poems deserve mention because of their associations with female characters. The first, like the "Song of Deborah," is one of the oldest passages of the Bible: the "Song of the Sea" in Exodus 15, a victory hymn attributed to and led by Moses after Yhwh destroyed Pharaoh's chariots by drowning his army. "Song of the Sea" is a Jahwist (J) composition that celebrates Yhwh as a warrior and portrays the indigenous peoples of the region trembling in fear at the news of the Deity's power.

Though eloquent and joyful, the poem is a typical celebration of masculine war making. But a curious coda, probably from the Elohist (E), was appended to the poem. Notice how it shifts the focus from Moses to Miriam.

> Then the prophet Miriam, Aaron's sister, took a tambourine in her hand; and all the women went out after her with tambourines and with dancing. And Miriam sang to them:

> > "Sing to the LORD, for he has triumphed gloriously;
> > Horse and rider he has thrown into the sea." (EX. 15:20–21)

The Elohist called Miriam a prophet and a sister of Aaron (though not of Moses). Her single verse of song replicates the opening verse of the song attributed to Moses.

Women in the ancient Mediterranean world often led the communal songs, drumming, and dancing. Some scholars believe these groups of female performers held a high status within their communities.[16] Still others see the curious appendix to "Song of the Sea" as evidence that Miriam was the Song's actual author. They blame the Bible's redactors for suppressing Miriam's leadership so as to exalt Moses.[17]

Are these verses in Exodus an historical remnant that points toward Miriam as one of the Israelite leaders? Do women have in Miriam a heroine with the stature of a Moses or David?

Unfortunately, probably not. The Exodus story was composed to create a new national identity for the runaway slaves of Egypt, says Hebrew Bible scholar Alice Bach. The narrator put the victory song into the mouth of Moses because he was the acknowledged leader of the new Israel.[18] We may yearn for another version of events, but what we have is the text at hand.

As for the rest of Miriam's story, we must use our imaginations, as Julia Stein showed us in chapter 3 with her poem "Miriam's Song."

Even if the Jahwist could not envision Miriam leading the community in song, we can do so now. And we can lead the songs of celebration ourselves.

Hannah's Song

A second poem attributed to a woman turns up in 1 Samuel. Known as the "Song of Hannah," it is attached to a poignant story about a barren wife named Hannah who was ridiculed by her husband's second wife for her infertility. After pleading with Yhwh for a son, Hannah finally gave birth and then dedicated the child to God. The boy became the great prophet and kingmaker Samuel.

Following the prose story, 1 Samuel 2 introduces a song of praise in gratitude for God's help.

> My heart exults in the LORD,
> My strength is exalted in my God.
> My mouth derides my enemies,
> Because I rejoice in my victory.
> There is no Holy One like the LORD, no one besides you;
> There is no Rock like our God.

There is so little that authentically reflects women's experiences in the Bible that it's tempting to take the "Song of Hannah" at face value. But scholars agree that it dates from a period later than the story and was inserted where it was because its fifth verse says, "The barren has borne seven." It does not specifically refer to Hannah or her situation, however, and the Bible says she bore a total of six children, not seven.

The song does contain beautiful language about God redeeming "the poor from the dust . . . the needy from the ash heap," a theme picked up much later in the New Testament and woven into another poem also attributed to a woman: Mary, the mother of Jesus.

There's no reason not to use and enjoy both praise songs. The difficulty comes when we substitute their understanding of God for our own. We can lose our voice that way, or, worse, fail to develop it at all.

Tutorial: The Art of the Lament

Women are supposed to be cheerful. If you don't believe me, consider the study I read about in the *Psychology of Women Quarterly*.[19] Participants were shown pictures of men and women and asked to comment on the emotional states of the individuals depicted. Smiling men were deemed to be friendly, but men who were not smiling were seen as emotionally neutral. Unsmiling women, however, were said to be angry; smiling women were viewed as emotionally neutral. Apparently, our culture expects women to smile as their default expression, and if they don't ascribes negative emotions to them. Many of us strive to live up to society's expectations and present a cheerful demeanor.

Yet every woman I've ever met has suffered trauma, loss, abuse, or tragedy. Behind the smiles, we all have something to complain about, if not for ourselves, then for the state of the world. Because complaining women are labeled "bitches," however, we may sit on our discontent. Our pain then creeps out indirectly; we get catty or we whine, a sign of the despair created by a sense of powerlessness.

In this exercise, we're going to give full voice to our sorrow and rage: We are going to lament. Lamenting is different than whining. In a lament, you acknowledge that your pain matters, that life is not fair, that you and those you care about deserve better. You assert that you are not life's victim. A true lament fosters a feeling of power because contained within it is a recognition that things can be different.

Formulating a lament is much simpler than it sounds, because laments, like other psalms, follow a formula. Laments by individuals, for example, usually have the following components:

- A salutation or address
- The complaint or lament
- A request for assistance, often quite specific, called the *petition*
- An expression of confidence in God, which may include memories of past help
- A vow to make an offering or to praise God once the crisis has passed
- Sometimes, an affirmation that God will hear and respond

In laments, the speaker may direct her complaint at God ("You!"), or speak in the first person. At other times, the object of complaint is "them," the enemy. Petitions are framed not as mere requests but as demands in the imperative: "hear!" "turn!" "intervene!" And while biblical psalmists turned to God for their help, you are free to write a nontheistic lament.

Using Psalm 13 as a template, let's look at how an individual lament is structured.

Address	1 How long, O LORD?
Complaint	Will you forget me forever?
	How long will you hide your face from me?
	2 How long must I bear pain in my soul?
	and have sorrow in my heart all day long?
	How long shall my enemy be exalted over me?
Petition	3 Consider and answer me, O LORD my God!
	Give light to my eyes, or I will sleep the sleep of death.
	4 and my enemy will say, "I have prevailed";
	my foes will rejoice because I am shaken.
Confidence	5 But I trusted in your steadfast love;
Vow of Praise	my heart shall rejoice in your salvation.
	6 I will sing to the LORD,
Affirmation	because he has dealt bountifully with me.

When you write your lament, direct, simple language is fine. You can try parallelism if you feel up to it, but expressing your heart's message is more important than stylish language. By bringing out what's been lurking in the shadows, you open yourself to transformation. When you say, "This is wrong!" inside you a vision of something better is growing, even if you have no sense of what it is. The psalmists refer to this emerging vision as "light to my eyes." Without such light, we are consigned to the death-sleep of fear, victimhood, and *can't*. You may not be able to see it now, but this vision will lead you. Even if your material circumstances do not change, lamenting will renew your inner world.

For inspiration, check out some of the Bible's individual laments, which include: Psalms 3–7, 10–14, 25–28, 35, 36, 38, 39, 41–43, 51–59, 61–64, 69, 71, 73, 86, 88, 102, 109, and 130, and Jeremiah 11, 15, 17, and 20. Complaining to God has a long and eloquent history!

Table 8.1: Poetic Works in the Bible

BIBLICAL BOOKS WRITTEN PRIMARILY IN POETRY
Ecclesiastes
Job
Lamentations*
Proverbs*
Psalms
Song of Songs*
The prophetic books of Isaiah, Jeremiah, Hosea, Joel, Amos, Obadiah, Micah, Nahum, Habakkuk, and Zephaniah.

POEMS INSERTED INTO PROSE NARRATIVES	
Gen. 49	"Testament of Jacob": Before he dies, Jacob commends some of the twelve tribes and condemns others.
Ex. 15:1–21*	"Song of the Sea": When the Egyptian army drowns, the Israelites celebrate.

(continued)

Nu. 23	"Sayings of Balaam": A pagan prophet praises Yhwh and Israel.
Deu. 32	"Song of Moses": Moses speaks to the people before he dies, in the form of a lawsuit that indicts Israel for disloyalty to Yhwh.
Deu. 33	"Testament of Moses": In a second deathbed speech, Moses blesses the tribes as if they were his offspring.
Judg. 5*	"Song of Deborah": Celebrants praise Yhwh for Deborah and Jael's victory over the Canaanite general Sisera.
1 Sam. 2	"Song of Hannah": A barren wife praises the Deity.
2 Sam. 22	"David's Song": David thanks God for delivering him from his enemies. The same poem appears as Ps. 18.
Judith 16:1–17*	The people celebrate their victory over the Assyrians and Judith's part in it.
	*Indicates that women are mentioned.

9

PROPHECY:

THE SPIRIT POURING OUT

*A country woman, one large basket clutched under her arm and an-
other balanced on her head, walked through Jerusalem's just-opened
gates. The sun had not yet crested the surrounding hills and the air,
though still, was cold.*

*But the woman did not feel the cold. In fact she sweated beneath
the cloak draped over her head and around her shoulders, perhaps because she had started walking before the stars had faded in the sky. The
girl striding beside her—a young woman, actually, of twelve or thirteen—
had tossed her cloak into the stiff pack of woven rushes strapped to her
shoulders. Her strong, sun-browned arms, filled with a cloth-wrapped
bundle, were bare.*

*"Haggith," the woman said, her words forming small white puffs in
the chilly air, "I want to set out the fruit next to Adi, the herb woman.
Everyone stops to visit her—for the gossip, if not for her salves—and I
always sell more when I'm next to her. She makes people laugh, so they
feel good and are looser with their coins."*

"Yes, Mama," said the girl who was almost a woman. But she wasn't

listening, not really. Her eyes were roving over the massive stone blocks of the city walls, the sturdy houses built into the walls, the other people walking toward the market area. In the soft morning light, everything she saw seemed fresh, new, and a little dreamlike.

The woman-child lagged behind her mother. Not that she hadn't been to Jerusalem before. She had, though her brother Benyamin usually came with their mother to the market to sell or trade the pomegranates and olives and other extra fruit, if there were any, which was not often. But this year's harvest had been surprisingly good.

Haggith's attention suddenly snapped forward. Her mother had abruptly stopped and Haggith peered over the older woman's shoulder to see why. Coming toward them was a man—a naked man. Not an especially tall man, but one whose broad shoulders and broad chest suggested strength and power.

Around them, people drew back to let the man pass as if his touch meant defilement. Yet their eyes followed his progress down the lane. Haggith heard a whisper pass through the crowd—a name, Isaiah. She felt chilled, the sweat now clammy on her skin. She had seen slaves driven naked through the village by the men taking them to Egypt to sell. Public nakedness, like the slavery it accompanied, was shameful but not unknown. But this man walked alone: He was a free man, he carried a staff, and, like her brother Benyamin, he was a member of the tribe. Any fool could see the marks of circumcision.

The man was now upon them. Haggith could hear what he said in an oddly gentle voice. "See, this is what will happen to those in whom we entrust our hopes and to whom we flee for help and deliverance from the king of Assyria! And we, how shall we escape?"

As the man passed, Haggith, like the others around her, turned to stare. Suddenly, the man looked back and held the young woman's gaze. Then he moved out of view. Though aware that her mother was now speaking and moving, Haggith stood looking back. She was thinking about the strength apparent in that chest, the deceptively calm voice, but most of all, the eyes. How could such beauty be so fierce?

No one knows if the prophet known as Isaiah actually walked through Jerusalem naked like a slave as he was commanded to do by Yhwh (Isa. 20:1–6), to chastise the people for imagining that an alliance with Egypt could save them from their common enemy, Assyria. But with the Hebrew prophets, almost anything was possible.

Prophets were not the kind of people you'd want as neighbors. They spoke cryptically, behaved strangely, and most frightening of all, lived dangerously close to Divine power. In a world where people believed that Yhwh determined if kings ruled or crops grew, anyone claiming to speak for God had special influence. To be a prophet in ancient Israel was not necessarily to be loved, but you were respected. Mostly.

To modern Westerners, the word "prophecy" suggests the ability to foretell the future, chiefly about events relating to the End of Time. Biblical prophets, however, were engaged with the here-and-now. Their *oracles*—messages from God—pertained to the immediate concerns of the people and their leaders. Treaties with foreign princes, the price of grain, the plight of widows and orphans: All were grist for the mill. Prophets were known for the tongue-lashings they delivered to those who defied God's will, but they also conveyed God's great love for the people of Israel.

Most prophets were men, but the Bible depicts a few women prophets playing crucial roles in the life of early Israel. Recovering their stories is one of the goals of this chapter.

Our other major task is to sort through the good, the bad, and the just plain ugly news for women in the prophetic books. The prophets vigorously defended the vulnerable members of society—yet they also used sexualized language that turned women into objects of scorn. We will look at examples of both kinds of oracles, dissecting the dyspeptic diatribes and recovering the strong voice for justice that shines through Israelite prophecy.

Initially, the prophets can all sound alike: some angry guy yelling about this or that obscure event. In fact, the prophets were quite different from one another. Every one of them promoted loyalty to Yhwh, but beyond that, there was no single party line; the daily news, local and international, shaped their utterances. Their messages were intensely political, which is why they often fell afoul of the powers-that-be. To help you make sense of their rants, I'll tell you a little about the contemporary events that triggered them.

Let's start by defining prophecy and talking about the biblical women who were called prophets.

Seers, Announcers, and Women of God

The various words and phrases used to refer to prophets in the Bible tell us a great deal about who they were and what they did. The common designations were *navi,* "one who is called" or "one who announces"; *hozeh,* "visionary"; *ro'eh,* "seer"; and the general term "man of God." Women prophets were called *nevi'ah* (the feminine form of *navi*).

In other words, prophets were people *called* by God to *announce* God's will, which they often received through *dreams or visions.* "Prophet" comes from *prophētēs,* the Greek word that was used to translate all the Hebrew words for prophet when the Bible was translated into Greek starting in the third century BCE.

Prophecy was an integral part of the social and political life of Israel by the eleventh century BCE, but prophecy did not originate in ancient Israel, nor did it flourish only there. Divine messengers, "shouters," and "revealers" were known throughout Mesopotamia, Egypt, Phoenicia, Assyria, and elsewhere in the eastern Mediterranean. Nor did all of the Bible's prophets speak for Yhwh. The Book of Kings mentions prophets for Baal and Asherah, indigenous Canaanite deities who were popular among the Israelites.

Yes-Men Need Not Apply
The Bible contains numerous references to prophets who were members of a professional guild that served the royal court or the temple. They were members of the ruling elite and most likely inherited their

positions. The prophets we know through their recorded oracles, however, were mostly countercultural types. Their words and deeds ruffled feathers at court and the temple.

When Amos prophesied in the northern kingdom that Israel would know God's wrath, the high priest there charged the prophet with treason and told him to get out of town and never come back. The priest, a government spokesman, did not like the fact that Amos agitated against the king—and in the king's own temple!

Amos was lucky; he lived to tell his tale. According to the book of Jeremiah, a prophet named Uriah fled to Egypt to escape a death sentence against him, but the king sent men to Egypt to kidnap him and drag him back to Judah. Uriah was executed and his body thrown into a common grave (Jer. 26:20–23).

Some of the prophets antagonized the folks in charge by enacting their divine messages much like Isaiah, who walked naked through Jerusalem. Scholars argue about whether prophets actually did the things they said they did or whether the descriptions were meant to be understood metaphorically. Either way, they brought the message home.

Women prophets, alas, were not nearly as outrageous.

NEVI'IM

In both Jewish and Christian Bibles, the set of books known collectively as "The Prophets" (nevi'im in Hebrew, the plural of navi) is devoted to the recorded words of ancient Israelite prophets. But the two traditions differ about which books fit that category and where they should be positioned within the Bible.

The Jewish Bible—the Tanakh—designates fifteen books of oracles as prophetic works. They appear in the following order: Isaiah, Jeremiah, Ezekial, Hosea, Joel, Amos, Obadiah, Jonah, Micah, Nahum, Habakkuk, Zephaniah, Haggai, Zechariah, Malachi.

In the Jewish tradition, the books of Joshua, Judges, Samuel, and Kings also are included within the broad category of *nevi'im*. Subtitled the Former Prophets, they tell the story of how Israel was favored by Yhwh but came to grief because the people and their leaders turned away from God. The fifteen books attributed to the men who tried to pull Israel from this downward spiral are designated the Latter Prophets.

Christians, on the other hand, think of Joshua, Judges, Samuel, and Kings (as well as a few other books such as Ruth) as histories. Furthermore, they insert additional books into the collection *they* call "The Prophets." The Book of Daniel is one, along with Lamentations (positioned after Jeremiah, because tradition said he wrote it). In Roman Catholic and Orthodox Bibles, the Deuterocanonical Book of Baruch follows Lamentations because a man named Baruch was Jeremiah's secretary.

Miriam, Deborah, Huldah, and Mrs. Isaiah.

Two of the oldest texts in the Bible—lengthy poems that celebrate great military victories—involve *women* prophets, as the previous chapter related. Judges 5 praises the prophet Deborah; in Exodus 15, Miriam led the revelries after the Israelites were safely out of Egypt. These songs testify to women acting as prophets at critical moments in Israel's history. And yet, the history of women and prophecy is decidedly ambiguous, as Esther Fuchs, professor of Judaic studies, points out.[1] We do not have the collected oracles of women prophets, and when women are portrayed as prophets, their features are blurred, distorted, or weakly rendered.

Leaving aside the negative depictions of female seers who were not advocates of Yhwh, just four women in the Hebrew Bible earned the title *nevi'ah*: Miriam, Deborah, Huldah, and the unnamed wife of the prophet Isaiah. Miriam's role following the victory at the Red Sea is unclear. She did not deliver a message from God; she led the women in song. Perhaps leading communal revelries had a heroic status of its own, but it was not a prophet's usual task. Furthermore, Yhwh declared only that Moses was a prophet and that Aaron was to be Moses' prophet for the times when he could not speak for himself. Miriam never received a divine appointment; an unnamed scribe merely recorded the tradition that she, too, was a prophet.

Miriam's standing became even murkier after she and Aaron challenged Moses over his wife, who was not an Israelite. "Has the LORD spoken only through Moses?" they asked, asserting their prophetic authority. "Has He not spoken through us as well?" (Nu. 12:2).

Rather than authenticating their status as prophets, however, Yhwh personally delivered a stinging rebuke to the brother and sister for their audacity in questioning Moses' judgment. God then afflicted Miriam—but not Aaron—with a defiling skin disease that required seven days of purifying isolation.

Fuchs notes that the narrator never explained the reasons why Miriam and Aaron complained about Moses' wife in the first place. As a result, Miriam came off looking merely jealous and petty.[2] Some readers find consolation in the story's ending: the entire tribe waited until Miriam was "clean" before setting out again on their march through the desert.

Deborah's identity as a prophet is similarly vague (Ju. 4–5). The Bible tells us she was a noted judge, but, like Miriam, she delivered no pronouncements that marked her as *nevi'ah*. Nor was she shown receiving a commission or message directly from Yhwh, although she told her general, Barak, that Yhwh commanded *him* to march against the Canaanite king.

Our third woman prophet, Huldah, was said to have played a vital role in formulating the Hebrew scriptures as we now know them. Her story is found in 2 Kings 22 and goes like this:

A king of Judah named Josiah, who ruled from 640 to 609 BCE, determined that the temple needed a thorough refurbishing. He ordered tax money to be given to carpenters and masons to repair the

building. As the workmen went about their remodeling, lo and behold, the high priest discovered a scroll called the "Book of the Law"
in a dusty corner of the building. The high priest gave the book to the
king's secretary, who gave it to the king. When the king saw the
scroll, he tore his clothes—a sign of grief—because he realized that
it contained statutes from Yhwh that neither he nor the people were
following. Josiah was sure that God was angry about this state of
affairs.

Before announcing the discovery, however, the king wanted to
make sure the book was authentic. He sent delegates to the *nevi'ah*
Huldah, married to the keeper of the king's wardrobe, to "inquire of
the LORD for me" (22:13). Huldah read the book and declared that it
was indeed authentic.

Additionally, Huldah delivered a powerful oracle from Yhwh, saying disaster would strike Jerusalem because its inhabitants had abandoned God and not kept the law. But Huldah said Yhwh would see to
it that Josiah would die in peace, because his "heart was penitent" and
he humbled himself before God. Most scholars believe that the "Book
of the Law" that Huldah read and certified became the nucleus of the
book of Deuteronomy, as chapter 2 related.

Huldah is the only one of the women designated a prophet who
acts like one. Even so, she was not quite correct about Josiah's death.
The reforming king did not die in peace but in battle against the Egyptians. Huldah was half right, however: She also predicted that his "eyes
shall not see all the disaster that [the LORD] will bring on this place"
(23:20). Indeed, Josiah had been dead for more than a decade before
the Babylonians swept into Jerusalem, sacked the city, and drove thousands into exile.

Bible scholar Diana Edelman, who doubts that the "Book of the
Law" was discovered as reported, believes that after the Israelites returned from exile, biblical authors added Huldah to the narrative about
the "Book of the Law" in order to lend verisimilitude. If a female

prophet named Huldah did live at the time of Josiah, Edelman speculates, it's more likely she would have been a conduit for the goddess
Asherah than for Yhwh.[3]

And the fourth woman *nevi'ah*, Isaiah's unnamed wife? She is
hardly worth mentioning, since Isaiah scarcely did so. The only reference to her, Isaiah 8:3–4, notes that the prophet "went to the prophetess, and she conceived and bore a son." The point of the story is not
the *nevi'ah*, but the birth, used as occasion for bestowing a symbolic
name on the son as a means of announcing the imminent fall of Dam-
ascus and Samaria. The designation "prophetess" in this case merely
was an honorific conferred on the wife of a prophet.

All in all, the few women prophets allowed into the canon do not
confront kings directly or chastise "the people," unlike the many male
prophets. Their speech is minimal or nonexistent and they do not
speak with God or perform miracles. In fact, women are more likely to
be the recipients of miracles, especially in the stories about the prophets
Elijah and Elisha in the Book of Kings.

And yet, the Bible's redactors maintained the tradition that Miriam,
Deborah, Huldah, and Isaiah's wife were prophets. Perhaps the title
referred less to what they did than their status within their communities. Only "prophet" was adequate to the task of expressing the esteem
in which they were held. This high regard should give us courage. Even
when constrained from living fully into roles so casually occupied by
men, good work will be recognized, subverting exclusive categories.

Do Justice, Love Kindness, Walk Humbly

Although women prophets got the short end of the stick, and male members of the profession never made gender equity a priority, prophets
repeatedly called for protection of the most vulnerable members of
society—including widows, orphans, and strangers—and vociferously
protested misuse of power and unequal distribution of wealth.

The prophet Micah summarized these prophetic values in simple terms. "With what shall I come before the LORD, and bow myself before God on high?" he asked. "Shall I come before him with burnt offerings, with calves a year old?" No, came the answer:

> He has told you, O mortal, what is good; and what does the LORD require of you but to do justice, and to love kindness, and to walk humbly with your God? (MIC. 6:8)

This is the heart of the Bible's prophetic message. Justice is not a concept but an act, something we are to *do*. It is linked to acts of kindness, which we must *love*, to do properly. And the prophet admonishes us not just to walk with God, but to walk *humbly*. We can't pretend to know what's best; God gets the last word.

The prophetic tradition of advocating for justice does not provide us with a fixed set of beliefs that we must adhere to; rather it functions as "a plumb line of truth and untruth, justice and injustice" that we apply in dynamic fashion, says Rosemary Radford Ruether, author of *Sexism and God-Talk*.[4]

The prophets articulated four primary principles, she says:

1. God defends and vindicates the oppressed.
2. God challenges the powerful when they dominate rather than serve.
3. God will overcome injustice and install a new age of peace and justice.
4. We must resist to any system of belief—including religion—if it fails to be empathic and in solidarity with the poor.[5]

Even though the prophets themselves could be misogynists, as we'll see in the next chapter, we can use their "prophetic principles" to challenge injustice—including sexism—wherever we find it. This includes the injustices—such as slavery, imperial pride, and the diminishment of women—that are embedded within the biblical texts. We can also assess interpretations of the Bible and religious traditions for their justice, kindness, and humility. Paradoxically, the Bible itself has provided us with a measuring stick to assess the worth of what's contained within it and all that flows from it.

Defending the Oppressed

Amos, active in the northern kingdom of Israel during the first half of the eighth century BCE, typified the prophets' scorn for those who oppressed the less fortunate.

> Hear this, you that trample on the needy,/and bring to ruin
>   the poor of the land,
> saying, "When will the new moon be over so that we may sell grain;
>   and the Sabbath so that we may offer wheat for sale?
> We will make the ephah small and the shekel great,/and
>   practice deceit with false balances, buying
>   the poor for silver and the needy for a pair of sandals,
>   and selling the sweepings of the wheat. (AMOS 8:4–6)

Amos was pointing his finger at merchants who were impatient for the Sabbath to end so they could return to making money by cheating the poor. Ironically, he prophesized during a particularly properous time in Israel's history, spurred by Assyrian political dominance. Israel's population had grown astronomically; it became the most densely settled area in the region, with perhaps 350,000 residents. Production of olive oil and wine soared, and merchants shipped these commodities not only from the hinterlands to the capital but quite possibly to Assyria and Egypt as well. Amos typifies the prophets' tendency to take their messages from current events.

Yet Amos also criticized women of the upper class, whom he saw as no less culpable than their husbands for their ill-gotten wealth:

Hear this word, you cows of Bashan who are on Mount Samaria,
who oppress the poor, who crush the needy,
who say to their husbands, "Bring something to drink!" (AMOS 4:1)

Bashan was a particularly fertile region northeast of Judah known for its sleek cattle. Amos's metaphor eloquently evokes the image of overindulged, pleasure-seeking Samarian women.

Certain prophets noted the special vulnerabilities of women, especially widows, who often were grouped with orphans or aliens as those most likely to be abused. "The alien residing within you suffers extortion; the orphan and the widow are wronged in you," Ezekiel lamented (Ezek. 22:7). Micah complained about rich landlords who foreclosed on creditors.

Alas for those who devise wickedness and evil deeds on their beds!
When the morning dawns, they perform it, because it is in their power.
They covet fields, and seize them; houses, and take them away;
they oppress householder and house, people and their inheritance.

(MIC. 2:1–2)

Like Amos, Micah lived at a time of increased affluence, but in Judah, which experienced something of a renaissance after the fall of the northern kingdom. Refugees flowed south and within a generation, the population may have reached 120,000. Literacy increased, stonework on public buildings became more refined, pottery and other goods were manufactured in bulk, oil and wine production emerged as a state industry, and urban centers developed to facilitate trade. The economic boom clearly did not benefit everyone equally, however. Ezekiel complained that Israel and Judah "had pride, excess of food, and prosperous ease, but did not aid the poor and needy" (Ezek. 16:49).

Both Micah and Amos criticized the religious establishment for playacting at religion without tending to its ethical provisos. Speaking for Yhwh, Amos proclaimed,

> I hate, I despise your festivals, and I take no delight in your
>   solemn assemblies.
> Even though you offer me your burnt offerings and grain offerings
>   I will not accept them;
>   and the offerings of well-being of your fatted animals
>   I will not look upon.
> Take away from me the noise of your songs; I will not listen to the
>   melody of your harps.
> But let justice roll down like waters,/and righteousness like an
>   ever-flowing stream. (AMOS 5:21–24).

The prophets recognized that God views religious rituals as meaning-
less if we are not working for justice.

Eden Restored

In response to injustice and false religion, prophets frequently evoked
the coming "Day of Yhwh," a time of retribution when, as Obadiah
said, "As you have done, it shall be done to you;/your deeds shall return
on your own head" (Ob. 15). For Obadiah, the guilty party in need of
chastisement was Edom, one of Israel's neighbors who did not come to
her aid during the Babylonian onslaught and later picked through the
leavings. But the object of Yhwh's wrath might also be the people of
Israel (in whole or in part), or Assyria, or other nations.

The prophets' depictions of life postretribution were powerful visions
of a new age of peace and prosperity. Joel prophesied that an outpouring
of the Spirit would erase differences between the sexes, between generations, and even between slaves and the free.

> I will pour out my spirit on all flesh;
> your sons and your daughters shall prophesy,
> your old men shall dream dreams,
> and your young men shall see visions.

> Even on the male and female slaves, in those days,
> I will pour out my spirit. (JOEL 2:28–29)

Joel also reassured the people that "you shall eat in plenty and be satisfied" (Joel 2:26), a promise that spoke to their more immediate needs.

Ezekiel described a lengthy vision of Jerusalem as a renewed Eden: water flowing in all directions from a rebuilt Temple, with fish, fruit trees, and land for all the tribes (Ezek. 40–48). Third Isaiah (see "The Three Isaiahs" on page 159), active after the end of the Exile, announced Yhwh's intention "to create new heavens and a new earth" and offered a compelling image of universal peace and harmony.

> I will rejoice in Jerusalem, and delight in my people;
> no more shall the sound of weeping be heard in it, or the cry of distress.
> No more shall there be in it an infant that lives but a few days,
>> or an old person who does not live out a lifetime; . . .
> The wolf and the lamb shall feed together, the lion shall eat straw like
>> the ox;
>> but the serpent—its food shall be dust.
> They shall not hurt or destroy on all my holy mountain.
>
>> (ISA. 65:19–20, 25)

There is a curious circuitousness to these promises of redemption, however. Every one of the prophets—from Miriam to Malachi—depicted Yhwh restoring Israel's fortunes by devastating and dominating its enemies within and without. Nahum declared, "The LORD is a passionate, avenging God;/The LORD is vengeful and fierce in wrath" (Nah. 1:2, JPS). In the seventh century BCE, Zephaniah said of the Day of Yhwh,

> That day will be a day of wrath, a day of distress and anguish,
> a day of ruin and devastation, a day of darkness and gloom, a day of
>> clouds and thick darkness,

a day of trumpet blast and battle cry against the fortified cities and
against the lofty battlements. (ZEPH. 1:15–16)

I read these prophetic promises of divine retribution with mixed
feelings. How can the problem of misused power—whether we're talking about merchants cheating the poor back then or an employer demanding sexual favors from an employee today—be corrected through
more violence and coercion?

And yet, as a woman I know what it is to be a victim and to yearn
for a stronger power to come to my aid. Some years ago as I walked
home from the grocery store at night, two teenage boys jumped me,
pulled me to the ground, and demanded my money. I had only a little
change left from my shopping, which did not satisfy them. Suddenly,
several cars drove up the street. The boys faded into the shadows between the houses and disappeared.

When I reached my apartment, I called the police—even though I
was pretty sure they would never find those boys—because I needed
some assurance that I was more than a victim. I still remember how re-
lieved I felt when a hefty policeman arrived to take the crime report.
Seeing a gun in his holster and mace on his belt, I felt safer, which
even at the time I thought was odd, because I don't like guns and what
they can do. I also understood that the reasons adolescent boys undertake petty crime are not best answered with firepower. But at that moment, I was grateful for the display of brute force on my behalf.

I wonder if indigent Israelites greeted the prophets' violent rhetoric
in the same way that I welcomed that police officer into my home.
Were they, too, flooded with relief knowing that they had been heard
and would be protected? Were they grateful for the promise of a better
tomorrow? We can't know for sure, but the prophets' calls for retribution suggest they found an eager audience for such sentiments.

The difficulty with these images of a warrior God swooping in on
clouds of glory to smite our enemies is that once they become en-
shrined in scripture, they take on an equivocal force. We assume that

God will use power justly. Then humans model their behavior on God's, take power into their own hands, and things quickly go awry. We all know of the enormous harm done by combatants acting in the name of God.

The prophets tell us to attend to the root causes of social problems. If we do that, perhaps we will have fewer opportunities to (mis)use coercive power and to force change.

THE THREE ISAIAHS

Although there is only one Book of Isaiah, most likely its oracles came from several different prophets. Whether they all were actually named Isaiah we don't know, but scholars have detected three distinct styles and preoccupations in the text.

The first Isaiah is also called "Isaiah of Jerusalem." He probably lived and prophesied in that city in the second half of the eighth century BCE. Chapters 1–23, 28–33, and 36–39 of the Book of Isaiah generally are credited to this man.

Second Isaiah (a.k.a. Deutero-Isaiah, from the Greek word for "second"), most likely lived in Babylon and worked within the community of Judean exiles during and after Exile in the late sixth to early fifth centuries BCE. Chapters 34–35 and 40–66 are said to be the work of Second Isaiah.

Some scholars see the hand of a Third Isaiah in Chapters 24–27 and 56–66; others say the writings in question were written by followers of Second Isaiah. These chapters were written after 538 BCE, most likely in Jerusalem.

Table 9.1: Major Prophets of the Bible

Dates (BCE)	Political Period	Name	Message	Book/Chapter(s)
~1200–1000	Tribal Confederacy	Deborah	A judge in Israel and military leader against the Canaanites as well as a prophet.	Judges 4–5
~1000	End of confederacy; beginning of monarchy	Samuel	Dedicated by his mother to Yahweh's service before his birth. Cautioned Israelites against monarchy but anointed Saul as first king of Israel and selected David as his successor	1 Samuel 1–25
~1000	Reign of King David	Nathan	Successor to Samuel. Pressed David to name Solomon as heir and helped Solomon consolidate his power.	2 Samuel 7–1 Kings 1
860–840	Assyrian empire	Elijah	Campaigned against the worship of Baal, raised the dead, prophesied doom for the king, ascended to heaven in a whirlwind.	1 Kings 19–2 Kings 2
860–840	Assyrian empire	Elisha	Linked to Elijah as successor. Healed and raised the dead, aided Israel militarily. Called Israel to repentance.	1 Kings 19–2 Kings 13

Dates (BCE)	Political Period	Name	Message	Book/Chapter(s)
750	Hiatus between periods of Assyrian domination	Amos	From Judah, but a prophet in Israel. Preached that the "Day of Yahweh" would include judgment of Israel. Denounced upper classes' luxury, spoke on behalf of the poor.	Amos
750	Hiatus between periods of Assyrian domination	Hosea	Born and prophesied in Israel. Focused on social corruption. Stressed Yahweh's loving kindness.	Hosea
740–701	Assyrian empire	Isaiah of Jerusalem	Associated with Jerusalem Temple and Davidic dynasty. Denounced ruling-class greed. Counseled total reliance on Yahweh rather than diplomatic alliances.	Isaiah 1–23, 28–33, 36–39
740–700	Assyrian empire	Micah	Judean peasant. Condemned rich urban landowners. Predicted city and Temple would be destroyed.	Micah
640–609	Reign of King Josiah, reformer in Judah	Zephaniah	Condemned Israel's neighbors and predicted end of life on earth. Shifted to repeal of Yahweh's sentence against Judah.	Zephaniah

(continued)

Table 9.1 (continued)

Dates (BCE)	Political Period	Name	Message	Book/ Chapter(s)
626–587	Babylonian conquest of Judah	Jeremiah	Viewed Babylon as Yahweh's tool for chastising Judah. Urged submission to Babylon and Yahweh. Though a priest, saw little merit in Temple cult or Davidic monarchy.	Jeremiah
~625–600	Demise of Assyria, rise of Babylonia	Habakkuk	Faced with Babylon's imminent conquest of Judah, concluded that the righteous must have faith in Yahweh's ultimate justice.	Habakkuk
621	Reign of King Josiah, reformer in Judah	Huldah	Authenticated the Book of the Law, found during Josiah's reign as the Temple was being refurbished.	2 Kings 21:3–29
~612	Demise of Assyria	Nahum	Judean. Gloated over Assyria's destruction.	Nahum
587	Babylonian conquest of Judah	Obadiah	Condemned Judah's neighbor Edom for helping Babylonians sack Jerusalem.	Obadiah
after 587	Babylonian Exile	Ezekiel	Priest and mystic exiled to Babylon. Preached that Yahweh was too holy to continue dwelling with unjust and violent people. Foresaw rebuilt Temple and divinely protected new Jerusalem.	Ezekiel

Dates (BCE)	Political Period	Name	Message	Book/ Chapter(s)
550–539	Babylonian Exile	Second Isaiah	Described Yahweh as working to restore faithful remnant to Judah. Composed "servant" songs celebrating redemptive role of Yahweh's chosen people, Israel.	Isaiah 34–35, 40–66
after 538	Persian Empire	Haggai	In Judah following the return from Exile. Carried the message that the Temple must be rebuilt. Only then would Jerusalem's fortunes be restored.	Haggai
~520	Persian Empire	Zechariah	In Judah following the return from Exile. Had mythical visions of rebuilt Temple and proclaimed Yahweh's messianic intentions for Israel.	Zechariah
~500–450	Persian Empire	Third Isaiah	In Judah following the rebuilding of the Temple. Sharply critical of the community's religious failures.	Isaiah 24–27, 56–66
~490–400	Persian Empire	Joel	Had apocalyptic visions signaling the Day of Yahweh. Called for repentance and foretold outpouring of divine spirit.	Joel
~490–400	Persian Empire	Malachi (Messenger)	Predicted judgment on Yahweh's day of visitation. Announced future reappearance of Elijah.	

10

LEWDNESS, WHORING, AND "WOMB LOVE": A LEXICON OF PROPHETIC SPEECH

Can a woman forget her nursing child,
or show no compassion for the child of her womb?
Even these may forget, yet I will not forget you.

—ISA. 49:15

Adulterous wife [Israel], who receives strangers instead of her husband! Gifts are given to all whores; but you gave your gifts to all your lovers, bribing them to come to you from all around for your whorings.

—EZEK. 16:32–33

When prophets spoke on behalf of God, they used powerful images to stir their listeners into action. As Isaiah and Ezekiel demonstrate, prophetic metaphors ranged from the profound to profane. Isaiah evoked the love of a mother for her infant to characterize Yhwh's devotion to Israel. Ezekiel, on the other hand, called Judah an "adulterous wife"—thus making God the cuckolded husband—for relying upon an alliance with Egypt for "her" defense.

Lamentably, a number of other prophets got stuck in the profane band of the spectrum. Isaiah, Jeremiah, Nahum, Hosea, and Micah all called Israel and the other nations "harlot," "sorceress," "witch," and "adulteress." Additionally, prophets depicted these "unfaithful wives" and "harlots" being publicly humiliated and sexually violated by God in the role of divine warrior or by the prophets themselves.

Not only did prophets treat women's sexuality as a quality that could be negatively applied to other objects, they also linked women and their sexuality with evil. Although the wider society undoubtedly accepted such views, the prophetic writings are the earliest instances in which such depictions find their way into scripture. The prophets did not use similarly forceful—and negative—masculine images.

What are we to do with this prophetic trash talk? My visceral response is to slam the Bible shut. I don't let anyone talk to me that way. But this would mean turning my back on the prophets' pleas for justice as well. Am I overreacting? They're just metaphors, after all.

No, if we pretend we're not squirming inside we're not listening wholeheartedly, and what is not whole cannot be holy. We need to find a way to handle the nasty language. Words *can* hurt us; that's why I've studiously avoided calling the Deity "he." Let's bring the objectionable passages out into the light of day, talk about why they hurt, and defuse them. This is different from justifying such statements or explaining them away. They will never be okay, but we can learn from them.

Fortunately, the prophets behave themselves a lot of the time, so this chapter also provides shortcuts to understanding recurring themes in prophetic writings.

Prophetic Trash Talk

Israel as Unfaithful Wife

The most egregious example of the unfaithful-wife motif is in Hosea, although Ezekiel and Jeremiah also used it (Hos. 1–3; Ezek. 16, 23; Jer. 3). Hosea tells us that God commanded him to "take for yourself a wife of whoredom and have children of whoredom, for the land commits great whoredom by forsaking the LORD" (Hos. 1:2). Hosea said he did as ordered: He married a woman named Gomer who had "played the whore." With her, he had three children whom he named God Sows, Not Pitied, and Not My People.

Metaphors such as Hosea's work as analogies. Just as Gomer was out of control, so, too, were the people of Israel. By "whoring" with Canaanite gods, they became "not my people."

If you read Hosea carefully, however, you will see that the prophet did not say Gomer was a whore; rather, she was "a wife of whoredom," an expression meaning "promiscuous." Women in those days were not to have independent ideas about their sexuality, which was always under the control of fathers, husbands, or other male relatives. The prophet was describing Gomer as out of control sexually, and that was very bad—for him. It indicated that he, as a husband, could not contain his wife's sexuality, and so he lost honor.

Scholars argue about whether Hosea spoke literally or figuratively, but that misses the point. A metaphor that uses the sexual behavior of Hosea and Gomer both reflects and reinforces contemporary gender attitudes, says T. Drorah Setel, Hebrew Bible scholar. Theologically, it says that God possesses and controls Israel as a husband ought to possess and control his wife.

Unfortunately, analogies can work in either direction. Reverse Hosea's schema, and men become analogous to God whereas women are the promiscuous people. More important, the man is right, and the woman is wrong, just as God is good, but the people are "whoring."

Alas, there's more to Hosea's disagreeable characterizations. A lengthy poem in Hosea 2 portrays God instructing Hosea's children to plead with their mother to change her promiscuous behavior. If she did not, God threatened,

> I will strip her naked and expose her as in the day she was born,
>   and make her like a wilderness, and turn her into a parched land,
>   and kill her with thirst . . .

Now I will uncover her shame in the sight of her lovers,
and no one shall rescue her out of my hand. (HOS. 2:3, 10)

Hosea portrayed God metaphorically, saying that "He" will reverse history by taking the people back to the wilderness, in the days before they came into the land flowing with milk and honey. Lamentably, the meaning of this passage relies on images of sexualized violence. The husband, who had been dishonored by his wife's behavior, must regain his honor by reasserting control of her. He would do this by taking her to a public place and stripping her naked. Her shame restores his honor.

Cycles of love and abuse. Hosea also said that God would separate Israel from "her" lovers—the *baals* (idols) to whom she had offered incense—and "put an end to all her mirth" (Hos. 2:11) because she did not acknowledge that Yhwh, not her idolatrous lovers, provided her with wine, grain, and flax. But God then said, "I will now allure her . . . and speak tenderly to her" (Hos. 2:14), winning her back so that she is faithful to God alone.

This sequence—separating, humiliating, then seducing a feminized Israel—mimics the cycle of domestic violence. Typically, a perpetrator isolates then abuses the victim, repents, and finally seeks reconciliation—and the cycle begins again. Apparently this pattern of abuse was known in ancient Israel, for how would readers have grasped the significance of Hosea's prophecy if they hadn't seen or experienced it?

Marriage could have been a useful metaphor for the intimacy of God's covenant relationship with Israel. Regrettably, Hosea—and also Jeremiah and Ezekiel—sullied the beauty of this image by dragging into it the violence that permeates too many intimate relationships. More than one commentator has accused Hosea of writing "pornography" because he objectified women and promoted male dominance.

To be fair, Hosea's intent was not necessarily to denigrate women. Gale A. Yee of the Episcopal Divinity School argues that Hosea's prophecy was aimed at Israel's leadership and male elite, who were oppressing their own people by amassing large fiefdoms sustained by onerous tributes from tenant farmers. By correlating the aristocracy's behavior with that of sexually deviant women, Hosea hoped to shame the elite into ending their economic and political entanglements with Egypt and other nations (their *baals*) and to worship Yhwh alone.

Even if we grant that Hosea's cause was just, nevertheless what stays with us is a metaphor that reinforces the notion that men are dominant and women should be subordinate to them. Unfortunately, Hosea was not the only prophet to call Israel an unfaithful wife.

Israel as Harlot, Sorceress, and Adulterer

Whereas Hosea charged Gomer with merely acting like a harlot, other prophets claimed Israel (or the people, other nations, or [fill in the blank]) *was* a harlot. Isaiah lamented that Jerusalem "has become a harlot, the faithful city that was filled with justice" (Isa. 1:21, JPS). Micah reported that Yhwh warned Samaria, "I will make a waste heap of all her idols, for they were amassed from fees for harlotry" (Mic. 1:7, JPS).

"You have polluted the land with your whoring and wickedness," thundered Jeremiah, and, "as a faithless wife leaves her husband, so you have been faithless to me, O house of Israel" (Jer. 3:2, 20). He then evoked statutes forbidding divorced couples to remarry if either partner had married another person in the interim. This was his way of warning that Yhwh would not "remarry" the "sisters" Israel and Judah, the two kingdoms created by the division of Solomon's empire, both of whom "went and whored" with other gods after leaving Yhwh (Jer. 3).

Ezekiel said God clothed "his" bride Jerusalem with embroidered garments and fine linen, gave "her" choice foods and adorned her with precious metals, yet she took the gold and silver, made "phallic images and fornicated with them" (Ezek. 16:17, JPS).

Ezekiel also gave readers an X-rated vignette involving two female figures, Oholibah and Oholah, who were not actual women but stand-ins for the ancient capitals of Jerusalem and Samaria, respectively. They "played the whore in Egypt," said Ezekiel, where "their breasts were caressed . . . and their virgin bosoms were fondled" by paramours "whose members were like those of donkeys, and whose emission was that of stallions" (Ezek. 23:3, 20). The women then "lusted" after Assyrians and Chaldeans and "defiled" themselves with the foreigners. Yhwh promised to end this "lewdness" by sending the Assyrians and Chaldeans to cut off the nose and ears of Oholibah and to devour the remaining Israelites by fire, so that "the nakedness of your whorings shall be exposed" (Ezek. 23:29).

Most disturbing of all, at the end of his rant references to harlotry blurred into images of actual women. Ezekiel, or a later editor, added the advisory, "Thus will I put an end to lewdness in the land, so that all women may take warning and not commit lewdness as you have done" (Ezek. 23:48). Imagine how many have read this as a warrant to "punish" women for perceived transgressions, using the humiliations that were meant to be figures of speech.

Reading Ezekiel, with his repeated denunciations of "lewdness" and "whoring," I have to wonder about the man's psyche. He seems to have been quite preoccupied by sex in an unhealthy way. Unfortunately, his language was as virile as the lovers he imagined Israel possessed: By repeating key phrases he builds a tower of condemnation that crashes down with the force of a tsunami. The Book of Ezekiel is a good place to use the "plumb line" of prophetic tradition and argue that this sort of smutty language is *not* the word of God.

Witchcraft and sorcery. Then there were the prophets who linked "harlotry" with charges of sorcery and witchcraft, as Nahum did in excoriating Nineveh, capital city of the predatory Assyrian empire.

> Because of the countless debaucheries of the prostitute,
> gracefully alluring, mistress of sorcery,

who enslaves nations through her debaucheries, and peoples
   through her sorcery,
I am against you, says the LORD of hosts, and will lift up your
   skirts over your face;
and I will let nations look on your nakedness and
   kingdoms on your shame. (NAH. 3:4–5)

Nahum called Nineveh a prostitute because women who charged
for sex were considered dangerous, mercenary, predatory, and self-
interested. These adjectives might have described the Assyrian empire
accurately, but such language did not extend compassion or understanding toward prostitutes as marginalized members of a culture
whose women had little economic independence.

Nahum claimed that not only did Nineveh use "her" sexual charms
to lure nations into her orbit, she also used sorcery. Magic symbolized
yet another power—like women's sexuality—that was hazardous if not
controlled.

While we might scoff at the idea of using magic to control entire
nations, sorcery was a fact of life for the ancients. Israelites simply
wanted to know if it was the work of Yhwh or the indigenous god Baal.
To Nahum, Nineveh's sorcery was used on behalf of Baal.

Cakes for the Queen of Heaven

Nothing popped the cork on a prophet's bile like worship directed toward
someone or something other than Yhwh. Women especially came under
fire for aberrant religious enthusiasms. (Never mind that they were shut
out of the official temple hierarchy and limited in what they could legiti-
mately do.) Several prophetic reprimands actually provide a fascinating
glimpse into the world of women's spiritual practices.

Ezekiel, known for his otherworldly visions while an exile in Babylonia, reported that during a visionary tour of the Jerusalem temple, he
spied men worshiping fetishes, and women at the gates of the inner
court "weeping for Tammuz" (Ezek. 8:14). Tammuz, known as Dumuzi

in ancient Sumer, was a Mesopotamian god who brought life to the infant developing in its mother's womb and, seasonally, to the fields and vines. When the fecundity of spring was lost to the dead heat of summer, statues of Tammuz would be bathed, anointed, and allowed to lie in state for a period of mourning. Apparently, women had adopted the tradition of grieving for Tammuz at the temple, which Ezekiel called a "vile abomination."

Ezekiel also railed against women "who prophesy out of their own imagination" (Ezek. 13:17). Presumably he thought the women were out of line not only because they were unauthorized to speak on behalf of Yhwh, but also because they employed divination methods learned from the Babylonians. One of his other complaints against these women was that they worked "for handfuls of barley and for pieces of bread" (Ezek. 13:19). Ezekiel believed taking wages for prophecy was improper, even though this meager recompense may have been the exiles' only source of income.

Jeremiah lodged his complaints about non-Yahwistic worship against entire families. Speaking in Jerusalem not long before it fell, he charged that

> the children gather sticks, the fathers build the fire, and the mothers knead dough, to make cakes for the Queen of Heaven, and they pour libations to other gods, to vex Me. Is it Me they are vexing?— says the LORD. It is rather themselves, to their own disgrace. (JER. 7:18–19, JPS)

Exactly which deity Jeremiah meant by "Queen of Heaven" is debated vigorously. Was he referring to Ishtar, the Mesopotamian goddess of war and love, or the Canaanite Astarte, who was identified with fertility? Susan Ackerman believes the Queen's cult was syncretistic, a form of worship that combined elements of both those goddesses into a third configuration.[1]

Whoever She was, She was immensely popular, as Jeremiah learned when the Babylonians triumphed over Judah and he fled to Egypt with other Judeans. There, he attempted to persuade "all the people and all the women" to cease their worship of the Queen, but the other exiles vowed to continue the practice, telling him, "We used to have plenty of food, and prospered, and saw no misfortune" when they made offerings to the Queen, and now they had nothing but misfortune (Jer. 44:17). Blaming the Queen's worshipers for the entirety of Judah's ill fortune, Jeremiah prophesied that "all the people of Judah who are in the land of Egypt shall perish by the sword and by famine, until not one is left" (Jer. 44:27).

A century after Jeremiah made his prediction, a temple to the Queen still stood in Egypt, and the Jewish community thrived there for another six hundred years.

Zechariah also attacked women's worship, but in an oblique way that's easy to miss. In the seventh of the eight visions that constitute his oeuvre, an angel guided Zechariah to a basket symbolizing the people's iniquity. When the lid was lifted, the prophet saw a woman in the basket. "This is Wickedness," said the angel (Zech. 5:8). Two women with wings "like the wings of a stork" then lifted the basket into the sky, taking it "to the land of Shinar, to build a house for it" (Zech. 5:9, 11).

What is this all about? First of all, the word translated as "basket" is *ephah* in Hebrew. An *ephah* was a unit of dry measure equaling a little more than twenty quarts. But *ephah* also was the word for a room set aside for cultic practices in Mesopotamia. Shinar was another name for Babylon, and by "house," the prophet meant a temple. The vision thus signified removing idolatry from the restored Judah and returning it to where it belonged.

The woman in the ephah could also represent foreign women married to Israelites who tainted worship of Yhwh with alien practices, suggests Beth Glazier-McDonald in *The Women's Bible Commentary*. She notes that the Hebrew for "stork" (*chasidah*) is related to the word for "faithful" (*chasid*). The women with wings of faith removed foreign influences, just as men in Judah following the Exile were being instructed to divorce their non-Israelite wives.

Although the faithful female creatures with wings could counterbalance the woman in the *ephah*, Zechariah's pronouncement—"This is Wickedness"—is so stark, so definitive, that the association of women and evil remains. Was it the worship of female deities that so incensed Zechariah or that women were the practitioners? Either way, he saw a female figure as representative of all that defiled Judah and he wanted her OUT!

The God Who Mothers

Difficult though it may be to believe, the same prophets who used male language for God and portrayed God as an abusive spouse, also employed nurturing metaphors for the Deity. Isaiah offered reassurance to the returning exiles by personifying Jerusalem as a woman, Zion, and making a direct comparison between God and a doting mother:

> But Zion said, "The LORD has forsaken me,
> my Lord has forgotten me."
> Can a woman forget her nursing child,
> or show no compassion for the child of her womb?
> Even these may forget, yet I will not forget you. (ISA. 49:14–15)

This same prophet reminded Israel that it had been "borne by [God] from your birth, carried from the womb" (Isa. 46:3). He even said, mixing metaphors, that Yhwh would go forth like a soldier and "cry out like a woman in labor" (Isa. 42:14).

Some prophetic images of God are not plainly feminine, yet offer relief from the relentlessly alpha male characterizations. Jeremiah depicted God in great anguish over the fate of Judah.

> O that my head were a spring of water,
> and my eyes a fountain of tears,
> so that I might weep day and night for the slain of my poor people.
> (JER. 9:1)

Jeremiah also suggested God acts as a nurse: "For I will restore health to you, and your wounds I will heal" (Jer. 30:17).

Isaiah portrayed God in the familiar role of chastising the chosen ones, but, uncustomarily, in the guise of a potter.

> Woe to you who strive with your Maker,
>
> earthen vessels with the potter!
>
> Does the clay say to the one who fashions it, "What are you making"?
>
> or "Your work has no handles"? (ISA. 45:9)

One of the Bible's most potent female images for God is hidden from view. The Bible repeatedly describes God as merciful and gracious, two adjectives reserved exclusively for the Deity. Phyllis Trible, author of *God and the Rhetoric of Sexuality*, points out that the Hebrew word for "merciful" is *rahûm*, which emerges from the same root (*rhm*) as "womb" (*rahmah*), "compassion" (*rahem*), and verbs such as "to show compassion." So, for example, when Jeremiah proclaims, "Thus says the LORD: I am going to restore the fortunes of the tents of Jacob, and have compassion on his dwellings," God's compassionate acts emanate from the womb. Since God does not have a literal womb, we can say God's "compassion" is an idealized version of maternal love, empathy, and caring. God's love is "womb love."

From whores to "womb love" and back again; is there any way to integrate these competing characterizations of the Divine?

Yes and no. Whether elevating mother-love or trashing faithless "harlots," the prophets idealized all qualities associated with females, some for the good and some for the worse. In that sense, at least, the images are consistent. Yet neither end of the spectrum accurately reflects the totality of women's lives and experiences. We may be able to salvage a few prophetic metaphors, but more likely, we need to create our own. This requires us to live into our experiences of the Divine and dig deep for the words—or visual images, movements, sounds, or tastes—to express what we know. The prophets have their testimonies, and we can have ours.

Theme Songs: Recurring Motifs in Prophetic Utterances

Prophetic oracles were idiosyncratic, but certain themes cropped up again and again. One major motif was the demand for ethical behavior and social justice that I discussed in chapter 9. The prophetic vision of a future of peace and prosperity—of the wolf and the lamb lying down together—was another. Here are eight other themes you will often see in prophetic writings.

Exclusivity. Over and over, prophets insisted that people must worship only Yhwh. A corollary was the recognition that all good things—good harvests, political stability, offspring—came through God.

Denunciation of idols. In reaction to the practices of neighboring kingdoms, prophets issued strong prohibitions against idol worship. They repeatedly asserted that Yhwh could not be embodied in a material image and that representations of any deity—they often cited Baal, Asherah, and Chemosh—were false gods.

Calls for repentance. The prophets never wearied of calling upon the people to mend their ways. Often, prophets enticed the people to repent with reminders of how Yhwh is a god who "is gracious and merciful/slow to anger, and abounding in steadfast love/and relents from punishing" (Joel 2:13).

Indisputable destruction. When the people worshiped idols or gods other than Yhwh, the prophets threatened them with God's wrath. Given events of the times—wars, assassinations, deportations, sieges, and famine—prophets had no difficulty summoning images of destruction that conveyed a sense of doom.

Israel as Chosen. Prophets assumed that Yhwh had a special relationship with the people of Israel. Perhaps because of this, prophets vacillated between righteous indignation and bewildered despair over the people's disinclination to hold up their end of the bargain with God.

The Jerusalem temple and David's dynasty. Certain prophets preached that the only way to regain God's good graces was to reinstate faithful worship in the temple and restore to the throne of Judah kings descended from David, the model monarch. Others mocked those who believed worship alone brought salvation.

Comfort. The same prophets who sputtered and fumed and rained down curses from God also delivered messages of comfort and hope. Usually this took the form of promising that God would once again look favorably upon the Israelites.

Miraculous powers. Prophets generally inspired others by the power of their words. A few, such as Samuel, were accorded the power to choose and anoint kings. In rare instances, a prophet demonstrated miraculous powers. Elijah and his successor Elisha (1 Kgs. 17–2 Kgs. 9) raised the dead, provided a never-empty jar of oil for a starving widow, and enabled an elderly, barren woman to bear a son, among other remarkable deeds.

Tutorial: Ephraim Returns (Jer. 31:18–20)

Jeremiah was a priest and prophet in Jerusalem when the Babylonians subdued Judah at the beginning of the sixth century BCE. (This was many years after the Assyrians had vanquished the northern kingdom of Israel, often referred to in the Bible as "Ephraim" from the name of the region's dominant tribe.) Although Jeremiah could use harsh words against the Judeans for their transgressions, in this passage he evoked a different mood.

The verses here are the center point of a larger passage, Jer. 31:15–22, that begins with a description of Rachel, beloved of Jacob, crying for her children—metaphorically the Judeans—who have gone into exile.

There are two voices in this excerpt: God's (the "I" in verses 18 and 20) and Ephraim's.

> 18 I can hear Ephraim lamenting:
> You have chastised me, and I am chastised; Like a calf that has
>   not been broken.
> Receive me back, let me return,/For you, O LORD are my God.
> 19 Now that I have turned back, I am filled with remorse;
> Now that I am made aware, I strike my thigh.
> I am ashamed and humiliated,/For I bear the disgrace of my youth.
> 20 Truly, Ephraim is a dear son to Me,/A child that is dandled!
> Whenever I have turned against him, My thoughts would dwell
>   on him still.
> That is why My heart yearns for him; I will receive him back in
>   love—declares the LORD. (JPS)

How would you describe the tone of this passage? What elements provide that feeling?

Ephraim attributes his waywardness to his youth. What metaphor does he use to describe how he has been chastised? What feelings does that evoke?

What arguments does Ephraim marshal in favor of letting "him" return?

How does Yhwh characterize the relationship with Ephraim? Phyllis Trible believes the last line of v. 20 could read, "Therefore, my womb trembles for him," and "I will truly show motherly-compassion upon him."[2] How does that affect your reading of these verses?

If you read the entire passage, you'll see that Yhwh's speech about Ephraim parallels Rachel's tenderness toward her children. Yet there is a critical difference between the two. Rachel inconsolably grieves for those who have been lost. God is present to forgive and receive back those who once were lost.

Perhaps you have experienced—or at least can imagine—the degree of grief carried by Rachel. In light of these deep feelings, how do you hear these words of promise and consolation? Does the possibility of a feminine compassion attributed to Yahweh influence how you hear this passage?

Jeremiah goes on to say in v. 22 that Yhwh "has created something new on earth: A woman courts a man." (The Hebrew literally reads, "a woman surrounds a man.") What is the "something new" that you would like God to create in the world?

PROPHECY, CONTINUED

Did prophecy end with the biblical prophets? Some would say no and point to the many Jews and Christians from the first century CE to our own who, inspired by the prophets, risked their lives and reputations to speak the truth they believed God had given them to proclaim. Like the Hebrew prophets before them, these women and men championed justice for the poor and dispossessed and called upon society to take up the burden of caring for the least among us.

Lillian Wald (1867–1940) was born into a well-to-do Jewish family soon after the end of the American Civil War. Though she later described herself as "spoiled," at sixteen Wald entered nurses training, beginning a lengthy career that would include:

- Helping to establish the field of public health nursing
- Founding the Henry Street Settlement House on New York's Lower East Side (in 1895)
- Agitating for public playgrounds, public school nurses, and special education classes

- Promoting trade unions for women workers
- Advocating for the rights of immigrants
- Helping, in 1909, to found the NAACP
- Campaigning to create the Federal Children's Bureau, a goal finally realized in 1912

Wald also worked with other women to oppose militarism and America's entry into World War I, efforts that led to her being branded as an "undesirable citizen." Wald subsequently served as a leader of the Women's International League for Peace and Freedom and lobbied for women's suffrage. More than one hundred years later, the Henry Street Settlement and the Visiting Nurse Service of New York continue Wald's pioneering work.

Another outspoken critic of the status quo and activist on behalf of the poor was Dorothy Day (1897–1980). A journalist and Roman Catholic lay woman, in 1933 Day cofounded the *Catholic Worker* newspaper, which agitated for a just society freed from the excesses of industrial capitalism. Day and her associates put their principles into practice: They housed and cared for women and men made homeless by the Great Depression. This practice developed into a network of Catholic Worker soup kitchens and "houses of hospitality" in urban and rural areas. Today, Catholic Worker volunteers maintain more than 130 facilities in the United States, open to all who have fallen through the holes in society's safety net. Catholic Workers also campaign for the rights of the poor and dispossessed, and against war and militarism. They act as a thorn in the flesh of the Roman Catholic hierarchy when it sides with the powerful against the poor.

Justine Wise Polier (1903–1987), daughter of the champion of Reform Judaism, Rabbi Stephen Wise, was the first woman judge in New York, serving on the Family Court for nearly forty years. During that time, Polier was a feisty advocate on behalf of children because, she said, "I saw the vast chasms between our rhetoric of freedom, equality and charity, and what we were doing to, or not doing for, poor people, especially children."

In 1958, Polier ruled that the New York Board of Education provided nonwhite children with an inferior education, and she later initiated a class action suit to end religious and race discrimination in foster care placements. Off the bench, she led organizations that promoted the cause of troubled youngsters and helped create interracial, interreligious facilities to care for them.

Polier almost did not get her judgeship. While still a temporary appointee, she publicly criticized the city's Depression-era relief efforts. Called upon to recant by the mayor who named her to the bench, she refused. The mayor later backed down and swore her in.

Then there was Dorothy Stang (1931–2005), assassinated at the age of seventy-three because she would not stop speaking out on behalf of the rural workers and peasants with whom she lived in Brazil's Amazon rain forest. Despite death threats, Dot, as she was known, said, "I don't want to flee, nor do I want to abandon the battle of these farmers who live without any protection in the forest. They have the sacrosanct right to aspire to a better life on land where they can live and work with dignity while respecting the environment." Dot was a sister of Notre Dame de Namur, a Roman Catholic religious order, and had been working in Brazil for twenty-two years when she was murdered.

Christian and Jew: What these women held in common was the conviction that faith is about action as well as belief. Taking unpopular positions, these champions of justice drew upon biblical sources as models and sources of strength. None walked through the streets naked, but they did lobby, write letters, demonstrate, fast, pray, go to jail, and sit in endless meetings. They did not always accomplish what they set out to do; sometimes their victories were only moral ones. They all faced public outrage and opposition from their peers for doing the work they did. Stang died because of what she said and did. But all carried the prophetic mantle.

Now that they are gone, who will take their place? Will you?

WHERE ARE THE WOMEN IN PROPHECY?

Deborah	Judg. 4–5
Miriam	Ex. 15:20–21; Nu. 12; Mic. 6:4
Huldah	2 Kgs. 22:14–20
Isaiah's wife	Isa. 8:3–4
Israel as unfaithful wife	Hos. 1–3
	Ezek. 16, 23
	Jer. 2:1–4:44
Israel as harlot, sorceress,	Isa. 1:21–23,
adulteress	Jer. 3, 4:30, 13:22–27, 22:20–23
	Ezek. 16, 22:1–16, 23
	Mic. 1:7
	Nah. 3:4–6
Women's apostasy	Jer. 7:18–19
	Ezek. 8:14–15,13:17–23
	Zech. 5:5–11
Daughters of Zion	Isa. 3:16–4:1, 54:1–10, 66:7–9

WISDOM:

THE LISTENING HEART

Take my instruction instead of silver,/and knowledge rather
than choice gold;
For wisdom is better than jewels,/and all that you may desire
cannot compare with her.

—"WOMAN WISDOM" SPEAKING IN PROV. 8:10–11

I would rather live with a lion and a dragon/ than live with an
evil woman.

—THE SCRIBE YESHUA BEN EL-AZAR BEN SIRA

SPEAKING IN SIR. 25:16

Prophecy had ended. The kings of Israel and Judah were dust.
Yhwh's chosen people were scattered from Egypt to Anatolia, and
Persia controlled their homeland. Religion was reduced to temple rit-
uals performed by long-robed priests.

After the Exile, ca. 500 BCE, where could one go to find meaning
and moral instruction?

For the faithful remnant of Israelites clinging to their traditions in
Jerusalem and a few foreign strongholds, the new voices of authority
were professional sages and teachers who schooled disciples in what
they called "Wisdom," *hokma* in Hebrew.

Wisdom teachings did not dwell on the laws given at Sinai or even on Yhwh. Instead, writings such as those found in Proverbs, Sirach, the Wisdom of Solomon, and numerous psalms offered prescriptions for how to do well and live ethically, musings on the cycles of the human and natural world, and promises of wealth to the wise and ruin to the foolish.

Unlike most of the Bible, Wisdom was not addressed to the community of Israel. Rather, Wisdom's precepts were directed to individuals, generally ambitious young men seeking to make their way in the world—a sort of self-help literature for the upwardly mobile. Alongside exhortations to worship Yhwh, sages counseled their pupils to be sober, honest, and sexually restrained, and offered ways to impress social superiors.

Certain collections of Wisdom literature, however, were more complex. The authors of Job and Ecclesiastes questioned whether the righteous received their rewards and evildoers their just desserts as other sages (and the Deuteronomistic Historian) asserted. These works avoid easy conclusions and provide profound reflections on the meaning of life.

Wisdom teachings are compulsory reading for women for several reasons.

First, Wisdom teachers observed and reflected upon life itself. We can't always trust *what* they said, since often they were misogynist. (Yeshua ben El-azar ben Sira's proverb is typical.) But we can learn from *how* they went about their work. They relied on lived experience rather than abstract speculation as the starting point for reflection— and in Wisdom teachings common sense and our hard-earned insights about humankind have a place to thrive. On Wisdom's path, we drink from the deep wellsprings of our own truth.

Additionally, a provocative duo of feminine presences appears in many Wisdom books. "Woman Wisdom" is a majestic counterpart to Yhwh. The "Strange Woman" is the embodiment of evil and scourge of innocent young men. Each is a complex creation of men's imaginations (and fears!); both present difficulties for women.

Yet even as the Strange Woman reduces women to their worst characteristics, the figure of Woman Wisdom hints at an alternative understanding of divinity more than a little influenced by the goddess traditions of Egypt and the Mediterranean region. Woman Wisdom is worth knowing more about—and we'd better become acquainted with the Strange Woman so we can counteract her image.

Outside of the designated Wisdom books are stories within the Former and Latter Prophets that provide tantalizing glimpses of "wise women" who commanded widespread respect in ancient Israel. These tales suggest that at certain times and places actual women had more influence than is ordinarily recognized. Their stories allow us to savor the possibilities.

We will explore all three of these facets in the chapter ahead. First, let's learn a little more about what constitutes Wisdom.

Wisdom's Beginnings and Myriad Forms

No one really knows when the Wisdom tradition became part of Israel's heritage. Biblical legends about Solomon say that after he was crowned successor to David, he dreamed one night that he had an audience with Yhwh, who asked the new king what he wanted for himself. Solomon admitted that he did not have what it would take to rule Israel; he asked God to "grant, then, Your servant an understanding mind to judge Your people, to distinguish between good and bad; for who can judge this vast people of Yours?" (1 Kgs. 3:9, JPS).

Yhwh imparted to Solomon what he requested and the rest, as they say, is history. Immediately following Solomon's dream, 1 Kings recounts the famous story involving the king and two mothers claiming one baby. Solomon, you may remember, used his gift from Yhwh to reveal the false claimant by ordering the child cut in two with a sword, then awarded the baby to the woman who rushed to save it. People were awed by the king, "because they perceived that the wisdom of God was in him, to execute justice" (1 Kgs. 3:28). Solomon became known as the father of the Wisdom tradition, and editors attached his name to several collections of Wisdom. Did he write them? Probably not.

In these stories about Solomon, I'm struck by how the king asked for an "understanding mind," a Hebrew phrase that could be better translated as "a listening heart," which is a lovely metaphor for wisdom. Compassion paired with the humility to know that we need to listen to others is what distinguishes wisdom from mere knowledge or intelligence. Not all biblical Wisdom teachings are redolent of "a listening heart," but we can adopt the metaphor for our own brand of wisdom.

Long before Solomon's time, Wisdom was an international phenomenon found throughout the courts and academies of Egypt and the ancient Near East. When Israel's sages wrote, they drew from a common pool of teachings that they amended according to their understanding of Yhwh's dictates.[1]

Certain Wisdom writings in Hebrew, for example, bear a striking resemblance to admonitions penned much, much earlier by Ankhsheshonqy, a priest of Ra who lived in Egypt sometime between 945 and 712 BCE. Ankhsheshonqy wrote, "Divine plans are one thing. Human thoughts are another (26:14)."[2] Proverbs 16:1 says, "The plans of the mind belong to mortals, but the answer of the tongue is from the LORD."

Scholars have located numerous parallels among the works of Egyptian, Assyrian, Israelite, and other ancient scribes. Wisdom was probably the first international intellectual trend.

Long before any scribe put his thoughts about Wisdom into permanent form, the common folk had their own brand of Wisdom that they expressed in forms similar to those used by the professionals. For years, scholars tried to distinguish between "folk" traditions and the (supposedly) more artful renderings of sages. That effort eventually collapsed when scholars realized that then, as now, ordinary women and men also articulated life's memorable truths in pungent ways. With the exception of the writings of Yeshua ben El-azar ben Sirac (his writings are known simply as Sirach), whose author has been identified, we can hold open the possibility therefore that the Wisdom we're imbibing may have had humble origins.

WISDOM IN THE BIBLE

Ecclesiastes (also called Qohelet, which means the Teacher, Gatherer, or Assembler)—ca. 450–330 BCE
A mordant reflection, mostly in prose, grounded in the author's view of life as *hebel*—a Hebrew word translated as "vanity" but best viewed as futility or something insubstantial that cannot last. Ecclesiastes challenges easy assumptions regarding righteousness and rewards, the value of wealth, and the possibility of love. Its poem, "For everything there is a season,/and a time for every matter under heaven," catalogs the polarities of life (Eccl. 3:1–8).

Job—ca. 539–332 BCE
When God allows one of the lesser gods to strip the righteous Job of his wealth and health, we get a lesson in the nature of God. Like Ecclesiastes, Job upends common wisdom about divine retribution. Its eloquent and sometimes enigmatic poetry follows a brief prose introduction presumably taken from a more ancient work.

Proverbs—ca. 450–350 BCE
In contrast to the two previous works, Proverbs wholeheartedly delivers the message that wisdom leads to success and folly to downfall. The book is composed of six collections by unknown authors written over several centuries, and includes lectures, admonitions, hymns, prayers, examples, autobiographical narrative, and, yes, proverbs.

Psalms 37, 49, 73, 112, 127, 128, 133 and 1, 19, 119—various dates
This first group of psalms reflects on the issues of life in the manner of the longer Wisdom writings, occasionally in series of short sayings. The latter group tells us to meditate on the law—*torah*—and that Yhwh's precepts are "sweeter than honey." Psalms 37, 112, and 119 are acrostics.

The Wisdom of Jesus son of Sirach (also called **Ecclesiasticus**)—
180 BCE
Though well known among contemporaries, included in the Septuagint,
and cited in the Talmud, Sirach was not incorporated into Jewish scriptures, and so is part of the Apocrypha. Unlike other Wisdom writings,
Sirach includes a lengthy review of biblical history.

Wisdom of Solomon—37–41 CE
Writing in Greek, the anonymous author of this work assumed the persona of Solomon for a series of didactic exhortations in verse. Directed
toward Jews in the diaspora during the Greco-Roman period, Wisdom
of Solomon borrows cultural references from the surrounding pagan
culture to argue for the superiority of Judaism over paganism. Wisdom—
sophia in Greek—was cast in terms compatible with Greek philosophy.
This is the only Wisdom book to hint at an afterlife other than the traditional Sheol; it suggests judgment awaits all—but in a far distant future.

Wisdom's Two-Faced Women

Woman Wisdom

> Wisdom, the fashioner of all things, taught me. (WIS. 7:22)

The Bible's Woman Wisdom was not a person but a personification
of all the best qualities men sought to cultivate in themselves. Described in lofty terms that bore little relationship to flesh-and-blood
women, Woman Wisdom never lost the insubstantial quality of an abstract ideal. Lavished with the virtues of various ancient goddesses,
Woman Wisdom was a feminine counterpoint to Yhwh, exalted though
never quite deified.

She also was ubiquitous: Woman Wisdom appears as a significant
figure in the books of Proverbs, Sirach, and the Wisdom of Solomon.

Table 11.1: Wisdom Calls in Many Forms

Wisdom can be identified by its subject matter as well as certain elements of style: brevity, simplicity, wordplay, direct address, and moral earnestness expressed in basic terms. Additionally, certain kinds of writing are commonly associated with Wisdom.	
Admonition	An admonishment, usually in verse form, imparted by an authoritative teacher to a student. Can appear as a positive *command* (Prov. 8:33) or negative *prohibition*. (Prov. 22:22–23)
Allegory	A narrative that presents two levels of meanings: the literal or surface meaning; and a secondary, symbolic meaning that turns the characters and action into representatives of something else, often abstract ideas or historical events. (2 Sam. 12:1–12)
Autobiographical narrative or reflection	A sage's personal story used to enrich his teachings. (Sir. 33:16–18)
Diatribe	A Hellenistic rhetorical form in which a speaker engages an imaginary interlocutor and then responds to his reasoning. (Wis. 1:16–5:23)
Disputation	In Job, the lengthy monologues used to debate traditional assumptions about Wisdom are called disputations. Laments and legal language are part of the mix. (Job 4–31)
Fable	A type of allegory in the form of a short story that succinctly imparts an abstract moral thesis or truth about human behavior, often using plants or animals as characters. The moral may be summed up at the end in an epigram. (2 Kgs. 14:8–10)
Example	An illustration used to clarify a point. (Eccl. 4:13–16)
Exhortation	An urgent appeal or admonishment to learn Wisdom and to act accordingly. (Prov. 1:8)
Hymn	A psalm that praises a personification of wisdom. (Sir. 24:1–22)
Lecture	In Proverbs 1–9, a sage transmits his message in three-part blocks of verse composed of (1) a call to attention; (2) the lesson; and 3) a conclusion that sums up the lesson. (Prov. 1:8–19)

(continued)

Proverb	A statement of "truth" gained through personal experience, which is expressed in terse, imagistic, and memorable language. Used to instill values or to comment upon the past or present. (Sir. 20:20)	
Name list or *Onomasticon*	Lists of geographical, cosmological, or meteorological phenomena presented in verse form. (Wis. 7:17–20, 22–23)	
Riddle	A question requiring thought, often with an ambiguous answer. (Judg. 14:10–18)	
Saying, maxim	Like a proverb, a pithy statement of truth, but often without the metaphorical language. A maxim may be an ad hoc aphorism specific to a situation. (Judg. 8:2)	

Her attributes changed according to the time and place of composition, but sages universally portrayed her as a seductress who implored men to pursue her—solely for the wealth and status she endowed, of course.

We, too, will follow Woman Wisdom's trail through the books in which she prominently figures.

Woman Wisdom in Proverbs: Present at the Creation. In Proverbs, Wisdom plays "God's girl Friday." She declares,

> The LORD created me at the beginning of his work,
> the first of his acts of long ago.
> Ages ago I was set up,
> at the first, before the beginning of the earth.
> When he established the heavens, I was there,
> when he drew a circle on the face of the deep,
> then I was beside him, like a master worker;
> and I was daily his delight, (PROV. 8:22–23, 27, 30).

If Wisdom was the first of Yhwh's creations and a "master worker" involved in establishing the heavens, doesn't this suggest she has a quasi-divine nature? She was created by Yhwh, but she also was God's deputy or adjutant in further acts of creation. It's hard to know exactly what the sage who penned these verses was thinking, but two ideas are plain: the "listening heart" of Wisdom has been beating from the beginning and is best embodied by a woman.

As we will see, "God's girl Friday" is not the only hint of Wisdom's exalted status.

Woman Wisdom also is credited with making righteous monarchs possible. "By me kings reign, and rulers decree what is just; by me rulers rule, and nobles, all who govern rightly" (Prov. 8:15–16). To understand the significance of this declaration, it helps to know that the Egyptian goddess Ma'at was the source of Egypt's justice system. "Doing Ma'at" entailed being truthful, just, and righteous, and accepting the social order. Proverbs' rendition of Wisdom contains distinct echoes of Ma'at.

Furthermore, an Egyptian hymn to Ma'at, from the era when Proverbs was compiled, urged her to take up residence in the tongue and head of the king so that he would act justly. Doesn't that seem strangely similar to Solomon's request for "a listening heart"?

Proverbs also declares:

I, wisdom, live with prudence, and I attain knowledge and discretion.
I have good advice and sound wisdom;/I have insight, I have strength.
I love those who love me, and those who seek me diligently find me.

(PROV. 8:12, 14, 17)

Talk of this sort suggests that women had "relatively high status" in society during the period when Persia ruled Judah, and that wise women may have had "real social influence," says Bible scholar Claudia V. Camp.[3] Camp speculates that in the early years following the Exile, when society was re-forming around the family rather than the monarchy, mothers were equally as important as fathers in transmitting values and instructing offspring.

Camp also notes Proverbs' declaration that Wisdom can be found "beside the gates in front of the town" (Prov. 8:3), where the elders sat to hear lawsuits and render judgments. From this, Camp deduces that women's voices were heard and respected in the public arena.

I wish I could agree, but I'm skeptical. Women undoubtedly helped to shape future generations as returning exiles struggled to regroup; that is social influence of a sort. But were they publicly esteemed for this role? I doubt it. Women often serve as a kind of frontier between men and social chaos, notes Carol A. Newsom, coeditor of the *Women's Bible Commentary*. Yet men tend to view this civilizing force with ambivalence. Women are both "seen as part of chaos and a shield for the symbolic order against chaos."[4] As part of the threatening "chaos," they are reviled and pushed to the margins. Meanwhile, idealized feminine abstractions such as Woman Wisdom that arrest the chaos are venerated.

The simultaneous reviling and revering of women is a theme to which we will return.

Woman Wisdom in Sirach. The sage Yeshua ben El-azar ben Sira was greatly vexed by what he perceived as the dangers inherent in female sexuality. "Do you have daughters?" he asked. "Be concerned for their chastity" (Sir. 7:24). And he advised,

> Turn away your eyes from a shapely woman,
> and do not gaze at beauty belonging to another;
> many have been seduced by a woman's beauty,
> and by it passion is kindled like a fire. (SIR. 9:8)

Yet even as ben Sira counseled men to keep their distance from "loose" women, singing girls, virgins, prostitutes, and other men's wives (Sir. 9:1–9), his Woman Wisdom spoke like a seductive vixen.

> Come to me, you who desire me, and eat your fill of my fruits.
> For the memory of me is sweeter than honey,
>   and the possession of me sweeter than the honeycomb.

> Those who eat of me will hunger for more and those who
>   drink of me will thirst for more. (SIR. 24:19–21)

Passion, apparently, was okay *if* it was reserved for the (safely) disembodied Woman Wisdom, whom ben Sira called, variously, a bride, a mother, a wife, and Torah. Sirach advised those in search of Wisdom to

> put your feet into her fetters,
> and your neck into her collar . . .
> Come to her with all your soul (SIR. 6:24, 26).

Sirach's version of Woman Wisdom "sometimes takes on dangerous characteristics that men experience as problematic in ordinary women," notes Pamela M. Eisenbaum of the Iliff School of Theology.[5]

Notwithstanding his otherwise orthodox (and rather prudish) views, pagan goddess imagery also slipped into the sage's work. By the time that ben Sira wrote (around 180 BCE), devotion to the Egyptian goddess Isis had usurped much of Ma'at's prestige, and the sage's representation of Wisdom reflects this ascendancy of Isis as an international cult figure. Isis had long been Egypt's "throne goddess," and was considered the "mother" of the Egyptian king, much as ben Sira depicted Wisdom as a mother to the wise. Isis also was considered cunning, clever, and determined, not unlike Wisdom.

Furthermore, ben Sira's lengthy poem, "Praise of Wisdom," bears a strong resemblance to Greco-Roman hymns of the period that lauded Isis as creator of the world. Wisdom, among "the assembly of the Most High . . . and in the presence of his hosts," sings of her glory, asserting,

I came forth from the mouth of the Most High,
and covered the earth like a mist.

I dwelt in the highest heavens,
and my throne was in a pillar of cloud.
Alone I compassed the vault of heaven
and traversed the depths of the abyss.
Over waves of the sea, over all the earth,
and over every people and nation I have held sway." (SIR. 24:3–6)

Although ben Sira ultimately identified Wisdom with Torah, "the book of the covenant of the Most High God" (Sir. 24:23), the goddess imagery is unmistakable.

Wisdom as Sophia in the Wisdom of Solomon. Surrounded by multiple religious choices—from pagan gods and goddess cults to schools of Greek philosophy—Jews living outside of Judah in the first century CE found it difficult to remain loyal to their heritage. To counter these baleful influences, the unknown author (or authors) of the Wisdom of Solomon borrowed heavily from Hellenistic culture and Greek philosophy to promote Judaism as superior to all other religious paths.

In these writings, Woman Wisdom appeared quite openly in the garb of Isis. She mimicked Isis's patronage of the pharaoh and her relationship to the Egyptian sun god, Re.

Just as the Egyptian king reigned through the grace of Isis, Wisdom counseled, "If you delight in thrones and scepters, O monarchs over the peoples, honor wisdom, so that you may reign forever" (Wis. 6:21). "Solomon" acknowledged her Isis-like influence.

Because of her I shall have glory among the multitudes
and honor in the presence of the elders, though I am young.
I shall be found keen in judgment,
and in the sight of rulers I shall be admired. (WIS. 8:10–11)

Isis accompanied the sun god Re in his royal ship, and "[Wisdom] glorifies her noble birth by living with God,/and the Lord of all loves her" (Wis. 8:3). Woman Wisdom even appeared to share the throne of Yhwh: "Solomon" appealed to God to "give me the wisdom that sits by your throne . . . she who knows your works and was present when you made the world" (Wis. 9:4,9).

What is more, a lengthy narrative poem depicted Wisdom intervening on behalf of Yhwh's righteous followers throughout the ages— Adam, Noah, Abraham, and Jacob, among others—thus displacing Yhwh as ultimate liberator. Even the story of the Israelites escaping from Egypt underwent radical revision:

A holy people and blameless race wisdom delivered from a nation
    of oppressors.
She brought them over the Red Sea, and led them through deep waters;
but she drowned their enemies, and cast them up from the depth of
    the sea. (WIS. 10:15, 18–19)

"Solomon's" litany of Wisdom's saving acts is all the more remarkable because it emphasized certain details to demonstrate just how Isis-like Wisdom was.

"Solomon's" version of Woman Wisdom also reflected the influence of Hellenistic philosophy.[6] Although Proverbs and ben Sira said Woman Wisdom was created "at the beginning of [Yhwh's] work, the first of his acts of long ago" (Prov. 8:22), now she was "all-powerful, overseeing all, and penetrating through all spirits that are intelligent, pure, and altogether subtle" (Wis. 7:23). These ideas derived from the Stoic belief that God is not separate from the world but pervades it, acting as its mind.

Why did "Solomon" adopt the vernacular of Egyptian popular religion and Hellenistic philosophy in depicting Wisdom? Writings that employed a philosophical framework conferred intellectual respectability on Egyptian Jews and endowed them with the status of their gentile peers, says Sarah J. Tanzer in the *Women's Bible Commentary*. Clothing Wisdom in the garb of a goddess also offered Jews the sort of personal relationship with a deity that had come into vogue throughout the Mediterranean region by the first century CE.

Perhaps it was this prevalence of *thea-logy*—goddess-talk—that left no room in the wisdom of Solomon for the other female figure ordinarily found in Wisdom teachings: the Strange Woman. To her, we now turn.

The Strange Woman

Creeping through the pages of Proverbs and Sirach is an icon of ill-repute so evil that her "feet go down to death; her steps follow the path to Sheol" (Prov. 5:5). She was said to prey upon the naive young men whose reputations, careers, and future wealth sages labored so hard to protect. Bible translators give this creature multiple designations—strange, loose, forbidden—or simply call her "the adulteress." (The Hebrew word is *zarah*.) Whatever her name, she was the paradigmatic floozy, especially dangerous because she used language exceptionally well to trap her prey.

> For the lips of a forbidden woman drip honey;
> Her mouth is smoother than oil;
> But in the end she is as bitter as wormwood,
> Sharp as a two-edged sword. (PROV. 5:3–4)

The Strange Woman was so powerful that "those who go to her never come back" (Prov. 2:19). "She is loud and wayward," waiting in the street to entrap young men "without sense," enticing them to return home with her by saying, "My husband is not at home" (Prov. 7:11,7,19).

Linked to the Strange Woman, often in the same verses, is the alien or foreign woman (*nokriyyah* in Hebrew). In the minds of the sages, these two deviant women merged together into one monstrous enemy.

Where did they get this stuff? What were they so afraid of?

Some scholars believe that the sages who wrote Proverbs were simply rabid on the subject of "foreignness." As a colony of Persia following the Exile, Judea was host to all manner of alien practices. Intermarriage was a particularly prickly matter. The priest Ezra reported that when he arrived in Jerusalem with fellow exiles around 458 BCE and discovered that Israelites had married local women, he promptly forced the men to divorce their "foreign" wives (Ezra 9–10).

"Foreign" husbands were not at issue, which suggests that although men ruled, women were credited with teaching children basic values. Foreign wives might infect their offspring with alien ideas, pagan worship in particular. Male children of aliens might inherit family land that could, in another generation of intermarriage, pass into the hands of non-Israelite tribes.

Other scholars focus on the uncontrolled sexuality implied by the epithets "strange" and "alien." They speculate that the sages were concerned about adulterous practices that could have resulted in one man's child being born to another man's wife. Bastards created all sorts of inheritance and status problems in the ancient world.

Or, perhaps the strange-alien woman was merely one who lacked a proper social category. She might have been a divorcee, or separated from or abandoned by her husband. With her sexuality no longer guarded or regulated by a man, she was a threat to the social order.

To Carol Newsom, the Strange Woman was less about real women, foreign or otherwise, and more about a convenient symbol for everything that was "other," out of bounds, and socially lethal.

To argue *for* a particular path also means you are arguing *against* another way of being, Newsom points out. The sages contrasted virtue and evildoing the better to define the meaning of virtue and declare its superiority. They designated the Strange Woman as most fully embodying the path not taken.

Wisdom writings, therefore, offer us sexual politics at its most re-fined: a world constructed by and for men where virtue was represented by an unattainable feminine ideal (Woman Wisdom) and evil by ordi-nary female allure.

Good Wives and Wise Women

As if to balance the derogatory figure of the Strange Woman in Proverbs, an editor appended to the end of the collection an "oracle" ascribed to the mother of a king named Lemuel and addressed to her son. (Neither figure is historical.) The first nine verses of this oracle, Proverbs 31:1–9, advise the king to stay away from women and wine, and to speak on behalf of the poor. These are the only instructions in Proverbs attributed to a mother.

Then, suddenly, the point of view shifts to praise for the "capable wife."

> What a rare find is a capable wife!
> Her worth is far beyond that of rubies.
> Her husband puts his confidence in her,
> And lacks no good thing. (PROV. 31:10–11, JPS)

The poem goes on to describe all that a good wife does for her husband and family—from a man's perspective. "Capable wife" often is trans-lated as "woman of valor," though the Hebrew (*eshet hayil*) actually de-notes strength, perhaps meaning strength of character.[7]

The "capable wife" of the poem is more of a flesh-and-blood woman than Woman Wisdom, yet she, too, appears to be an ideal type. This wife sees to it that her family never wants for food or clothing. She sells her weavings and is generous to the poor. In fact, this woman is so energetic, she seems completely unreal—until I think of my great-grandmother Ana Lydia Walter. Ana gave birth to twelve children, eleven of whom survived childhood. When her husband died young, she became the head of the household, supported by her grown children who worked in the local textile/mills. She kept a cow, pigs, and chickens; foraged for wild greens, nuts, and mushrooms; and knew how to heal with herbs. She began every day by baking bread in her kitchen's massive coal stove and served a full dinner at noon to her offspring. Ana continued to preside over the family home until one day, at the age of eighty-six, she set out two freshly baked pies to cool, took off her apron, sat down in the parlor rocker for her morning repose, and did not get up again.

"Let her works praise her in the city gates" (Prov. 31:31).

To see Wisdom actually enacted by a woman in the Bible, however, we must turn from the designated Wisdom books and look in the Former Prophets (2 Sam. 14 and 20), where characters described as "wise women" appear in tales from both the north and south, Israel and Judah. If biblical authors could use the term "wise woman" (the JPS translators say "clever") and assume that their audiences would not find it odd, then we may safely assume that actual women played such a role in their towns or clans.

Consider, for example, the wise woman of the city of Abel in Beth-maacah (2 Sam 20:14–22), who prevented the destruction of her town by negotiating with the general laying siege to it. The "wise woman"— otherwise unidentified—shouted to the general, Joab, from the city wall to get his attention, then presented her credentials: "I am one of those who are peaceable and faithful in Israel" (v. 19). With great persuasive power, she argued that to destroy their town was to destroy "a city that is a mother in Israel" (v. 19).

Joab, for his part, seemed to have no problem bargaining with a woman; he simply laid out his terms. To save her town, she must aid his mission: find and kill the pretender to King David's throne who had taken refuge in Abel of Beth-maacah.

So confident was the woman that the townspeople would follow her lead that she said to Joab, "His head shall be thrown over the wall to you" (20:21). And, without further discussion, the townspeople did exactly that. Joab then decamped, leaving the town walls intact.

From this we can deduce that some matriarchs assumed the roles of town elders, royal diplomats, and court sages, says Claudia V. Camp, who goes so far as to suggest that "we should infer a significant degree of training and experience in positions of leadership."[8]

The possibility that there were female sages truly has a worth "far beyond that of rubies."

Ecclesiastes: A Message for Our Time

What do people gain from all the toil at which they toil under the sun?

A generation goes, and a generation comes, but the earth remains forever.

(ECCL. 1:3–4)

Experience has taught me that just when I begin to think the Bible is too far removed from the twenty-first century to be of any use, I'll find something that fits like a glove. Ecclesiastes is like that. It challenges the commonplaces promulgated in other Wisdom books (Job excepted). There is no Strange Women or Woman Wisdom in Ecclesiastes; just profound reflections on the meaning of life.

Perhaps the key to Ecclesiastes' relevance is that it was written in an era not unlike our own.

Its author, who took the pen name of the Teacher (*Qohelet* in Hebrew), lived sometime between 250 and 200 BCE. Although he repeatedly said, "There is nothing new under the sun," barely a century earlier Alexander the Great and his armies had pushed the Persians out of power and established new empires ruled over by Alexander's generals.

The Greeks brought a new international culture called Hellenism, an amalgam of Greek values, languages, and modes of thinking blended with local cultures. An influx of cosmopolitan Greek speakers began to remake the conquered territories with Greek architecture, philosophy, and social norms. Entire cities—Alexandria in Egypt, for example—sprang up or were remade on the Greek model, with amphitheaters, temples, market squares, and gymnasia.

Hellenism also introduced agricultural technologies that required slaves to maintain. Commerce and commercial manufacturing burgeoned, making independent artisans and household production of goods superfluous. The provincial elite embraced these exciting new trends that had the potential to make them even wealthier.

Many Jews in Palestine, Egypt, and other Greek colonies drank deeply of Hellenism. In reaction, theocrats in Jerusalem circled the wagons and tightened boundaries against religious "outsiders." They also appropriated the meager resources of the peasantry to maintain their entrenched temple hierarchy. Ordinary people ended up with few choices.

Perhaps this is why the Teacher sounded so weary of life, which he proclaimed to be *hebel,* a word translated as "vanity" or "utter futility," but which literally means "breath, air, or vapor." "Vanity of vanities," says the Teacher, "vanity of vanities! All is vanity" (Eccl. 1:1).

Apparently the teacher found life ephemeral, without substance, and inexplicable. He also grumbled over the burdens of life, such as the enslaving toil that took the product of one's work and handed it over to others. He lamented that "in the place of justice, wickedness was there" (Eccl. 3:16) and that the system of divine retribution, whereby good and evil people are rewarded or punished according to their deeds, was broken. He wept for the oppressed and wailed at the power of their oppressors. He even kvetched that a good woman was hard to find!

And then you die. "All go to one place; all are from the dust, and all turn to dust again" (Eccl. 3:20).

The Teacher was angry with a society in thrall to Hellenism, and he found the traditional theological answers inadequate. Yet he could not quite envision an alternative. How, then, was he to live? His ultimate conclusion—reiterated six times throughout the book—may surprise you.

> There is nothing better for mortals than to eat and drink, and find
> enjoyment in their toil. This also, I saw, is from the hand of God.
>
> (ECCL. 2:24)[9]

Although the Teacher's response might not sound deep or imaginative, Mexican theologian Elsa Tamez finds in the Teacher's words a radical response to the dehumanizing reality in which he lived. To take pleasure in the small details of life entails living "by a contrary logic. That is, to live as human beings who feel that they are alive, in a society that does not allow them to live because of its demands for productivity and efficiency."[10] The Teacher asserted that even in the midst of the *hebel* of exploited labor, we *can* live a meaningful life.

Temple piety was noticeably absent from the Teacher's prescription. While he spoke earnestly of God, he said that "God has long ago approved what you do" (Eccl. 9:7). His logic cut the legs out from under the rationale for the temple hierarchy and its rituals.

As the Teacher worked his way through to his radical conclusion, he did not ignore the value of Wisdom nor counsel indifference to suffering. Nor was he fatalistic; yet, he saw that "the race is not to the swift, nor the battle to the strong . . . but time and chance happen to them all" (Eccl. 9:11).

Initially, the Teacher blamed his feeling of *hebel* on humankind, who spoiled God's perfect creation. Then he announced that God was responsible for everything, including his own misery. Ultimately, the Teacher recognized "how the righteous and the wise and their deeds are in the hand of God" (Eccl. 9:1). Humans cannot penetrate the mystery that is God but must learn to fear God (Eccl. 5:7), that is, to cultivate respect and awe. As Tamez points out, when we "fear" God—acknowledge God's power—we can live fully, because God is in control. Any worry on our part is unnecessary.

Though the Teacher had little use for traditional pieties, his profound faith and pragmatic prescription to live fully in the face of futility can be invaluable to us in the twenty-first century. Although our world is smaller, in many ways, than ever before, the problems facing us are monumental. The Teacher tells us to enjoy what we do not *despite* the suffering but *because* of it. For most Westerners, his advice to appreciate life's simple pleasures is an antidote to our excessive materialism. To those who could benefit from more material security, the Teacher extends a safety line of trust in God. Not a passive trust, but one deeply aware that there is a power greater than the world's princes and principalities. Life may be *hebel*, the Teacher says, but God's justice ultimately will prevail.

Tutorial: "The End of an Unrighteous Generation is Grievous"

One of the sages' most oft-repeated teachings was that the righteous were rewarded and evildoers received their just desserts. Here's how the author of the Wisdom of Solomon expressed this belief.

> But the ungodly will be punished as their reasoning deserves,
> those who disregarded the righteous and rebelled against the Lord;
> for those who despise wisdom and instruction are miserable.
> Their hope is vain, their labors are unprofitable, and their works
>   are useless.
> Their wives are foolish, and their children evil; their offspring are
>   accursed. (WIS. 3:10–13)

He went on to assert that "the end of an unrighteous generation is grievous" (Wis. 3:19).

Do you believe the wrongdoers are inevitably punished? Is this the way you have seen things play out in the lives of those you know? Do you see the hand of God in what you have observed?

As in the excerpt above, "Solomon" maintains that even the offspring of the "foolish" will not prosper.

> But children of adulterers will not come to maturity,
> and the offspring of an unlawful union will perish.
> Even if they live long they will be held of no account,
> and finally their old age will be without honor. (WIS. 3:16–17)

Do you agree with this? Why do you believe as you do? Why do you think "Solomon" focused on adultery as "ungodly"?

The other side of the sages' equation was that "the fruit of good labors is renowned, and the root of understanding does not fail" (Wis. 3:15). "Solomon" noted that the godly may be afflicted,

> But the souls of the righteous are in the hand of God, and no
> torment will ever touch them.
> For though in the sight of others they were punished, their hope
> is full of immortality.
> Having been disciplined a little, they will receive great good,
> because God tested them and found them worthy of himself.
>
> (WIS. 3:1, 4–5)

Do you think hardship is an expression of God's discipline? How do you explain suffering? Are there rewards for living righteously? What might they be?

Punishment and rewards are provocative topics. Ask others what they think about these teachings, just to see what responses you get. You won't be known for boring conversations.

WISDOM'S HALL OF SHAME

The Bible's Wisdom teachings were gold mines of guidance for social climbers. Take this example—one of hundreds—from Sirach: "When an influential person invites you, be reserved, and he will invite you more insistently" (Sir. 13:9). Proverbs and Sirach also contain numerous nuggets of common sense, such as, "Fools think their own way is right, but the wise listen to advice" (Prov. 12:15).

Alas, the sages could be wildly misogynist as well. Believing that forewarned is forearmed, here are ten of their worst insults.

If you get ticked off by their cavalier manner, then respond to them in kind. Celebrate women with pithy sayings or, if it will make you feel better, turn the tables and come up with something equally sexist about men. Why not write your contribution on a sticky note and cover over the passages in the Bible that belittle women.

> It is a disgrace to be the father of an undisciplined son,/and the birth of a daughter is a loss. (Sir. 22:3)
> There is no venom worse than a snake's venom/and no anger worse than a woman's wrath. (Sir. 25:15)
> Any iniquity is small compared to a woman's iniquity;/may a sinner's lot befall her! (Sir. 25:19)
> Like a gold ring in a pig's snout is/a beautiful woman without good sense. (Prov. 11:22)
> A continual dripping on a rainy day/and a contentious wife are alike;/to restrain her is to restrain the wind/or to grasp oil in the right hand. (Prov. 27:15–16)
> It is better to live in a corner of the housetop/than in a house shared with a contentious wife. (Prov. 21:9)
> Drooping hands and weak knees/come from the wife who does not make her husband happy. (Sir. 25:23)
> A sandy ascent for the feet of the aged—/such is a garrulous wife to a quiet husband. (Sir. 25:20)
> Any wickedness, but not the wickedness of a woman! (Sir. 25:13)
> The mouth of a loose woman is a deep pit;/he with whom the LORD is angry falls into it. (Prov. 22:14)

WHERE ARE THE WOMEN IN WISDOM?

Woman Wisdom	Prov. 1:20–33; 8:1–9:6
	Sir. 1:1–20; 4:11–19; 6:18–31;
	14:20–15:10, 24:1–29
	Wisdom 6:12–25; 7:7–9:18
	Baruch 3:9–4:4
The Strange Woman	Prov. 2:16–19; 5:1–23;
	6:20–35; 7:1–27; 23:27–28
	Sir. 9:1–9
Wives and Mothers	Prov. 1:8–9; 14:1; 15:25; 18:22;
	19:13–14; 19:26; 20:20; 23:22–25;
	29:15; 30:21–23; 31:10–31
	Sir. 7:26; 23:22–27; 25:16–26; 26:1–9,
	13–18; 36:26–30; 42:6
	Wisdom. 3:10–13
Daughters	Sir. 7:24–25; 22:3–5; 26:10–12; 42:9–14
Children	Prov. 13:1, 24; 19:18
	Sir. 7:23; 30:1–13

12

THE OTHER HALF
OF HISTORY

Some years ago, I read of an extraordinary discovery of dinosaur remains in China. It was notable because the skeleton was 90 percent intact. Typically, to locate 60 percent of a specimen is considered good. "Sixty percent," I thought at the time. "What if women had 60 percent of their story in the Bible?" And then I wondered how much of our story is in the Bible: 5 percent? 2 percent? 0.5 percent?

On good days, I say 5 percent. In an attempt to account for the other 95 percent, this chapter draws on archaeological discoveries, research on preindustrial societies, and the Bible itself to depict the daily life of women in Ancient Israel.

Regrettably, there are large gaps—particularly when it comes to women's religious practices—and because society changed over time, no one model suffices. Most women, perhaps 90 percent, however, lived on the land in extended families that farmed and herded for subsistence. While they were undoubtedly affected by regional shifts in power, fundamentally they survived by doing the same things year in and year out for much of the first millennium BCE.

Let's imagine what village life might have been like for an Israelite woman.

A Day in the Life

First of all, the average woman would be young, because females generally did not live past thirty due to the stresses of childbearing. Her husband might live until he was forty, but not her or his other wives. Let's say she is seventeen. She probably has conceived twice already, but, most likely, only one child still lives. That's how it was: Only half the babies lived to conceive babies themselves. Yhwh willing, more babies would come (although Israelite women had, on average, only four children), because many hands were needed to help farm the arid, rocky land and tend the flocks of sheep and goats. Boy children especially were valued, since they could drive the oxen that pulled the plow on the steep, terraced slopes.

We'll suppose this woman has lived on a wooded plateau in the highlands north of Jerusalem ever since she was married at fourteen to a man at least ten years older than she was. The marriage was arranged by an aunt who knew of the man through her husband's family. He was, of course, a member of the same clan, and her father was pleased with the nice bride price the groom was able to pay—livestock, a sickle, and several other iron implements.

The woman lives with her husband's family now, because that's what women do after marrying. Their small hamlet contains almost one hundred inhabitants, all of them related in some fashion to her husband's father, now deceased, or his uncle, who has assumed leadership of the family. It is a prosperous community: They have good water year round and Uncle is careful to set grain aside from each harvest, in case of a drought. They are close enough to Jerusalem that they can trade surplus oil or wine for such things as knife blades, beads, and scented oils.

The young woman and her husband live in a plastered, two-story house along with two young nephews and their widowed mother.

The first floor of the house is native stone, the second story of mud-brick, and it shares a courtyard, bounded by a low stone wall, with two adjacent residences. These are occupied by her husband's married brothers, their wives, and children. Her widowed mother-in-law, who is now blind, lives with one of the brothers. The priest who sees to the family's religious rituals lives with Uncle, who also has several servants.

She doesn't see her own family very often; it is a half day's walk to their village and, even if she didn't have the baby, her mother-in-law wants her close by. The old woman may be blind, but she still directs the work that the other women do, including Uncle's wife, who thinks she ought to be overseeing things now. Anyway, her mother died last year, along with her younger brother, in the pestilence that took a third of the village children.

The workday begins early. Her husband rises first to feed and water the oxen and donkey. Afterwards, he mucks out their stalls while the older nephew milks the nanny goats. The young woman, meanwhile, nurses and cleans up the baby, then assembles the breakfast of dried figs, goat cheese, and flatbread made the previous evening. When she sets the food out on mats in the courtyard, household members eat quickly, dipping their dry bread into shallow bowls of olive oil.

While her aunt clears away the remains of the meal and her younger boy watches the baby, the young woman takes a goatskin pouch and a *kad* (a pottery water jar) and begins the walk uphill from the village to the spring. In the summer, she will rely on well water and the stored rainwater in their cistern, but the rainy season has just ended, and the spring still flows. The walk is worth it: The water there is sweet, unlike the harsh well water.

Besides, she will probably meet her sisters-in-law on the way, giving them an opportunity to talk without the presence of the older women.

By the time the young woman returns to the compound, her husband has yoked the oxen and her nephew has herded the sheep and goats into the courtyard. She gives the skin of water to her husband. Barley harvest is underway. It's hot and dusty work, but its yield will carry the livestock through the hot months when the pasture dries up. Meanwhile, the many varieties of wheat—emmer and eikorn, hard and soft wheat—are ripening.

The young woman nurses the baby again, then turns him over to one of her young nieces, who has arrived leading her mother-in-law. The girl will watch the baby in the shade of the fig tree, where they've rolled out a mat. She brings her niece a reed fan to swat away the flies that buzz around the baby, and hopes the child remembers to use it.

Her mother-in-law will share the shade, swinging a skin full of goat's milk suspended by rope from a tree branch. This churning action will produce *leban*, the protein-rich curds that will be used for lunch. It's a spring treat: The goats recently gave birth and still have their milk. The older woman will also be listening to the comings and goings in the courtyard, questioning everyone on what they are doing to make sure it's done right.

The other women in the family, along with their daughters, have started to work in the garden adjacent to the compound where the family grows their leeks, greens, lentils, chickpeas, and fava beans. (The nephew who isn't yet old enough to follow the herds helps by picking caterpillars and other pests off the plants.)

The young woman's job for the morning, however, is to make bread for everyone's lunch. Pushing open the heavy wooden door to her house, she steps over the raised block of native limestone that serves as a threshold and enters the ground floor. It takes a moment for her eyes to adjust to the dimness. Not much sunlight can find its way through the narrow slits in the stone walls that serve as windows, but even blindfolded she'd know where she was from the odor of livestock combined with damp earth and old wood.

The oak beam ceiling is low, a little over six feet high, and supported by two rows of five stone pillars. On her right, large stone troughs occupy the spaces between pillars, crafting off a corral for the animals. The donkey is tethered there now; the oxen will join him when they are returned from the field in the evening. The remainder of the area provides a nighttime home for the sheep and goats. A rounded stone bin built into the stall wall holds barley for the livestock. While the main part of the room has a floor of packed earth, the corral is paved with flagstones lined with straw.

The young woman walks past a cooking pit in the floor, marked by a broad hearth stone perhaps three feet wide. It is cold and dark; in good weather, she cooks outside where the smoke from the fire can go up, and not into her eyes. Lined up against the adjacent wall are dozens of tall, four-handled ceramic jars, called *nebels,* each big enough to hold about seven gallons of oil or a bushel of grain. Most are empty, waiting for this year's harvest. But she is looking for one of the smaller, shorter jars, a *kad,* that holds the flour she and her sisters-in-law ground yesterday.

A doorway at the back of the main room leads into a mud-plastered room that runs the width of the house, although it is only as deep as the span of her arms. Tools and ropes are stacked to the right, and tack hangs from pegs in the wall. To the left are *kads,* jugs, and pitchers, some containing foodstuffs, others waiting to be filled. Locating the flour, she takes an ample wooden bowl, pours the flour into it, and adds salt from another container. She rests the bowl against her hip and picks up a small jar containing leaven, then goes out into the courtyard again. With water from the *kad* that she filled earlier, she kneads the flour, salt, and leaven into dough, covers it with a rush mat, and leaves it to rise.

Now it's time to build the fire in the depression under the clay oven in the courtyard, using scraps of thorn bushes and olive pits left from last season's oil pressing. When the fire burns down to coals, the oven will be ready. Momentarily, she sits by her baby's grandmother in the shade and takes her turn swinging the churn. The baby naps under a coverlet of wool. (Her mother carded and washed that wool again and again to make it soft enough for the child.)

Two of her "sisters" come into the compound from the garden. Time to make the bread! The young woman punches down the dough in the bowl, then she and the others pinch off large balls. One by one, she flattens the balls on a smooth, wooden frame, which she hands to the others. One has already removed the stone seal from the top of the oven, which is shaped like a beehive and stands about waist high. With a swift movement, her sister-in-law presses the flattened dough onto an interior wall of the oven, where it adheres and quickly bakes. Her nephew has fetched a shallow basket, and he helps her pile the finished breads into it.

The baby is awake and crying, so the young mother nurses him while the others finish the baking. Then they disappear into their houses to assemble the other ingredients of the lunch: more figs, perhaps some parched grain, olives, and the spring onions just pulled from the garden. Most of the curds will go into jugs for the men and boys to share. Her older nephew appears, sent by the men from the fields to gather lunch. Her sisters-in-law will help him carry the food, stay to eat, then return with the empty containers.

The young woman has just enough time before her own lunch to start preparing the grain for tonight's dinner and tomorrow's bread. She drags the heavy basalt grinding slabs out of the house and into the shade of the fig tree. Using bread wheat retrieved from one of the underground storage pits in the courtyard, she places several handfuls on the concave lower stone. Then she places the upper stone on top and pushes it back and forth to husk, crack, and crush the grain. Later, she or another one of the women will turn most of the crushed grain into flour, using the three-legged basalt mortar and pestle.

Finally she stops for lunch with the others, nursing the baby as she drinks *leban* from a small wooden bowl. One of the girls is helping the old woman with her food. Afterward, while her mother-in-law naps and the baby sleeps, her nephew helps her clear away the dishes. Then he, too, lies down for a nap. Her sister-in-law takes over the grinding, the hardest chore, which requires hours of work each day. The younger woman picks up the pestle. At least she can work in the shade. It's early in the year, and the heat is not at its worst. When the other women return, they will help.

By midafternoon, the grinding is done, she has fetched water again, and dinner is under way, sending the scent of spice and smoke into the breeze. The cracked wheat that did not become flour has gone into a large copper kettle along with leeks, coriander leaves, and black cumin. She's added some pungent spring greens that grow near the spring. The food will simmer over the fire in the courtyard cooking pit until the men return from the fields. In the meantime, her nephew is busy at the dung heap at the far end of the garden, shaping dung into round, flat cakes. Dried in the sun, the cakes will make good cooking fuel.

Once again, the young woman mixes dough and sets it to rise. Now comes the least favorite of her chores. She approaches her mother-in-law, who hands her a fine-toothed comb made of bone. As she kneels, the old woman loosens her hair and the younger woman begins to pull the comb through the long, gray locks. She's looking for lice and their eggs, and Mother is not very patient with her work.

Before long, however, the baby wakes, and she stops to feed him. Afterward, Mother gives her permission to go work on her weaving. So, the young woman takes the baby and goes up the steep flight of stone steps alongside the house to the second story, where the family sleeps and takes shelter during the rainy season. Without the columns and with slightly larger windows, the room seems larger and airier than the ground floor. Yet she could cover the length of its plastered floor in ten paces, and the ceiling height is no more than seven feet.

A loom leans against the far wall, its partially completed weaving stretched from the horizontal beam supported by two wooden uprights. The woolen warp threads run from the top beam to the bottom, threaded through clay weights that hold them taut. After placing the baby on a blanket on the floor, the young woman sits on a low stool made of split rush woven over a wooden frame. She's always enjoyed weaving. It's a peaceful occupation and it creates a thing of lasting beauty, not like the meals that must be made over and over again.

Carding and spinning are more tedious, but they help pass the long hours of the rainy season, when the courtyard becomes a sea of mud. Plus, the oil in the wool soothes the cracked skin of her hands. Next to the loom is a tall basket of yarn skeins that she has spun. Another basket is full of carded wool that is as puffy as the clouds. She hopes to turn it into yarn fine enough for her husband to trade for dates from Jordan River palms when he travels to the Jerusalem market with lambs for the spring festival.

Keeping one eye on the baby, the young woman sends the coil of weft yarn back and forth, until her mother-in-law's sharp voice calls her name. Time to join the other women, who by the smell of things must be baking bread. The men and boys will be back soon, she thinks and as she rounds the corner of the house she hears the sheep and goats making their way toward the compound. Suddenly, the courtyard is filled with the bleats and barks of livestock and dogs. Her husband, his brothers, and the field servants have returned. The oxen drink from the courtyard trough where the men splash themselves to remove a coating of dust from the barley fields. Dinnertime!

The young woman rushes to nurse the baby before joining the other women, who are lifting the kettle off the fire. They pour its thick stew-like contents onto a large platter, then top it with the remains of the curds. Two of them carry the platter to an assortment of rush mats. The men and boys eat; then the women finish the stew by scooping it up with pieces of the fresh bread that they wash down with cups of wine.

Tonight there is a treat following the meal. One of the sisters-in-law has made small cakes with the last of her raisins and *dibs,* a syrup made from figs. With thick clusters of grapes already appearing on the vines, a good harvest seems likely, so using up last year's crop doesn't seem too extravagant.

Sundown approaches as the women clear away the food and put aside the bread for tomorrow's breakfast. The young woman has the baby in her arms, her mother-in-law having left for her night's rest, so it is slow going. As she works, her husband and nephew bed down the livestock by the light of small olive oil lamps set into wall niches. Later in the spring, when the flocks must travel far afield for good grazing, the men will sleep under the stars. But tonight, they will unroll mats and coverlets inside. The widow and her boys are already stretched out upstairs. Perhaps there will be a few moments to exchange news with her husband before they drift off to sleep. There's not much time, however; the sun rises early and so must she.

Not every day was like this one. Some days there was *more* work. When the figs ripened all at once, they had to be laid out to dry and protected from animals and pests. There would be olives to harvest and cure or press into oil, grapes to turn into wine, and nuts to sort or shell or store. From time to time, when a goat or sheep was slaughtered, its hide had to be scraped, soaked, cured, and then cut and stitched, to repair a tent or to make a tool or container. And there would be no clothing or warm coverlets unless wool was carded, spun, and woven.

Certain chores may have felt less taxing, such as a day's outing with the other women and the children to the stream bed where rushes grew. Over the ensuing months, the women would peel long strips of the dried rushes, soak them, and weave them into storage baskets. On other occasions, the women sought out the thick and sticky clay, from which they shaped cooking vessels and storage jars. Dried in the sun, and perhaps burnished with red ocher, the pots would then be fired in a kiln of mud bricks, which took two to three days of round-the-clock fire tending. Periodically, women also made soap from plants or from fats mixed with natural sources of potassium and alkalis.

As you can see, there was rarely a time when women's hands were not occupied—spinning, or weeding, or cooking, or rubbing the soft belly of one of the babies to persuade her to sleep.

HEALTH AND HEALING IN ANCIENT ISRAEL

If, despite all the hard work, village existence sounds appealing in its simplicity, we should note other facts of ancient life. "Mother" would not have been the only one whose head and body hair was infested with lice. Archaeologists have recovered a number of fine-toothed combs of ivory and bone that were used to extract lice, some with lice eggs still embedded in the teeth.

Then there was the prevalence of tapeworms and whipworms, which caused diarrhea and malabsorption of food. "The combination of hot climate, poor hygiene, and polluted water created a breeding ground for parasitic diseases," say Philip J. Stager and Lawrence E. Page, the authors of *Life in Biblical Israel*.[1]

Blindness like "Mother's" is commonly mentioned in the Bible and was probably the result of trachoma, an infection of the conjunctiva and cornea, which was transmitted by poor hygiene and flies.[2] Acute infectious diseases (indicated by the Hebrew word *maggephah,* which is usually translated "plague" or "pestilence") might sweep through a village, decimating its population, as numerous plague stories in the Pentateuch suggest. Skeletons reveal that Israelites also suffered from arthritis, tuberculosis, septic infections, and cancer.

In general, ancient Israel did not have the same command of healing arts as did the cultures of Egypt and Mesopotamia. Stager and Page report that diagnoses were "left to the priests," and physicians did not gain respect until after the Exile.[3] Generally, the Bible presents illness as punishment for violating the commandments, and infertility as God's work.

Since by default the home was the center of health care, women may have stepped into the breach with herbal cures. (We know, for example, that the ancient Israelites used as medicines the resin of terebinth trees, myrrh, and the pulp of wild gourds, a powerful purgative.) For the most part, however, this is another area for which we lack information about women's contributions.

Israelite Women: The Facts of Life

As my portrait of rural village life suggests, women in ancient Israel did not have a place outside of the family, and their world generally was limited to the roles of worker, wife, and mother.

- Males (in ancient Israel called *ba'al,* "lord") headed the household, told its members what to do, and allocated its resources. This arrangement would later be called *patriarchy*.

- Israelites were expected to marry close blood relatives. Exceptions were so rare that they merited mention: for example, when Moses permitted Israelite warriors to spare every young Midianite women "who has not had carnal relations with a man" (Nu. 31:18, JPS), apparently with an eye to replenishing the supply of marriageable women.
- Women left their *bet 'ab*, father's house, for their husband's, and became members of the man's family.
- Descent and inheritance was reckoned through the man's family, just as it is in the modern West.
- The household might also shelter several wives. Polygeny seems to have diminished with urbanization, but kings such as David had multiple wives, and Israelite law accommodated the practice.
- Lastly, women lived with a *joint-family*: Several generations lived together or in adjacent houses and held property in common under the direction of the head male.[4] The strain of such arrangement should not be underestimated, and probably accounted for the stringent incest regulations encoded in Israelite law.

Given these conditions, it would be easy to assume that women were captives of male authority with little personal power. Yet while labor in the rural joint-family was divided along gender lines, "Israelite women exercised control over critical aspects of household life," says Carol Meyers, professor of Bible and archaeology at Duke University.[5] Their labor, she concludes, was necessary for survival and therefore valued equally with the men's. "Male authority existed in certain spheres but there was no connotation of misogyny, the oppression of females, or the notion of female inferiority."[6]

Power, Authority, and Influence

Myers's work refers to "female power" and "male authority," and it's important to note that power and authority are not synonymous. Authority is "the right to make a particular decision and to command obedience."[7] Power "is the ability to act effectively on persons or things"— even though one might not have been given the right to do so.[8] In other words, there is a difference between authority legitimated by others and power gained through informal influence.[9]

In the Bible, we find women exercising considerable power despite lack of authority. Bathsheba, for example one of King David's wives, enlisted a court prophet and a general to lobby David to appoint her son, Solomon, as his successor. Only David had the authority to designate his heir, but the wife used what power she had to influence his choice. (She succeeded.)

Sociologist Michelle Zimbalist Rosaldo reminds us that male authority generally is taken for granted, but when women exercise power they frequently are viewed as "manipulative, disruptive, illegitimate, or unimportant."[10] This accounts for the prominence in the Bible of female *trickster figures,* morally ambiguous folktale characters of low status who use any means necessary to get what they want. The midwives in Exodus who lied to the pharaoh, for example, were classic tricksters, as was Tamar, who solicited sex from her father-in-law.

City Women

As urban centers grew in size and importance and the royal court weakened the power of the clans, a new social structure developed. Some women became the equivalent of employees, living near royal palaces or the homes of the elite and serving as personal maids, bakers, perfume makers, seamstresses, and, yes, concubines.

Then there were the wives of the cooks, scribes, metalworkers, potters, horse wranglers, leatherworkers, and others who supplied the palace with its goods. The village household was self-sufficient, but households in town could not be. Instead of having multigenerational families made up of people related by marriage or blood, urban households were relatively small. Women who played a critical role in the economy of village life found their influence limited in the towns and were at greater risk of being left without family to provide for them. Though city women's lives might have lacked some of the hardships of villages, Carol Meyers suggests that without the mutual interdependence of village life, gender differences became more sharply defined.[11]

After the Exile

The Exile may have reversed this trend. Israelites who returned to Judah after 539 BCE no longer had a king or royal court, and cities were smaller and less important. As a result, the self-sufficient, joint-family household reemerged as the centerpoint of society, argues Claudia V. Camp. Reclaiming a region depopulated by the Exile required the pioneering approach of an earlier period; with it came the kind of functional egalitarianism that existed in the early years of Israel's history.

In the fractured social landscape of Judah after the Exile, even women's right to inherit may have been acknowledged, says Tamara Cohn Eskenazi. When the priest Ezra made Israelite men divorce their "foreign" wives (Ezra 9–10), he may have been less concerned with ethnic purity than with the loss of inherited land. "Such loss would not be possible when women did not have legal rights to their husbands' or fathers' land."[12]

The Book of Nehemiah gives the clearest signal that women had new authority in the restored community of Israel, says Eskenazi. Ezra brought "the book of the law of Moses," the Torah, into a Jerusalem square to read before "the assembly, both men *and women* and all who could hear with understanding" (Neh. 8:1–2, emphasis added). The inclusion of women in the official assembly is deliberate, as the author repeats the phrase "men and women" again in verse 3—a pointed contrast to Moses at Sinai where the assembly was exclusively male.[13]

We know for certain that social mobility as well as property and inheritance rights were available after the Exile to at least one community of women: at Elephantine, on the Upper Nile in Egypt, where a significant Jewish colony existed from 525 to 400 BCE.

An ancient collection of papyri detail legal proceedings involving an Egyptian woman married to a Jewish man. (The woman was the slave of another man; her husband was free.) The documents depict a marriage that was very modern in its concerns: The division of property in case of divorce, the inheritance of each child, and the disposition of the couple's house, which appears to have been a fixer-upper that they improved over the years.

Written in Aramaic, the papyri tell us that although the woman was a slave, she was legally married and had property rights. She owned half of the house and willed it to her two children, a girl and a boy. Eventually, all three were granted their freedom. The daughter's marriage contract reveals that she was quite wealthy and that she retained rights to her property and possessions should she divorce. The girl's mother, the former slave, and her husband jointly sold property to their son-in-law. The former slave even became a titled member of the local Jewish temple through her husband's official position.

The World's Oldest Profession

Now you see her, now you don't: Prostitutes slip in and out of the shadows of the Hebrew Bible. They appear at critical junctures, then vanish. Their elusiveness in the narrative mirrors the Israelites' mixed feelings about these women who were both desired and despised, sought and shunned.

Scripture never outlawed prostitution per se. In a society where (female) chastity was highly valued but (male) lawgivers gave men permission to have sex with any unmarried woman, prostitution had to be tolerated.[14] And as a "tolerated specialist in an activity prohibited to every other woman," prostitutes helped to define the qualities of a "good woman" by comparison.[15]

Yet a priest could not marry a harlot (Lev. 21:7), a priest's daughter who sold her sexual favors was to be burned (Lev. 21:9), and money made from harlotry could not be paid to the temple priests to fulfill a vow (Deu. 23:18).

Prostitution in the Bible

Prostitutes take center stage in three stories.

Tamar. In chapter 4, we heard about the widow Tamar, who assumed the garb of a harlot to force her father-in-law, Judah, to fulfill his family's obligation to her: conception of an heir (Gen. 38). The narrative conflict in that story hinges on Judah's two different responses to harlotry, notes Phyllis Bird, professor of Hebrew Bible at Garrett Seminary. Seeing the harlot by the side of the road, he propositioned her. Hearing that his daughter-in-law had "played the whore" and become pregnant, he sentenced her to death. Yet "the two acts and the two women are one."[16]

Further irony awaits the reader. Tamar gave birth to twins. The eldest was named Perez, and elsewhere in the Hebrew Bible we learn that Perez became the ancestor of the man hailed as the greatest king of Israel: David. By her act of harlotry, Tamar made possible the entire line of David's Kings.

Genesis 38 suggests that male storytellers viewed harlotry as risky business—for the clients! Women controlled the transaction; clients, like Judah, risked exposure, humiliation, even intimidation. As women beyond the control of father or husband, prostitutes were viewed with distrust.

Rahab. Scripture credits another harlot with saving the I'sraelites when the tribes first arrived in Canaan. Camped in the desert on the far side of the Jordan River, the Israelites sent two spies into Canaan to gather intelligence (Josh. 2). The men made a beeline for a bordello in Jericho. When officials arrived looking for the spies, a prostitute named Rahab hid the Israelites at great risk to herself. Rahab then parlayed her loyalty into a promise: safety for herself and her family in the coming conflagration. When the Israelites besieged Jericho and exterminated the entire populace (Josh. 6), only Rahab's family was spared.

The story reveals several features of a harlot's life. First, that she lived on the margins, both figuratively and literally. Phyllis Bird suggests that the spies sought her out because as an outsider in her own society, she might be more likely to assist other outsiders, which in fact she did. Additionally, her house was located on the periphery, built into the town wall (as we learn when the spies climb out her window to safety). Her location afforded easy access for travelers and other strangers.

Second, as Bird points out, the story pleases us because of a plot twist that relied upon the popular understanding of a harlot's character as lacking in wisdom, morals, and religion. Rahab surprises us on all counts. She is shrewd, protects the spies, and professes devotion to Yahweh, but the story would not work if prostitutes didn't have a shady reputation.

Rahab's story also reminds us that prostitutes are the only truly independent women we meet in the Hebrew Bible. She did not ask her father, brother, husband, or other male before she struck a deal with the Israelite spies; she acted on her own authority.[17]

Two mothers, one infant. When Solomon was approached by two prostitutes arguing over one infant, their livelihood proved crucial to the king's choice of judicial method, which was not to question the women but to provoke the truth by threatening to cut the baby in half (1 Kgs. 3:16–27).

Harlots had a reputation for "smooth and self-serving speech," used to lure and gratify customers, notes Phyllis Bird. Such women routinely lie, the logic goes, so interrogating them would gain nothing. In his wisdom, Solomon looked beyond the stereotype of the harlot and appealed to the heart of a mother (another stereotype, alas). The ruse worked, and the false mother was revealed by her failure to protect the child.[18]

TEMPLE PROSTITUTES?

Certain biblical prophets inferred that Israel's neighbors mixed sex with their worship by employing "temple prostitutes." The Deuteronomist righteously decreed, "None of the daughters of Israel shall be a temple prostitute; none of the sons of Israel shall be a temple prostitute" (Deu. 23:17).

But the word translated as "temple prostitute," *kedesha*, is more precisely rendered as "one set aside." Its Hebrew root is also the basis for the word "holy," *kadosh*. (The generic word for "prostitute" is *zonah*.) Phyllis Bird translates *kedesha* as "hierodule" and suggests such women actually were some sort of non-sexual temple functionaries. Or, she says, perhaps their roles did include sexual activity—but calling them prostitutes demeaned an otherwise sacred function.[19]

Throughout the ages, interpreters of the Bible have seized upon the accusation of sacred prostitution to assert the superiority of Yahwism over the religions of Israel's neighbors. The charge is as false now as it was when first made.

The Religious Lives of Israelite Women

Trying to pin down the religious lives of Israelite women is a deeply dispiriting exercise. Women were only peripherally involved in official religious activities, and while it is certain that Israelite women expressed their understanding of the Sacred in profound and varied ways, we can only speculate about what those ways were.

Women's religious roles and status most likely corresponded to their roles and status in Israelite society, contends Phyllis Bird. "Since women's place in society is determined by their place within the family," she reasons that their roles in the official cult were impeded by their periodic "impurity," the necessity of deferring to men within the family, and the common understanding of women's roles as wife and mother.[20] Positions such as priest, which required continuous leadership, were out of the question.

The religious tasks that the Bible says women performed carried limited authority and honor, required little religious training, and mimicked their usual domestic responsibilities, says Bird: They wove and sewed vestments and hangings and cleaned the ritual implements, furniture and surroundings. Bird speculates that women also prepared ritual foods at the Temple because the Bible isn't specific about who cooked the meat not consumed by sacrificial fire. Although this task was assigned to men after the Exile, Bird imagines the women of the priests' families took on the job in an earlier period. Bird also suspects that both before and after the monarchy was instituted women may have been temple musicians or singers. (Later, this was probably a male profession.)

Leadership roles open to women were charismatic ones, such as prophecy, that did not depend upon social status or association with the official cult. Bird doubts that women could have exercised their prophetic gifts freely while also upholding their household responsibilities. (It seems the "second shift" is not an entirely modern idea.) Nor would women prophets have been members of the prophetic guilds, trained as apprentices, or permitted to serve at court.

Though barred from official positions, women could be part of the larger community of worshipers. Women partook of ritual meals, were bound by covenant law, sang, prayed, made and fulfilled vows, sought oracles, brought offerings, and underwent ritual cleansing. Given the number of biblical reports about women receiving direct communication from divine sources, Bird concludes that "women's communion with the Deity was common."[21]

Holy Women

Women's "communion" and unofficial religious roles are on display in a vignette from the life of Rebekah, Isaac's wife. Previously barren, Rebekah finally is pregnant with twins, but they "struggled together within her . . . so she went to inquire of the LORD" (Gen. 25:22). "Inquiring of Yhwh" usually meant going through an intermediary, although none is named. Perhaps Rebekah consulted a female religious functionary or prophet who dealt with women's concerns, suggests Nancy R. Bowen of the Earlham School of Religion. Even if Rebekah "inquired" directly, this was a "magical act to ensure the well-being of her pregnancy," for which she is rewarded with a prophecy regarding her sons.[22]

Israelite women may have relied upon holy women who assisted at births, performed rituals for maternal health, and answered questions regarding the course of disease, says Bowen. She points to the Book of Ezekiel in which the prophet excoriates three types of prophets, including "the daughters of your people, who prophesy out of their own imagination" (Ezek. 13:17). Ezekiel lived in Babylon during the Exile, and his description of the work these women prophets performed bore a striking resemblance to the rituals of Mesopotamian birth attendants.

Ezekiel charged the Israelite women with false visions and divination, but Bowen suggests he more likely feared their power. The future of the Exile community depended upon the fertility of Israelite women, and Ezekiel claimed that the unauthorized prophets harmed their patients. Perhaps he also doubted the abilities of unsanctioned women prophets.

Most scholars read Ezekiel and distinguish between what he did—authorized prophecy—and what the women were doing, which they label witchcraft or divination. Bowen shows, however, that functionally, Ezekiel and the women "who prophesy out of their own imagination" engaged in identical behavior. In seeking to nullify the power of the women prophets, Ezekiel pronounced a curse identical to Babylonian appeals to their god Shamash to put a witch to death. "What Ezekiel does is as much an act of magic or divination as what the female prophets are engaged in."[23]

Women's Devotions

For most women, religious life historically has been centered in the home or with groups of women in rituals that are particular to them. Phyllis Bird believes that may have been true for Israelite women as well. Surely there were ceremonies for each step of the life cycle, including menstruation and birthing. Were there women elders who led devotions? Did women make pilgrimages apart from those prescribed by the dominant cult? Did they endow shrines, consult mediums, participate in spirit-possession cults?

Archaeological discoveries support affirmative answers to some of these questions. Israelite figurines from the tenth century BCE depict women holding disks that might be tambourines, frame drums, or perhaps loaves of bread for a sacrifice. These small terra-cottas testify to women's participation in rituals of some sort.

More intriguing, however, are the terra-cotta "pillar figurines" that turned up by the hundreds in Judah during the seventh century BCE. They depict the upper torso of a naked woman with prominent, almond-shaped eyes and tear-drop curls, "a kind of tangible prayer for fertility and nourishment."[24] Her large, hanging breasts sometimes are supported by her thick arms. The base of her body is a simple, flared column. Molds for these figurines have been found in potters' workshops, so they were obviously mass produced.[25]

More than eight hundred of the figures have been found. Uncovered mostly in private homes and tombs, and rarely more than one per location, the figurines apparently played a part in personal or household devotions.

The figures lack symbols that would identify them as divine beings, and do not depict the pubic triangle, says Tikva Frymer-Kensky, author of *In the Wake of the Goddesses*. She thinks the pillar base evokes the sacred tree and the asherah poles, "the force of vegetation and nourishment," but not a distinct goddess. They "are a way of ensuring and demonstrating the fact that there really is a power of fertility, which can be seen and touched," Frymer-Kensky proposes, perhaps as a response to the vigorous efforts during this time to stamp out non-Yahwist worship.[26]

To better understand what the supposedly monotheistic Israelites were doing with these womanly idols, we need to know more about how the Israelites developed their ideas about God. In the next chapter, I unravel the curious history of the Deity called Yhwh, followed by an attempt to answer the question, "Is God male?"

13

GOD, GODS, AND

GODDESSES

M ore than one woman reading the Bible has concluded that its reigning Deity has a multiple personality disorder and that one or more of those personalities needs some serious anger-management training.

God, a.k.a. Elohim, Yhwh, Elyon, Yhwh Sabbaoth, and El Shaddai, is admittedly a complicated character, playing at least eight different (and sometimes conflicting) roles in the Bible (see "Now Starring God as _____!" on the next page). There's a good reason for the complexities: God has a history—and it's not the one you think you know.

Although the Bible claims that Israel pledged allegiance to only one Deity from the get-go, in actuality Israelites relied on the power of gods—and probably also goddesses—until at least the Exile in 587 BCE. Religious practices varied with time and place, but they operated along a continuum from *polytheism,* the worship of many gods; to exclusive worship of one god without denying the existence of other gods; to *monotheism,* the belief in only one god and exclusive worship of that god.[1] Universal acceptance of monotheism took centuries, and even after it was established images of other gods and goddesses continued to influence the language in which Yhwh was described.

In this chapter, we'll explore the ways in which traditions that honored many gods bled into Israelite religious beliefs and practices. Along the way, we will see how these vestiges of polytheism gave later scribes a bad case of indigestion, and they did their best to obliterate or downplay anything that veered from the worship of a single god.

We'll find out why God acted in such contradictory ways and how Yhwh acquired the characteristics described in the Bible. I promise you a much fuller understanding of the biblical God, one you can use as a springboard to devise your own conception of—and relationship to—the divine.

NOW STARRING GOD AS ____!

"The biblical God is an extremely complex, even contradictory, figure," says Stephen L. Harris in *Understanding the Bible*.[2] Consider the Deity's many roles:

Warrior God. The Warrior God is not a warm and fuzzy deity, but an avenger, someone you'd want watching your back in a bar brawl. In the triumphant victory song of Exodus 15, the Israelites praised this aspect of God: "In the greatness of your majesty you overthrew your adversaries;/you sent out your fury, it consumed them like stubble" (15:7). The Warrior God had much in common with the Canaanite storm god, Baal.

Lover. In contrast to the Warrior, God as Lover surfaces in the repeated refrain that God is "merciful and gracious, slow to anger, and abounding in steadfast love and faithfulness, keeping steadfast love for the thousandth generation" (Ex. 34:6–7).

Despite Israel's repeated failures, the loving God professes undying affection for its people, and backs this up with comfort and support. The deities of other ancient Near Eastern cultures might ask for respect or recognition, but they never asked for love.

Holy Being. In the Bible, God is not only powerful but so holy it's dangerous. Many of the priests' extravagantly detailed regulations were formulated so that Israelites could approach God without being consumed by the power of holiness.

God's *kavod* ("glory") was the most tangible manifestation of this holiness. It presented itself to the Israelites as a cloud and a pillar of fire during their wanderings in the wilderness. It also appeared as an invisible emanation within the Tabernacle, the portable shrine built especially to house the Ark of the Covenant, the gold-leafed wooden box holding the stone tablets inscribed with the Ten Commandments. The priests said that God's glory invisibly rested on the Ark's "mercy seat," between the golden statues of cherubim with outstretched wings on each side of the Ark (Ex. 37:1–9).

Object of Sacrificial System. Through their sacrificial system the Israelites acknowledged their dependence on God and displayed their gratitude. Ritual offerings of animals, grain, wine, and oil denoted their subordination to Yhwh and indicated that what they gave to God was merely what God had given them.

Lord of History and World Judge. The biblical "histories" we've explored feature many personalities, but numero uno is God. Israel's Deity appointed kings, decided the outcome of battles, and nudged reluctant heroes. In the time period covered by the Pentateuch, the Deity frequently was present visually and aurally; gradually, God's presence devolved to acting through designated intermediaries, such as prophets and kings who were modeled "after God's own heart."

God also served as the One who ultimately avenged victims, judged the faithless, and meted out punishment, even using foreign kings and armies as instruments of judgment.

King. Psalmists depicted God like a Near Eastern monarch, incorporating aspects of the Warrior and Judge. "The LORD is king, he is robed in majesty;/the LORD is robed, he is girded with strength," sings the anonymous poet of Psalm 93, one of a cluster of psalms (Ps. 93, 95–99) that celebrated this aspect of Israel's Deity. The seemingly arbitrary and capricious power that God sometimes exerted may stem from belief in the absolute power of the sovereign.

God as king had a special relationship with royal counterparts in Israel, promising David, "I will raise up your offspring after you, who shall come forth from your body, and I will establish his kingdom....I will be a father to him, and he shall be a son to me" (2 Sam. 7:12, 14).

Ultimate Reality. "To whom then will you liken God, or what likeness compare with him?" asked the prophet Isaiah (Isa. 40:18). God was not just an all-powerful deity but the only one. "I am the first and I am the last; besides me there is no god" (Isa. 44:6). God as Ultimate Reality was responsible for everything that exists: "I form light and create darkness,/I make weal and create woe" (Isa. 45:7). God also has everything under control: "I work and who can hinder it?" (Isa. 43:13). We may not be able to comprehend why things happen as they do because God's "understanding is unsearchable" (Isa. 40:28).

Ethical Puzzle. Depicting God as Ultimate Reality created a dilemma, no less for the Israelites than for us today: How is it that a Deity said to be benevolent and all-powerful allows so much suffering in the world? If God created suffering, then God is not supremely good. If God did not create suffering and cannot prevent it, then God is not all-powerful.

Despite many assurances in the Bible that the evil receive their just desserts, several biblical writers questioned this system of retribution. In the Book of Job, for example, God permitted *ha-satan,* the Adversary, to take everything from the pious Job and inflict him with a savage disease. Job's so-called friends, following the party line, believed Job's afflictions were a consequence of his sins. Despite their chastisements, Job refused to ask forgiveness for sins he knew he had not committed. In fact, Job demanded justice from God. The author of Job never entirely resolved this moral dilemma—God's response to Job was to point to the gap between divine and human capacities—and the ethical puzzle of the Bible's God remained.

The Origins of God

To understand Israel's God, we need to go back to a time before Israel even existed: the middle of the second millennium BCE, when Ugarit, a city-state on the Mediterranean coast in what is present-day Syria, dominated the region. Because of a major archaeological find there in the 1920s, we know a great deal about the religious traditions inherited by the tribes that later inhabited Canaan—including the Israelites.

Earlier Near Eastern cultures had extensive rosters of deities, but by the time Ugarit was in the ascendant, divine pantheons had become rather limited. El, an aged and kindly patriarch, ruled over his spiritual family along with His consort, the queen mother Athirat (Asherah, in Hebrew), who was called "procreatress of the gods." Baal, their son, was a young storm god and divine warrior. His sister—and sometime consort—was Anat. A goddess called Astarte (in Hebrew, Ashtaroth) was also a consort of Baal.

When the Israelites first appeared in Canaan, about 1200 BCE, they had their own tribal god named Yhwh, but they also shared in the Late Bronze Age religious culture of the other tribes in the region, just as they shared language and pottery styles and burial patterns. Like the other Canaanites, Israelites had priests, "dedicated servants," chief priests, and even a "tent of meeting." They all made "offerings of well-being," "tribute offerings," and "burnt offerings."[3]

There were differences between the Israelites and other tribes, of course. The Israelites believed that their origins lay in Egypt, and that Yhwh also came from the south, from a place referred to at different times as Sinai, Paran, Edom, or Teiman. Yet generally, Israel's religious perceptions—even their unique traditions regarding Yhwh—were shaped by Canaanite culture. As a result, not only is the Hebrew Bible filled with comparable practices, it is replete with echoes of El, Asherah, Baal, and perhaps even Anat.

Yhwh and El

Mention the biblical God to anyone and, unless they grew up on the dark side of the moon, the image that will come to mind is something like the muscular old man with flowing white hair and beard painted by Michelangelo on the ceiling of the Sistine Chapel. This is Yhwh in the guise of benevolent patriarch, a role played by El as well.

As "fathers," El and Yhwh both were compassionate toward humans. They visited their people in dreams and served as their divine patrons. They both lived in tents called tabernacles. El dwelt amidst the cosmic waters; Yhwh, alongside "a river whose streams make glad the city of God" (Ps. 46:4). El, like Yhwh, was called "creator of the earth."[4]

Israel's very name derived from "El." This suggests that originally the chief god of Israel *was* El. At some point, scholars speculate, Yhwh was added to the Israelite divine pantheon.

In *The Early History of God,* Mark S. Smith proposes that the Israelites identified El with Yhwh quite early on, and the two became one and the same. Smith has a useful framework to describe these sorts of changes. Israelite religion, he says, developed by means of two movements: *convergence* and *differentiation.* By convergence, he means the combination of various deities and their features to form Israel's one deity, called by various names (Yhwh, Elohim, El Shaddai, etc.). Differentiation involved distinguishing the Israelite cult from that of its neighbors. "Through conflict and compromise between the cults of Yahweh and other deities," Israel developed its own understanding of God.[5]

CONVERGENCE IN ACTION

A scene in Exodus displays convergence at work. The passage describes Moses tending flocks in the desert when a voice calls to him out of a burning bush. "I am the God of your father," the voice tells him, "the God of Abraham, the God of Isaac, and the God of Jacob" (Ex.3:6). When Moses asks this god its name, the voice cryptically answers, "*Ehyeh-Asher-Ehyeh*" (Ex. 3:14, JPS), which the NRSV translates as "I AM WHO I AM." The voice later explains to Moses, "I am the LORD [YHWH]. I appeared to Abraham, Isaac, and Jacob as El Shaddai, but I did not make Myself known to them by My name YHWH" (Ex. 6:2–3, JPS).

The Priestly writers inserted this explanation about God's name into a story about Moses in order to resolve any lingering confusion about the identity of the Deity who commissioned him. They wanted to make sure that Yhwh would be considered the very same god as the deity-formerly-known-as El Shaddai who spoke to Moses' ancestors. This clarification also established that there were no other gods—at least not any as important as Yhwh. No matter that the Exodus version of events conflicted with stories of the ancestors in Genesis, where God *does* use the name Yhwh. The Exodus author apparently was not familiar with those traditions—or didn't care.

Yhwh, "the Gods," and the Scribes

El presided over a multitiered divine "council" or "assembly" that loosely mirrored the royal court of Ugarit. At its head were El and his consort, Athirat. Their offspring—many of whom controlled natural phenomena and fertility—occupied the second rung. The third group, which included worker deities that served other gods, occupied the lowest rank. They were kin to the angels that emerged later in the history of Israelite religion.

Despite the best efforts of monotheist redactors, divine courtiers frequently popped up in the Hebrew scriptures, as in this poem from Deuteronomy, which also includes "divine warrior" imagery grafted onto Yhwh from Baal or the goddess Anat.

> Praise, O heavens, his people,
> worship him, all you gods!

> For he will avenge the blood of his children,
> and take vengeance on his adversaries;
> he will repay those who hate him,
> and cleanse the land for his people. (DEU. 32:43)

So distressing were the implications of these lines that the scribes responsible for faithfully copying and disseminating the Hebrew text of the Bible amended the text. The "official" Hebrew version that is the basis for all Jewish bibles reads like this:

> O nations, acclaim His people!
> For He'll avenge the blood of His servants,
> Wreak vengeance on His foes,
> And cleanse the land of His people. (DEU. 32:43, JPS)

Notice the differences? The call for praise goes out to the "nations" rather than the "heavens," which would have had to be full of divine beings subordinate to El. The official text also substituted "servants" for "children," lest there be any hint of a divine family in El's retinue. More egregiously, the later editors eliminated altogether part of the original first line, the call for "other" gods to worship El. And lastly, they axed "he will repay those who hate him."

Taken together, these changes tone down the warrior image and eradicate other divine beings.

This same poem in Deuteronomy demonstrates how Israelites integrated Yhwh into El's pantheon.

> Remember the days of old,
> Consider the years long past;
> Ask your father, and he will inform you;
> your elders, and they will tell you:
> When the Most High [Elyon] apportioned the nations
> when he divided humankind,

> He fixed the boundaries of the peoples according to the
>   number of the gods;
> the LORD's [YHWH] own portion was his people,
> Jacob [Israel] his allotted share. (DEU. 32: 7–9)

The epithet translated as "Most High" is Elyon in Hebrew, one of the formal titles for Ugarit's El. The poet was saying that when El distributed the Canaanite tribes among the various gods, Jacob (another name for Israel) was given to El's offspring, Yhwh.

The later editors apparently didn't like the idea that tribes were allotted "according to the number of the gods." The "official" version reads, "according to the number of the Israelites," which does not make much sense. Bernard M. Levinson speculates in *The Jewish Study Bible* that the copyists "corrected" the text to bring it into line with the strict monotheism of a later age.[6] The NRSV, quoted above, restored the "gods" based on wording found in the Greek translation of the Bible (the Septuagint) and the Dead Sea Scrolls. These references to a divine court and El and Yhwh's father-son relationship better reflects the early polytheism of the Israelites.

Differentiation

To be sure, the Israelites did not appropriate all of El's characteristics for Yhwh. Can you imagine the biblical God celebrated with the following verses?

> El drinks wine till sated,
> Vintage till inebriated.
> El staggers to his house.
> Stumbles in to his court.
> Thukamuna and Shunama carry him,
> Habayu then berates him,
> He of two horns and a tail.
> He slips in his dung and urine,

> El collapses like one dead
> El like those who descend to Earth.[7]

The Canaanite El, you see, was the patron of drinking. He also was quite the lover, as demonstrated by this description of an encounter with two of his wives:

> He bows down to kiss their lips,/Ah! their lips are sweet,/
>   sweet as succulent fruit.
> In kissing, conception,/In embracing, pregnant heat.
> The two travail and give birth/to the gods Dawn and Dusk.[8]

Yhwh might share many attributes with El, but they were not identical!

Yhwh and Baal

In contrast to beneficent El, his son Baal influenced the vengeful warrior side of Yhwh.

Baal was responsible for the fertility of the land through the rain that he brought. Frequently, he was called "rider of the clouds" and "the prince lord of the earth."[9] A typical Canaanite bas relief depicted Baal with a club in his right hand and a lance resembling a tree or stylized lightning in his left.

Baal's home was Mount Sapan, which was identified with the highest mountain in the region of Ugarit. Epic tales of Baal described him defeating the sea god Yamm, a victory that led to him being crowned king. Another described Baal's imprisonment by Mot ("Death"), which resulted in a drought. To free Baal, his consort Anat struggled with Mot, a battle that was described with agricultural metaphors evoking Baal's life-giving fertility. Anat was successful but, after seven years, Baal and Mot renewed their conflict and the sun goddess had to intervene before Mot would admit defeat.

Israelites worshipped Baal as a deity distinct from Yhwh right up to the Exile in the sixth century BCE. All the while, many of the Canaanite god's characteristics were being attached to Yhwh.

Unlike El, of whom not a harsh word was spoken, Baal got a lot of bad press in the Bible, perhaps because Baal competed with Yhwh for adherents. It is difficult to reconstruct Baal's history in Israel because biblical writers consistently portrayed Baal worship as a deviation from foundational monotheism, while we now recognize that Baal was an integral part of Israel's religious heritage.

When Canaanites depicted Baal, they typically included these elements:

- The divine warrior marched forth.
- Nature convulsed as the divine warrior displayed his power.
- The divine warrior returned to his holy mountain as king.
- The divine warrior thundered and initiated fertilizing rains.[10]

Psalm 18 eloquently demonstrates how Yhwh's followers appropriated Baal's characteristics.

In my distress I called upon the LORD;/to my God I cried for help.
From his temple he heard my voice,/
　　and my cry to him reached his ears.
Then the earth reeled and rocked;/
　　　　　the foundations also of the mountains trembled and quaked,
　　　　　because he was angry.
Smoke went up from his nostrils,/and devouring fire from
　　his mouth;/glowing coals flamed forth from him.
He bowed the heavens, and came down;/
　　thick darkness was under his feet.
He rode on a cherub, and flew;/
　　he came swiftly upon the wings of the wind.
He made darkness his covering around him,/
　　his canopy thick clouds dark with water.

Our of the brightness before him there broke through his
  clouds hailstones and coals of fire.
The LORD also thundered in the heavens,/
  and the Most High uttered his voice.
And he sent out his arrows, and scattered them;/
  he flashed forth lightnings, and routed them.
Then the channels of the sea were seen,/and the foundations
  of the world were laid bare at your rebuke, O LORD,/
  at the blast of the breath of your nostrils. (PS. 18:6–15)

The psalmist noted elsewhere that Yhwh saved the petitioner as requested. (After such a performance, anything less seems inconceiv-
able.)

Like Baal, Yhwh lived on a mountain (Zion) that was called a "holy
place," or his "inheritance." Zion was even said to be "in the far north"
as was Baal's abode (Ps. 48:2). Baal had a temple, as did Yhwh, which
later prophets identified with the temple in Jerusalem. Just as Baal defeated Yamm, Yhwh repeatedly wrestled with and overcame the sea, or
sea creatures such as the Leviathan, or the primeval chaos known as
Rahab.

You rule the raging of the sea;/when its waves rise, you still them.
You crushed Rahab like a carcass;/you scattered your enemies with
  your mighty arm. (PS. 89:9–10)

Yhwh, like Baal, was even able to vanquish Death (Mot). Is it any
wonder that sibling rivalry existed between the two?

Mark S. Smith speculates that the campaign—in word and deed—
against Baal erupted in the ninth or perhaps the eighth century BCE.
Biblical "historians" blamed King Ahab and his notorious wife, Jezebel,
for the upsurge in Baal worship. Yet as we now know, Ahab, who ruled
from 873 to 852 BCE, simply upheld tradition. Furthermore, his royal
patronage of Baal's cult was a savvy political gesture, since Baal worship

probably appealed to non-Israelite residents of the northern kingdom. As for Jezebel, she was merely worshiping the Deity she had grown up with as daughter of the king of Tyre (a sea coast city in what is now Lebanon).

Biblical writers, however, insisted that Jezebel led Ahab into this "foreign" cult and that she killed off Yhwh's prophets. In retaliation, the prophet Elijah supposedly saw to it that four hundred prophets of Baal were slaughtered (1 Kgs. 16, 18). Did any of this actually happen? We don't know. But it is clear that despite subsequent attempts to stamp out Baal worship, it remained a robust aspect of Israelite worship until the Exile.

Anat, Warrior Goddess

What about that other martial figure of the Urgaritic pantheon, Anat, the bloodthirsty warrior wife (or sister) of Baal? (Divine warriors of the female persuasion had a long history in the ancient Near East.) Anat herself never appears in the Bible, except as a component of a few names (Anathoth as a place name, for example, in Josh. 21:18 and elsewhere). But her legacy is present. Take a look at this selection from a series of sagas in which Anat engaged "the youth at the foot of the mountain":

> And look! Anat fights in the valley,/She battles between the two cities.
> She smites peoples of the wes[t],/Strikes the populace of the east.
> Under her, like balls, heads,/Above her, like locusts, hand(s),/
> > Like hoppers, heaps of warrior-hands.
> She fixed heads to her back,/Fastened hands to her waist.
> Knee-deep she gleans in warrior-blood, Neck-deep in the
> > gor[e] of soldiers.
> With darts she drives away captives,/With her bow-string, foes.[11]

By now, it should come as no surprise that the Bible, also, is replete with similarly savage imagery. Like Anat, Yhwh battles at or on mountains, becomes enraged and seeks revenge, produces corpses and heads galore (Isa. 34:2–4), feasts on captives (or makes them eat their own flesh [Isa. 49:26]), and wades in the blood of the defeated. Here is just one example, from Deuteronomy 32:

> For I lift up my hand to heaven, and swear: As I live forever,
> when I whet my flashing sword,/and my hand takes hold on judgment;
> I will take vengeance on my adversaries,/
>   and will repay those who hate me.
> I will make my arrows drunk with blood,/
>   and my sword shall devour flesh—
> with the blood of the slain and the captives,/
>   from the long-haired enemy. (DEU. 32:40–42)

And this from Psalm 58: "The righteous will rejoice when they see vengeance done; they will bathe their feet in the blood of the wicked" (v. 10).

Blood is so pervasive in encounters with Yhwh that biblical authors drew on the red color of wine and the wine harvest to craft a metaphor for Yhwh's confrontations with the enemies of Israel. In this example, the prophet Isaiah questions Yhwh as the Deity emerges from the killing fields:

> "Why are your robes red, and your garments like theirs who
>   tread the wine press?"
> "I have trodden the wine press alone,/
>   and from the peoples no one was with me;
> I trod them in anger/and trampled them in my wrath;
> their juice splattered on my garments,/
>   and stained all my robes." (ISA. 63:2–3)

Are you as ambivalent as I am about the legacy of Anat? I don't play video games with lots of murder and mayhem, so maybe I just can't appreciate her finer points. It's not that I don't approve of woman warriors; I'm just not fond of severed heads.

Without getting too psychological, Anat plays like an Oedipal fantasy gone bad, a boyhood fear of Mommy writ large. Surely there is a way of representing feminine power that doesn't entail crushing the opposition? We may be able to find this in the Asherah, Yhwh's female counterpart. Chapter 14 explores the Bible's intriguing traces of God's likely onetime consort.

Yhwh Who?

When and where the Israelites adopted Yhwh remains one of the great mysteries of the Bible, along with the exact meaning of the name. Editors working at the time when Yhwh was *the* national deity smoothed out the biblical story of this God, distorting the historical picture. The best information we have comes from inscriptions, which can be dated more precisely than biblical texts.

A victory stele from the very late ninth century BCE celebrates a Moabite monarch's recovery of territory from the Israelites, and brags that in addition to killing seven thousand captives, "I took thence the [altar-hearths] of YHWH, and I dragged them before Kamosh [primary Moabite deity]."[12] Graffiti on two large pots found in the northern Sinai also mention Yhwh; they date to around 800 BCE, as does a Hebrew tomb inscription in Hebron that includes Yhwh's name. Several other inscriptions exist, but like these, none of them date before the 800s BCE.

As for "where," the archaeological and biblical records strongly associate Yhwh with regions south of Canaan, such as Edom (also called Seir) and the Sinai. The Sinai graffiti refers to "Yhwh of Teiman," placing the deity's origins in either "the South, Country of the South," or a region of Edom, depending upon how one identifies Teiman.

Then there is the biblical story in which Moses fled to Midian, located south of Edom in northwest Arabia along the Gulf of Aqaba. There, Moses married the daughter of a priest, called Jethro in some places and Reuel in others. The Midian deserts are also the place where Moses first encountered Yhwh in the burning bush. Could this meeting have followed an introduction to the Deity by his Midianite father-in-law? Some scholars think so; others disagree.

As for what the name Yhwh means, even that is uncertain. It is written with the Hebrew letters יהוה *yod-he-vav-he*, which are transliterated as YHWH. With vowels added, the word was perhaps pronounced "Yahweh," although no one quite knows for sure.

The name Yhwh bears an enigmatic relationship to God's self-identification to Moses as *"Ehyeh-Asher-Ehyeh,"* which can be translated "I am what I am,"or, "I will be what I will be" (NRSV, Ex. 3:14). God tells Moses to say to the Israelites that "Ehyeh sent me to you," (3:14, JPS), then announces he is to tell them, "[YHWH] has sent me to you" (3:15, JPS). The name Yhwh thereby is associated with the God who declares, *"Ehyeh-Asher-Ehyeh,"* but the combinations of Hebrew consonants are different. Some scholars speculate that the name Yhwh derives from *"haway,"* an older form of the Hebrew verb "to be."[13]

Ultimately, we are left with speculation, at least until archaeologists give us something more substantial. What we know for sure is that the Israelites had adopted the tradition of a liberating God identified by the unpronounceable name of Yhwh by the ninth century BCE (and probably before), that this God eventually became the reigning national Deity and, ultimately, the only One.

14

THE LOST GODDESSES

s God male?

Theologians would answer that God is beyond gender. They'd point to the Priestly version of creation in Genesis—

> So God created humankind in his image,
> in the image of God he created them;
> male and female he created them. (GEN. 1:27)

—and contend that the Deity must therefore contain both male and female, but, being divine, transcends sexual identity altogether. As for "he" and "his," well, Hebrew has no genderless way of identifying anyone or anything.

These theological niceties notwithstanding, it's hard to read the Bible and think of the Deity as sexless. As we learned in the last chapter, God might not be called "father" in the Hebrew Bible, but "He" does take the role of one. Yhwh also functions as warrior, storm god, and king. This preoccupation with war and statecraft but not, say, birthing—other than "opening the womb" of childless women—suggests a Deity on the masculine end of the spectrum.

Then there's the matter of language. Though they can't be helped, all those masculine pronouns add up to an impression of God as an actual "He."

God's seeming maleness stems in part from the Bible's monotheism. For all that was gained by restricting worship to Yhwh alone, "eliminating other gods and jettisoning old religious practices changes fundamental ideas about the workings of the cosmos," writes Tikva Frymer-Kensky, a University of Chicago scholar of ancient Sumer and Assyria.[1]

In this chapter we will explore which fundamental ideas changed and in what ways by delving into the lost polytheistic world, especially Near Eastern goddesses. In doing so, we may discover new understandings of the divine and alternate possibilities for a relationship with culture and creation.

Unfortunately, polytheism has a bad name in the West. It's considered idolatry, which is worse than having no religious beliefs at all. But to comprehend the Bible, we have to accept the internal logic of ancient polytheistic religions. Like Yhwh, the gods and goddesses worshiped in Sumer and Babylonia, Egypt and Ugarit made the world's chaos explicable. They offered guidance for daily living and laws to govern society. They stimulated awe, reverence, prayers, ethical decision making, and philosophical disputations. They inspired hymns of praise, sacrifices, rituals, and festivals. In short, ancient polytheism comprised all the components of religions we may deem more acceptable.

Cradle of the Gods (and Goddesses)

Devotion to powers greater than human predates ancient Mesopotamian societies, but the religion of Sumer, founded more than forty-five hundred years ago, is among the oldest that we know very much about. (Al-

though Egypt, too, had a long and rich religious history, the "Land Between the Rivers" more directly influenced Israelite beliefs and practices.)

Each city-state of the southern Tigris–Euphrates River Valley had
its own cohort of deities, headed by a principal god or goddess in whose
name the local king ruled, says Frymer-Kensky, author of *In the Wake
of the Goddesses*. Family gods assured household members health and
prosperity, and individuals had special deities as well. Since the land
belonged to the city's chief god, this deity also was the major employer,
and temple functionaries oversaw the irrigation systems and agricultural surpluses.

Frymer-Kensky maintains that female and male deities in ancient
Mesopotamia were equally well regarded—yet sex roles were important.
With one major exception, Sumerian goddesses had functions that pertained to their femaleness. They were mothers, mothers-in-law, queens,
wives, daughters, and sisters, and they were associated with stereo-
typically female tasks. Goddesses guided the development of the child in
the womb, its safe delivery, and its growth to adulthood. They oversaw the
stores of food supplies and made sure the temple system that housed
them ran well. They were model stewards, managers, and housekeepers.

Sumerians also believed that goddesses brought them the skills that
sustained civilization, from writing, accounting, and surveying, to
pottery making, healing, and dream interpretation. The goddesses responsible for the grain, wool, and brewing that provided humankind's
basic sustenance occupied lofty places in the divine hierarchy. Goddesses also guided the art of song and gave voice to laments. The consort of the chief god ruled as queen and shared his power.

All these occupations and functions mirrored the roles that human
women assumed. Frymer-Kensky writes that the divine models likely
were empowering for Sumerian women. At the same time, she notes,
these models reinforced sex role stereotypes and elevated them to an
eternal ideal. Overall, the paradox of these divine figures reflected the
social paradox of Sumerian women: Continuation of the city-state de-

pended upon women to bear the next generation, yet women were never accorded the power to rule. Women might be authorities on numerous crafts and arts, but ultimately they had to accommodate their husbands and families.

The exception to this paradox was Inanna, Mistress of the Date Palm, the goddess of love, war, and rain. Enormously powerful, Inanna was married to Dumuzi, the god responsible for the fertility of fields and herds, yet she never took on wifely tasks. Nor was she maternal. Rather, Inanna lived the life of a young male: She roamed freely, sought out lovers, engaged in warfare. As the goddess of rain, which assured fertility, she oversaw the state storehouses that harbored the products of that fertility. Eternally the maiden, she was unencumbered and unattached, promiscuous and bloodthirsty—the model of everything a Sumerian woman was not permitted to be. Her restless, peripatetic nature also meant she had no place in society; she existed at the margins, both feared and exalted. Honored at festivals by cross-dressing devotees, Inanna actually reinforced gender roles by embodying a defiant exception to women's normal behavior.

Inanna played a major role in a key annual ritual designed to assure the agricultural abundance, known as *he-gal,* on which Sumer's existence depended. Each year the king undertook a "sacred marriage," becoming the "beloved spouse of Inanna," to assure good harvests. At the culmination of the ceremony, the king, in the role of Dumuzi, joined in sexual union with Inanna, a role assumed by one of the city's high-ranking women, perhaps a priestess.

No one can say whether this act actually brought about abundant harvests, but it did make sexuality the foundation of the cosmic order out of which all else flowed. Also, by imitating the cooperation required to sustain life—the combined effort of humans and the divine—the sacred marriage sanctified the mundane daily tasks of plowing, planting, irrigating, harvesting, and storing.

Above all, the sacred marriage exemplified a system that honored a female deity as the being who mediated between humans and the divine—and, more specifically, honored female sexuality as the means by which life was sustained. When modern commentators identify Inanna and her successors simply as "fertility" goddesses, they seriously underplay the goddesses' complex roles in ancient societies.

The Twilight of the Goddesses

As political and economic power in the lower Tigris–Euphrates River Valley shifted from the south to the north and back again, then was seized by invading westerners, the gods and goddesses of Sumer mutated. New ruling dynasties had their own divine pantheons and assimilated Sumer's into theirs. While the basic structures of Mesopotamian religions remained about the same, names changed (Inanna converged with Ishtar, an Akkadian goddess, for instance) and certain gods were displaced by others.

One constant, however, was a gradual erosion of the powers of goddesses. By the Old Babylonian period (1800–1550 BCE), there were few stories about female deities. When goddesses did appear, they were stereotypical—mothers, advisers, temptresses—and secondary, according to Frymer-Kensky. The primordial mother goddess had been demoted in rank even earlier, her function taken over by the head male god.

A creation hymn from Old Babylonia demonstrates how divine male dominance was making headway. Known as the "Enuma Elish," the poem describes how the new deity on the block, Marduk, established himself as the king of all the gods by taking on the mother goddess, Ti'amat, in bloody combat. Here is how an ancient poet described the outcome of their supernatural battle:

> [Marduk] sliced [Ti'amat] in half like a fish for drying:
> Half of her he put up to roof the sky,
> Drew a bolt across and made a guard hold it.
> Her waters he arranged so that they could not escape. . . .
> He opened the Euphrates and the Tigris from her eyes . . .

He piled up clear-cut mountains from her udder . . .
He set her thigh to make fast the sky,
With half of her he made a roof; he fixed the earth.[2]

With the other half of her body, Marduk created the earth. Ti'amat, the primal female force, was reduced to inert matter manipulated by others. She who had borne all the gods was now the prisoner of the high god, able to bless the earth with her fructifying waters only by command of the god-king Marduk.

The main religious festival in Old Babylonia became a New Year's ritual that reproduced Ti'amat's defeat by Marduk, who was played by the king. Babylonians held ceremonies to mark the union of Marduk and his consort, but they did not include human reenactments, which denied the people and their king an intimate interchange with the divine. In contrast with the old ritual of sacred marriage that glorified sexual union and fertility, the Babylonian state celebrated hierarchy, royal prerogative, and order. Human sexuality lost its divine status. Kings no longer claimed to be descendants of gods, or gods in their own right, but rather viewed themselves as the "image" of the head god.

Only Inanna, now known as Ishtar, escaped the general downsizing, but even she underwent radical surgery. Stories emphasized her lust for war, and one hymn depicted Ishtar as so savage that the other gods could not control her. (This development may have reflected the gradual militarization of the region, especially under the Assyrians.) Yet other hymns praised her grace, beauty, and joy. These two extremes were a sign of the mixed feelings engendered by the idea of a powerful, sexual female being.

Ugarit inherited this increasingly misogynistic religious culture around 1450 BCE and then passed it on to the Canaanites and, later, Israelites. Yet even Ugarit's divine patriarch, El, had a spouse, Athirat, who was called mother of the gods. And like El, Baal, and Anat, Athirat turned up in the Bible—more or less.

Yhwh and His Asherah

Athirat's Hebrew name was Asherah. Stories, commandments, and prophetic rants about "the *asherah*" and "the *asherim*" appear throughout all periods of biblical history.

For centuries, the *asherah* was believed to be a grove of trees, because the Greek translation of the Bible and the Latin Vulgate translated *asherah* as "grove." This language found its way into the King James Version (KJV), the first authorized English translation of the Bible. But in the original Hebrew, *asherah* was paired with verbs such as "made," "built," "set up," and "planted," which suggested that it was fabricated, not grown. Then, the archaeological finds at Ugarit in the 1920s revealed that there was, indeed, a goddess named Athirat/Asherah.

The physical object called the *asherah* in the Bible apparently was a wooden pole set up next to an altar or on a "high place" where worship took place (often, adjacent to altars dedicated to Baal). But scholars argue about what this pole and biblical references to *asherim* symbolized.

- Did "the *asherah*" mean the goddess herself?
- Or, did it refer to an object with a vestigial association with the goddess?
- Or, was it merely a cultic object associated with Yhwh?

Our understanding of *asherah* is complicated by the fact that the Bible recorded only denunciations of this object. One of the most vociferous anti-*asherah*s was the "historian" of the books of Samuel and Kings, who excoriated anyone trafficking in *asherim*. Here is a typical rant.

[King Manasseh] did what was evil in the sight of the LORD, following the abominable practices of the nations that the LORD drove out before the people of Israel. For he rebuilt the high places that his father Hezekiah had destroyed; he erected altars for Baal, made a sacred pole [*asherah*], as King Ahab of Israel had done, worshiped all the host of heaven, and served them. (2 KGS. 21:2–3)

The writer added that Manasseh set a "carved image of Asherah" in the Jerusalem temple, the only biblical reference to an actual image of the goddess.

None of these objects have been found, since wood decomposes over time, but even if an *asherah* turned up, it could not tell us how the Israelites used or thought of it. Archaeologists, however, have discovered three inscriptions in the northern Sinai that invoke Asherah's name and link her to Yhwh. Dated to about 800 BCE, they appear as graffiti on two large pots, along with a number of figure drawings. Here is a translation of one of the inscriptions:

> Thus says Amaryau:/ Say to my lord:/Is it well with you?
> I bless you (herewith—or: have blessed you)
> to/before Yhwh of Teiman and his *asherah*.
> May [Yhwh] bless (you) and keep you/and be with my lord . . . [3]

Then there is a tomb inscription from the same era found near Hebron, west of the Jordan River:

> Uriyahu the rich wrote it./Blessed be Uriyahu by Yhwh.
> For from his enemies by his Asherah he has saved him.
> by Oniyahu/and by his Asherah/ his A(she)rah.[4]

Yhwh and "his" asherah? What can this mean?

That depends upon whom you ask. The majority of scholars believe that the *asherahs* in the Hebrew scriptures refer to the goddess herself as well as her symbol, the sacred pole. They deduce from this that Israelites worshiped Asherah during the years of the monarchy—from about 1000 to 587 BCE—and, on the basis of the inscriptions, that at least some viewed her as Yhwh's consort.[5] Since Athirat partnered El and El converged with Yhwh, there was a certain logic to pairing the Hebrew version of Athirat with Yhwh.

Other scholars maintain that "Yhwh's *asherah*" indicates a being of lower rank than Yhwh, who "is rather a *mediating entity* that brings *his* blessing and is conceived in the mind in the shape of a stylized tree that was thus subordinate to Yahweh" (italics in original).[6] Still others believe that "the asherah continued with various functions in the cult of Yahweh without connection to the goddess who gave her name to the symbol."[7]

Clearly, it remains difficult for monotheists to admit to remnants of polytheism in the biblical tradition. Yet the Israelites' apparent celebration of Asherah as an adjunct of Yhwh speaks to a human yearning to balance the polarities of nature and to create religious symbols that mirror their own experiences. Yhwh, if conceived as father God, needed a mother goddess. As a husband, "He" needed a wife. Without this counterweight, half the human race was not represented.

From Words to Images

Chastened by later prohibitions against worshiping "idols," we forget that people in the ancient world were more likely to express their devotion through image making since few could read or write.

Archaeologists have uncovered a wealth of artifacts from the second and first millennia BCE in Canaan. These show that artisans placed images of divine beings on all manner of goods, including medallions, amulets, carved ivories, ointment spoons, tool handles, flasks, pillars, offering stands, incense burners, miniature shrines, scarabs, terra-cotta plaques, statuettes, and "stamp seals," small cylinders of fired clay that were used to mark property with the owner's identity.

These objects catalog the visual symbols that predominated in Canaan/Israel at any given time and tell us better than words could about the prevailing religious values, say the authors of *Gods, Goddesses, and Images of God in Ancient Israel,* Othmar Keel and Christoph Uehlinger. These discoveries confirm that monotheism was a long time in the making and that it only gradually shouldered aside female deities.

The Naked Goddess: Middle Bronze Age (1750–1550 BCE). Prior to Israel's appearance in Canaan, the dominant image on terra-cotta cylinder seals was a "Naked Goddess." This nude female form in frontal view with her arms at her sides usually appeared flanked by branches, with her pubic triangle emphasized. Metal statuettes about eight inches high as well as somewhat smaller figurines made from sheets of gold, silver, or bronze suggest the goddess's high rank. Seals also depicted lions and wild goats, sometimes with a female goddess serving as "Mistress of the Animals."

Warriors and Trees: Late Bronze Age (1550–1200 BCE). Peaceful images of fertility and abundance disappeared when Egypt became a major colonial power in the region. The naked, erotic goddess went undercover, symbolized instead by a tree. When goddesses appeared in human form, their martial power was emphasized, and they were likely to be sculpted from terra-cotta solely for personal devotions. Warrior deities came into vogue, but they were rarely shown interacting with female figures.

Domineering, Triumphant Gods: Early Iron Age (ca. 1250/1150–1000 BCE). When Israelites first appeared in Canaan, earlier trends continued. The Egyptian deity Seth converged with Canaanite Baal, now depicted with wings and a horned cap, and sometimes shown standing on a lion, symbolic of a vanquished opponent. Other than simple terra-cotta goddesses, deities in human form were exclusively masculine, domineering, and triumphant, as were images of rulers. The fertility connected with the goddess was symbolically represented—a suckling mother animal, for example—indicating that "blessing and fertility were no longer directly connected with a personal power who was acting consciously but was thought of increasingly as a numinous power and force."[8]

Lord of the Ostriches: Israelite Monarchy (ca. 1000–925 BCE). The trend during this period was away from female deities, in human or symbolic form. One of the figures taking their place was the "Lord of the Ostriches." Like Yhwh, ostriches were indigenous to the arid steppes south and southeast of Israel. Rarely domesticated, the ostrich "represents not only a deserted, dangerous and sinister world . . . but also a numinous power that commands respect and honor because it can survive mysteriously at the edge of habitable land."[9] Female figures reappeared as three-dimensional statuettes of clothed women, each holding a large disk, probably a tambourine or frame drum. The iconography of other artifacts suggests that these devotees were making offerings to the Canaanite goddess Anat.

Lords of Heaven: Assyrian and Egyptian Influence (925–722 BCE). Motifs associated with the heavens, the sun, and the stars, rather than the earth came along with foreign domination. Artisans borrowed Egyptian iconography, including solar disks representing the sun's power, falcons, scarabs, and the uraeus (a snake holding it own tail, an emblem of the circle of birth, death, and rebirth). The goddess's sacred tree was now guarded by griffins and cherubs, which symbolized royal power, not the divine female. All of these winged creatures served a "Most High God" or "Lord of Heaven"—Baal or Yhwh.

Ishtar, the Most High God, and Pillar Figurines: Assyrian Domination (722–600 BCE). Images of gods and goddesses—especially Ishtar or her eight-pointed star—now abounded, and influenced the Judean artisans producing objects for Yhwh's cult. The "Most High God" appeared in human form with lunar accoutrements such as crescent moons, stars, and moon disks. The naked, female "pillar figurines" described in chapter 12 appeared during this time, but, paradoxically, seal impressions were less likely to carry religious images, perhaps an out-growth of emerging prohibitions against making and worshiping idols.

The Ineffable: Exile and Return (sixth century BCE). During the Exile in the sixth century BCE, it becomes difficult to distinguish symbols adopted by indigenous Judeans from those of non-Judean immigrants. The prophetic oracles written at this time suggest that the overwhelming tendency among Judeans in exile was to move further away from a Deity with a visible form. Nearly three hundred years earlier, the prophet Isaiah had reported seeing a vision of Yhwh seated on a throne. Yet in Babylon during the Exile, the priest and prophet Ezekiel said he spoke with God but glimpsed only "the appearance of the likeness of the glory of the LORD" (Ezek. 1:28). By the time Judeans returned to their homeland, the prophet Zechariah, in his visions ca. 520–518 BCE, did not even speak with Yhwh, but with an angel deputized as go-between.

Subsequent to the Exile, God became remote, unapproachable, indescribable, and definitely not female as the Israelites, rejecting foreign influences, officially adopted monotheism.

Monotheism's Long Shadow

You may be perfectly satisfied with the God of the Bible—or not. Either way, you have to admit that the differences between ancient Near Eastern religious practices and Israel's later one-deity system are profound. The Hebrew Bible brings us extraordinary richness, notes Tikva Frymer-Kensky, but also leaves us with problematic attitudes toward nature, humanity, culture, and gender.[10]

The Un-greening of Religion

Creation is not celebrated for its own sake in the Hebrew Bible. Israelite priests converted traditional celebrations of the barley, wheat, and grape harvests into festivals designed to acknowledge Yhwh's gift of the land, not the miracle of the earth's sufficiency.

In the river valleys of ancient Egypt and Mesopotamia, human inge-
nuity made irrigation possible, but Canaan's dry, rocky highlands had
no rivers. The Israelites therefore were completely dependent upon rain
and, by extension, Yhwh—perhaps another reason why the storm god
Baal was such a fierce competitor for the Israelites' affections.

Yhwh's mastery of cosmic powers such as rainmaking gave the
Israelites confidence in God's ability to control history—particularly
their own. They told of how the Deity would even override the laws of
nature—holding back the Red Sea so the Israelites could escape the
Egyptian army, for instance—to protect their people.

The old theologies had a different take on Creation. People celebrated the rains and harvests and fertility for themselves. The ancient
deities mediated *between* humankind and nature, through dynamic relationships in which humans collaborated with various gods and goddesses. *This* god might withhold rain—or health or babies or victory in
war—but *that* god could be appealed to for redress. Before monotheism, humans were never without an advocate.[11]

Culture and Gender

According to the myths of other ancient Near Eastern cultures,
deities provided Homo sapiens with everything they needed to get
along on earth and in society, from music to skill in farming. Genesis,
to the contrary, tells us that the first humans developed culture on
their own. Adam and Eve's sons Cain and Abel were the first herder
and farmer, respectively. Their descendants developed the art of
music and the ability to make "all kinds of bronze and iron tools"
(Gen. 4:22).

What gifts did Yhwh bestow on the Israelites?

Laws and the priesthood, along with the sabbaths and festivals
unique to Israelite religion. Daily life was sanctified to the extent that
individuals adhered to the Yhwh's laws. Holiness resided solely in official religious undertakings and was radically disconnected from
ordinary human activities—winemaking, weaving and spinning, food

preparation, herding goats and sheep—which were deemed secular. Despite enormous responsibility for their realm, humans in many ways were on their own.

Frymer-Kensky points out that this arrangement had gender implications. The areas of human society that Mesopotamians viewed as the province of male gods—politics, hierarchy, and law—became gifts from Yhwh. The cultural spheres linked to goddesses, however, came under human jurisdiction. No rituals or festivals of thanksgiving marked their practice. "Throughout the Bible, in every aspect of biblical thought, human beings gain in prominence in—and because of—the absence of goddesses."[12]

Biblical Anthropology

A religious system in which just one Deity creates and controls the entire cosmos has to address the problem of why bad things happen to good people. How could God be all-powerful and all-good, yet permit the sort of suffering we see daily in our world?

The Bible explained this conundrum by making humans responsible for the evil that befell them. Rather than standing between humans and nature's harsh realities, Yhwh had a symbiotic relationship with Creation, using it to direct and discipline the Israelites.

When the Israelites misbehaved and violated the covenant, God used the powers of the natural world to enforce fidelity through drought or bad harvests. Good things came in proportion to the people's adherence to the covenant. The biblical worldview, therefore, "puts enormous responsibility in human hands, for the whole world depends on human behavior."[13]

Frymer-Kensky doubts that Israelite peasants would have made the connection between the lack of adequate harvest and failing "to do justice, and to love kindness" (Mic. 6:8), as the covenant required. Monotheism's difficult-to-grasp abstractions guaranteed that both Israelite monarchs and their people continued to appeal to the old gods to help them out.

This older pantheon included parent gods whose job it was to intercede on behalf of individuals before greater gods. In the biblical schema, however, "God-the-father is also the highest power of the cosmos."[14] Who, then, was to advocate for the people defined as Yhwh's children?

For otherwise monotheistic biblical writers, the answer was—surprisingly—feminine intercessors, such as Woman Wisdom, Lady Zion, and Mother Rachel. Each of these feminine figures mediated between Yhwh and the feckless people of Israel—more specifically, its men.

Woman Wisdom was approachable in a fashion that Yhwh was not and offered men an object for their devotion that was both orthodox and female. Lady Zion was the image prophets used to personify Jerusalem and to evoke the love that existed between God and God's people. She was "the sacred bridge that unites them."[15] This feminized Zion made it possible for men to express their love in a way that they could not with the distant, masculine Yhwh.

During the Exile, the prophet Jeremiah evoked the matriarch Rachel, legendary wife of Jacob, in a manner resembling Sumerian goddess-mothers.

> Thus says the LORD:
> A voice is heard in Ramah, lamentation and bitter weeping.
> Rachel is weeping for her children; she refuses to be
>   comforted for her children,
>   because they are no more. (JER. 31:15)

In response, Yhwh promised Mother Rachel that her children—the Israelites—"shall come back from the land of the enemy" to their own country. In much the same way, the Sumerian goddess Amageshtinanna, who bewailed the death of Dumuzi, was allowed to take his place in the Netherworld part of the year so that Dumuzi—and fertility—could return to Earth.[16]

Even the staunchest partisans of Yhwh, it seems, could not do without a female icon or two!

In Our Image

The actual history of Israelite religion, with the many polytheistic flourishes even in its most orthodox expressions, grant us the latitude to make choices for ourselves about what is sacred and how we conceive of divinity. Mulling over the following questions can help make use of this freedom to reimagine God.

- How do you feel about the Deity depicted in the Bible?
- What characteristics reassure you? What do you dislike or fear? What engenders ambivalence?
- Of the many qualities exhibited by the biblical Deity, which are characteristic of the One with whom you commune?
- How do you now define Holiness?
- Who or what do you worship?
- How is this Being active in your life?

When Snakes Could Fly

Millennia before Israel existed, snakes—often winged—and the uraeus were goddess figures, says Miriam Robbins Dexter in *Whence the Goddesses*. From at least 7500 BCE and probably earlier, *theacentric* (goddess-centered) civilizations throughout Eastern Europe, the Near East, and India portrayed goddesses as snakes and with snakes, as well as in human form, or as bird-women. More than mere "fertility" figures, these images represented goddesses of regeneration who may have been responsible for the entire cycle of life, from birth through death and into the afterlife.

One of the earliest recorded snake-goddesses was the Egyptian Uatchet, who "was represented both as a woman and as a large *winged serpent*" (emphasis in the original).[17] Her symbol was the uraeus, which the northern dynasties adopted as a sign of sovereignty. The uraeus adorned the headdresses of pharaohs for thousands of years. In Egyptian hieroglyphics, a stylized serpent denoted both "goddess" and "priestess."

Sumerian, Syrian, Minoan, Mycenaen, and Indic cultures all depicted snakes with goddesses. Classical Greece and Rome also adopted the serpent-goddess: Hygieia, the Roman goddess of health (and source of the word "hygiene") was depicted with a serpent around her shoulders and a caduceus at her side.

As societies moved away from earth-based religions, serpents were demoted to servants of the gods or, worse, their enemies. The Hebrew Bible evinces this trend.

In the eighth century BCE, the prophet Isaiah of Jerusalem envisioned Yhwh on a "high and lofty" heavenly throne.

> Seraphs were in attendance above him; each had six wings: with two they covered their faces, and with two they covered their legs, and with two they flew. And one called to another and said: "Holy, holy, holy is the lord of hosts; the whole earth is full of his glory." (ISA. 6:2–3)

Isaiah's description evoked the symbol of Uatchet if you know how to interpret it. The uraeus technically was a representation of Egypt's black-necked cobra, which spits as well as bites. In Hebrew, the name for both the actual snake and its mythological image is *saraf*, "the one that burns." Isaiah's seraphs therefore were winged serpents. In numinous zones, such as the heavenly precincts described by Isaiah, these creatures could appear with legs, hands, and even human voices.[18] Graphic depictions of uraei with two or four wings were very popular during Isaiah's lifetime.

Generally, however, the Hebrew Bible depicted serpents and snakelike creatures as enemies of Yhwh, or at least the object of God's wrath. Psalm 74 praises God by saying,

> You divided the sea by your might;/ you broke the heads of the dragons in the waters.

> You crushed the heads of Leviathan; you gave him as food for the
> creatures of the wilderness. (PS. 74:13–14)

The Leviathan was a sea monster that represented the forces of
chaos. Writing at the time of the Exile, the psalmist hoped to elicit
God's help against the Babylonians, but he did so by associating the
formerly noble serpent with chaos and monsters.

The legend of Adam and Eve (Gen. 2–3), however, remains the best
example of the Israelite campaign against the snake-goddess. The story
depicts Eve accepting an invitation from a serpent, "the shrewdest of
all the wild beasts," to eat from "the tree of knowledge of good and
bad" that Yhwh had put off-limits. Yhwh reacted to the news that Eve
acquiesced by cursing the serpent:

> Because you did this,/More cursed shall you be/
>   Than all cattle/And all the wild beasts:
> On your belly shall you crawl/And dirt shall you eat/
>   All the days of your life. (GEN. 3:14, JPS)

Assigning the serpent to crawl on its belly suggests that it had a
previous mode of transport. Wings, perhaps?

Although commentators later said that Eve brought sin into the
world, I've long thought that she did us a favor. Primal innocence is not
all it's cracked up to be. Once the first couple ate the fruit offered by
the serpent, they could do things they couldn't before—such as fashion clothes for themselves out of fig leaves. By getting thrown out of
the garden, they began the journey that eventually would produce all of
human culture, from farming and herding to metalworking and music.
Perhaps that's what Yhwh intended all along.

As I hope you've realized, reading the Bible through Eve's eyes provides
us with the opportunity to see the entire cosmos in a new and exuberant

way. We discover that we have choices about what we accept as Holy and how we image God. With the Teacher, we find that "there is nothing better for mortals than to eat and drink, and find enjoyment in their toil" (Eccl. 2:24). We learn to embrace our allotted years as a blessing rather than a curse. And we are empowered to seek justice for all of Creation.

May the Holy One bless your journey.

HOW TO READ THE BIBLE:
A TRAVEL GUIDE

Here's a bit of advice before we shove off on our Grand Tour of the Bible: You may not understand everything on first—or even second—reading, but clarity will come. You don't need to believe everything you read, and you can certainly disagree with it. A complex ancient manuscript does not easily reveal its secrets.

As you read the Bible, there may be times when you just want to cover territory and that's fine. To get the most out of the process, however, I suggest you read more slowly. Travel at a leisurely pace. Stop often. I recommend selecting short, cohesive units of the Bible and using the approaches outlined below. It will help you slow down and see all there is to see.

Selecting a Destination

"What to read?" is the first question. For each genre, I've provided lists of passages featuring women; the starred ones are good starting points. If the passage is lengthy, break it into smaller units. (Most Bible versions do this for you by dividing the text into paragraphs.) Allow your curiosity to guide your reading once you try a few of the starred readings.

You could select a passage from the weekly portions read by Jewish congregations. They read the first five books of the Bible each year from start to finish in weekly units called *"parashah,"* along with associated readings from the Prophets, called *"haftarah."* Christians, on the other hand, use a three-year cycle of weekly readings called the *lectionary,* which consists of small slices of the Bible keyed to the church calendar. These usually are small enough to chew thoroughly.

Reading with an Open Heart and Mind

Over the years, I've developed the following method for exploring a passage. It entails reading the Bible with pen and paper at the ready, and with an open mind and heart. (With time, you will develop your own method.) You might want to read through the following sections to get an overview of the process, then try it out when you're ready to dig deeper into a passage. You don't have to use all the tools I offer all at once and there won't be a quiz.

Working from the Center

I begin by centering myself. Usually, I close my eyes, take a couple of deep breaths, relax my shoulders, and for a minute or so follow my breath as it moves in and out of my body. I become aware of how I'm sitting and what my body feels like. I let go of tension with each breath. When I'm settled, I open my eyes and begin.

1. First, I read the passage carefully once or twice, then pause to note how it strikes me. I think about what feelings it evoked, however "unreasonable."

2. Then, I jot down a few words about these early impressions. If these impressions are linked to past encounters with the text, I note what they are about.

Sometimes, my first impressions won't seem to make sense; I have to trust that there will be value in them. I remember traveling to the Grand Canyon for the first time and thinking the vista looked flat, like a blurry, painted backdrop. The scale of the place was so immense—together with the myriad shapes of rock and earth, and colors that changed from moment to moment—that my brain could not register all of the sensations. (Don't be surprised if your first encounters with the Bible are similarly disorienting.) It took several days until I was able to see the landscape in 3-D, perceiving distances and picking out rock formations.

I've since learned that most visitors to the Grand Canyon respond as I first did. Back home thinking about my visit, I was tempted to discard my initial impressions and concentrate on my later memories as the "true" ones. After all, those were the picture-postcard images that I had journeyed hundred of miles to acquire.

But editing my memories would have been a mistake. My initial, incapacitating astonishment at the sight of the Grand Canyon told me something significant about the vastness I had encountered. At times, the comfort of ordinary perceptions must give way so that we can grasp what unsettling encounters have to offer.

I hope you will value your initial impressions of biblical texts in the same way. Your feelings, often fleeting and quickly replaced by reasoned conclusions, are pathways to meanings that you might not otherwise glean. They may seem contrary to what you think you "should" be feeling—but they are important. Please honor them.

YOUR TRAVEL KIT

Besides a Bible (appendix 2 helps you find one), your explorations will be aided by having:

- A notebook or journal
- Writing implements
- Sticky notes

To underline in your Bible, use a soft pencil, because highlighters bleed through the thin paper and so do most pens (except for the fine-point drafting pens found in art stores). A small plastic ruler or simply a piece of cardstock will ensure that your underlining is neat.

The sticky notes are for marking passages and annotating your Bible, if you'd like. It's a way to start a conversation with the text, a chance to think out loud, challenge, revel in, or simply remember something that moves you, confuses you, or raises your hackles.

Moving On

After you've recorded your first impressions:

1. Read your passage again—and again. Read out loud if you're in a place where you can do that. If there is dialogue in the passage, read it as if real people were conversing.
2. Watch out for elements that seem "off" in your passage: confusing descriptions, conflicting feelings, or perplexing lines of argument that make you wonder, "Huh?" Make a note of these and also a list of anything that is unclear—unfamiliar words, place names, allusions, or other questions of fact.
3. If women are mentioned, observe how they are presented, especially relative to men. In what ways does their representation feel authentic or distorted?

Then look for definitions and context:

4. Clarify the meaning of the items you listed as being unclear. The notes in your study Bible will help you. You also may have to consult a Bible dictionary or an atlas. (These tools are described in the next appendix.) Remember to read the introductory essay to your particular book of the Bible.
5. Read the passages before and after your selection to grasp its context. Is your passage a continuation or shift of topic or tone? Has the scene

or characters changed? How do the answers to these questions affect your understanding of the passage?

Survey the scene and determine what is still unclear. Keep your questions in mind as you move on to the next leg of the journey because they will guide your search.

Scenic Overlook Ahead

Now you can slow way down and find out in more detail how your passage is put together. Keep in mind that there's no taxi meter running, no race to win. This kind of close reading, exploring, and problem solving doesn't have to be done all at once. It's okay to pause, think, reflect, and proceed a little at a time. Remember, too, that basically you're asking the same two questions all the way through: What's going on here, and what does it mean to me?

Check out "What Do You See?" a checklist of compositional details on the following page. Start at the top of the list and read through your passage looking for each of these elements. Write down what you find— and anything else that catches your eye. These nitty-gritty details can provide surprising insights.

After you've gone through the list, take a moment to stop and review what you've discovered thus far.

* What stands out about the passage? Are there any telling details? (Verbs are a good indicator of what the writer hopes to communicate, so pay particular attention to them.)
* In twenty words or less, what do you think the writer intended to say?
* What questions remain? What emotional responses linger?

This doesn't have to be the end of your journey, but it's a good place to rest for now. Just as you stop for the night when traveling a great distance, it's useful to put your inquiry aside and pick it up later when fresh insights may arise.

Perhaps it will help you to know that scholars call this process of coming to an informed understanding of a text *exegesis* (ek´ sə-je´-sis). The word

Table A1.1: What Do You See?

Recurring words, phrases, and ideas	What words, phrases, or ideas recur? These may provide a key to what is most important or indicate the development of ideas.
Verbs	How is the action advanced? Underline or list all the verbs. Note if any are in the imperative (command) form.
Nouns and names	Who is named and how are they identified? Who is not named? What objects are mentioned and what is their function?
Mood	What is the atmosphere created by the passage? How is this mood created—through action, description, dialogue?
Assertions	Are there exhortations, admonitions, advice, warnings, or promises? Assertions of truth?
Cause and effect	Does the writer set forth advice in an "*if … then*" form? Is cause and effect present in the action itself? Or are reasons given for an action?
Examples, comparisons, or contrasts	Does the passage provide illustrations or examples, make comparisons, or offer contrasts?
Questions	If questions are part of the passage, what are their function? Do they introduce new ideas, provide a summary, or have a role in dialogue?
Connecting words	Connectives expose key ideas and relationships. "But" introduces a contrasting proposition; "if" is a conditional denoting something that may or may not occur; "for," "because," "therefore" precede explanations; "in order that" signals a statement of purpose.
Lists	Is there a list of items or ideas? Examine it for progressions (from larger to smaller, from ___ to ___) and the order of items. Is anything left out that should logically be there?
Description	What words are used descriptively? Adjectives and adverbs are sparse in the Bible; when they appear, they are significant.
Assumptions	What does the passage assume that you know or believe?
Point of View (POV)	From whose perspective is the passage written? Who is the presumed audience?

comes from a Greek verb meaning "to lead out of." You can think of your work as "leading the meaning out of a text."

Bringing It All Back Home

While we'll never know a writer's intention for certain, most of the time we can come up with a plausible explanation. The next step—determining what the passage means to you—is more open ended because meaning making is highly individual. Here's where all of your personal history comes into play. What I take away from a passage may be different than what you get from it; there is no one "correct" interpretation.

This art of interpretation is known as *hermeneutics* (hur´-mə-no´-tiks), a fact I am imparting not only so you have a fancy word with which to impress your friends. "Hermeneutics" is derived from the same root as the name of the Greek god Hermes, messenger of the gods and patron of travelers, who sported winged shoes, a broad-brimmed hat, and a herald's staff. I think of biblical interpretation as an attempt to intercept Divine messages like those Hermes carried.

A final set of questions helps bring meaning to the surface:

- In what ways is the text speaking to me? What new insights does it present?
- How does its pertain to my life or the world around me? Does it remind me of anything in my life or the wider world?
- Is there a character or an action or an insight that moves me?
- If the passage leaves me cold, where is the disconnect? If I disagree with the biblical writer, what do I want to say to him?
- What in the passage do I want to keep?
- How do I think my life experiences influence my understanding of the passage? Can I imagine other perspectives?
- What has this text added to my understanding of God or the Sacred?

Staying Open to Meaning

Time may pass before the meaning of a passage sinks in or has value. You may need to walk around with the passage rattling around in your head for a while. It may even subside into your subconscious, then suddenly, unexpectedly, pop up to illuminate an issue or a situation.

That's what happened one evening as a friend was telling me and some of her other friends about her grandfather's recent funeral. She was very sad, but she said, "I don't know why I'm still so bothered by this."

"Because this is how we honor our mothers and fathers," I said, the words of the Ten Commandments coming out of my mouth before I knew what I was saying. She was startled, and then the meaning sank in. I had never before thought of mourning as honoring our ancestors, but it suddenly made sense. And my friend felt more at ease with her grief.

Mapping Your Location

Sometimes after working with a passage there's something about it that still bugs me, so I diagram it to better see what's going on. By "diagram" I mean write it out in any form that helps me make connections visually or in a more right-brained way.

A story about Sarah and Abraham in Genesis 18, for instance, had me stuck. On its surface, the action was clear, but there were concealed undercurrents.

In the story, three "men"—it's unclear whether they are angels or Yhwh in disguise—appear at the tents of Abraham, who offers them hospitality. A conversation ensues during which the visitors announce that Sarah will bear a son. At that Sarah laughs, and then Yhwh challenges Abraham over his wife's response and Abraham challenges Sarah.[1] Here's what my diagram looks like:

They said to him, "Where is your wife Sarah?"

And he said, "There in the tent."

Then one said,   "I will surely return to you in due
                                    season, and your wife Sarah shall
                                    have a son."

And Sarah was listening at the
    tent entrance behind him.

Now Abraham and Sarah were
    old, advanced in age; it had
    ceased to be with Sarah after
    the manner of women.

So Sarah laughed to herself   "After I have grown old and my husband
    saying,   is old, Shall I have pleasure?"

The LORD said to Abraham,   "Why did Sarah laugh and say 'Shall I
                                    indeed bear a child, now that I am
                                    old?' Is anything too wonderful for
                                    the LORD? At the set time I will
                                    return to you, in due season, and
                                    Sarah shall have a son."

But Sarah denied, saying,   "I did not laugh";
for she was afraid.

He said,   "Oh yes, you did laugh."

Once I wrote out the passage in this manner, I could see more plainly
the explanatory remarks added by the narrator in this minidrama, the relative physical locations of the actors, the progression of the action, and the
dramatic tension surrounding Sarah's laughter. My diagram also graphically
illustrated the plot point on which everything hinged: that Sarah is quite
old. The narrator places this information dead center—"Now Abraham and

Sarah were old, advanced in age; it had ceased to be with Sarah after the manner of women"—then repeated it two more times. Here is the surprise, but also the crux of the matter: Sarah may be old, but Yhwh can do anything.

The diagram also helped me see more clearly that although the men were talking *about* Sarah, she was actively engaged in the conversation: She listened, then she laughed and spoke to herself. I also thought it interesting that while the passage began with the (male) visitors speaking with Abraham, it wrapped up with a spat between husband and wife. This combination of divine pronouncement and household tiff imbues the passage with engaging charm—and explained the emotional undercurrents I could sense but not locate.

I have diagrammed passages by outlining them using a standard academic format (I. A, B, II. A, B, etc.) as well as being more free-form, letting my hand take me where it will on a blank page, clustering phrases, then circling and linking them—connecting the dots, as it were.

Check Your Baggage

To get the most out of your reading, it helps to be aware of what you're bringing with you on your journey through the Bible.

Start by thinking about what role the Bible has played in your life. Was there a Bible in your house when you were growing up? Why or why not? Did anyone read it? If so, under what circumstances? Did you hear the Bible read during religious services? In what language? What impressions do you have of those experiences? What role has the Bible played in your life as an adult? Are particular passages special to you? Are there passages you respond to negatively? How do you feel about people for whom the Bible is a guiding force in their daily lives? Why?

As you jot down answers to these questions, you may discover preconceptions that you want to set aside. You may uncover unwarranted trust or distrust that holds you back from new insights. At the very least, your notes will make interesting reading after you have worked with the methods outlined in *Eve's Bible*.

A second set of conditions also needs attention: the social and cultural context in which you engage the Bible. One of life's truisms is that what you see depends upon where you are standing. When you travel into the Bible, the "where" does not refer so much to physical location as "social location." Social location includes all the variables that have made you *you*: religious upbringing, family background, race, sex, age, sexual preference, physical abilities, geography. All of these factors influence how you read and respond to biblical material.

Take a moment to write down some of the defining features of your life. Once you acknowledge that you approach the Bible from a distinctive standpoint and begin to consider how your ideas were formed, you gain a greater openness to other points of view. You also become less likely to worship at the altar of dogmatic biblical interpretations.

A SHOPPER'S GUIDE TO BUYING A BIBLE

When you shop for a Bible, you will find infinite variety. There are hardbound, leatherbound, and paperbound Bibles. You can buy tiny pocket Bibles and huge volumes that require a special stand to support them. You will find Bibles titled like novels: *The Message, A Passion for God, Good News for Modern Man*. Bibles with gilt-edged pages and ribbon bookmarks. Bibles with almost as many footnotes as text. And on and on.

How, then, do you make a choice?

The main thing to remember is that the color or kind of binding, the gilt-edged pages, or the size of the Bible are bells and whistles. You can decide later which of these particulars suits your needs. First, you need to answer this question: Which of the dozens of modern translations do you want to read?

Only they're not called translations; they are called *versions*.

Bible Versions

All of the English versions of the Bible are translations, but every translation from the original languages resulted in a different English version.

Why? Because translation comprises translating cultural beliefs as well as words.

Language and Culture

A language reflects the culture that brought it into being. Translating from one language into another entails moving back and forth between different ways of experiencing the world. A book such as the Bible presents additional difficulties because thousands of years have passed since its words were written.

Sometimes there simply are no words available to translate an experience or emotion common to one culture and language but not to another. And then there are idioms and puns and colloquialisms. How does a translator convey the humor, earthiness, or sarcasm that is bound up in wordplay? The writers of Genesis, for example, describe Adam, *ha adam,* as made from earth, *ha adamah.* The Hebrew pun points to how the first human was literally made of earth and suggests that we are rooted in the physical world, not the heavens. "Earth creature" might better approximate the meaning of *ha adam* than the proper noun Adam.

Knowing a little about how translators go about their work and how they try to bridge the gaps between languages (and cultures) will help you choose your version.

How Translators Translate

You will probably choose a version because it sounds good to you or feels comfortable to read. That's fine. But without knowing it, your choice expresses a preference that is fundamental to the act of translation. When translators work, they use one of two approaches. They translate either *word-for-word,* using English words that are closest to the original Hebrew, Greek, or Aramaic words, or they use a *thought-for-thought* approach that reaches for the overall sense of the sentence.

The word-for-word method is more literal. You may see it referred to as "formal equivalence" or "formal correspondence" because the translator searches for words or expressions that are *equivalent to* or *correspond* closely to the original, adjusting the choices according to context.

These translations provide a close rendering of the original text and the author's personal style, but they are not lyrical. They may even sound a little clunky in places. The New Revised Standard Version (NRSV) treads this path.

(Literal word-for-word translations of the ancient language into English can be found in *interlinears,* which print the original Hebrew, Aramaic, or Greek with a direct English translation above each word. The text of a standard English version runs alongside the original in a column.)

The thought-for-thought method of translation is called "dynamic transference" or "functional equivalence." These translations attempt to *transfer the dynamic qualities* of the original text into English. They are not formally equivalent but convey the sense of a passage in a way that *functions as equivalent* to the original. Translators who work by this method often use punchy contemporary language or a restricted vocabulary in order to make their version more accessible. The New International Version (NIV) is a popular thought-for-thought translation.

Here are examples of the two different approaches to translation. On the left is Gen. 3:1–3 from the NRSV (word-for-word) and on the right, the same verses from the NIV (thought-for-thought).

NRSV

NIV

Now the serpent was more crafty than any other wild animal that the LORD God had made. He said to the woman, "Did God say, 'You shall not eat from any tree in the garden'?" The woman said to the serpent, "We may eat of the fruit of the trees in the garden; but God said, 'You shall not eat of the fruit of the tree that is in the middle of the garden, nor shall you touch it, or you shall die.'"

Now the serpent was more crafty than any of the wild animals the LORD God had made. He said to the woman, "Did God really say, 'You must not eat from any tree in the garden'?" The woman said to the serpent, "We may eat fruit from the trees in the garden, but God did say, 'You must not eat fruit from the tree that is in the middle of the garden, and you must not touch it, or you will die.'"

Note that the NRSV language is more formal than the NIV's, which implies a more distant relationship between God and the woman. In the NIV, God, as quoted by the woman, sounds more like a parent speaking to a child: "You must not eat. . . ." The NRSV sounds stiff in places since it hews closely to the original language, while the NIV tends to flow more smoothly—but words not in the original are added to create this smoothness: "Did God *really* say . . . ?" The differences are subtle, but in subtlety lie nuances of meaning.

Both of these modes of translation are accurate; you won't find gross distortions in either. As a reader, you get to decide which approach you prefer. Or, you can purchase several versions and compare them as you read, which helps to illuminate the meanings behind the English words.

Paraphrases

A third option in biblical translating is a *paraphrase*. The author of a paraphrase usually takes an English version and puts it into contemporary or simpler language. These are not translations so much as they are retellings of the Bible. Here, for example, is how Eugene H. Peterson reworked Genesis 3:1–3 for his paraphrase of the Bible called *The Message*.

> The serpent was clever, more clever than any wild animal GOD had made. He spoke to the Woman: "Do I understand that God told you not to eat from any tree in the garden?" The Woman said to the serpent, "Not at all. We can eat from the trees in the garden. It's only about the tree in the middle of the garden that God said, 'Don't eat from it, don't even touch it or you'll die.'"

You can see that paraphrases are easy to read. They are not suitable by themselves for Bible study, however, because so much of the original has been changed.

He, She, or It

Women have another issue when it comes to Bible versions, and it's a hot one: gendered language. At one time, Americans accepted the use of "men" or "he"—generic masculine language—to refer to both women and men.

Nowadays, we expect inclusive language that explicitly acknowledges both men *and* women. But the Bible isn't written that way. Attempts to create more inclusive translations have been controversial because a lot of folks are touchy about tampering with scripture.

Modern translators have dealt with gendered language in a number of ways. When the National Council of Churches, the mainline Protestant group that holds the copyright to the Revised Standard Version (RSV), decided in the 1970s that it was time to update their earlier editions, their translators decided to make the language of the revision as inclusive as possible. After all, women in their member denominations now were ordained ministers and church leaders.

Some readers appreciate the new inclusivity, whereas others feel it distorts the meaning, even when amendments are clearly marked. A storm of protest greeted the Evangelical favorite, the New International Version, when it was offered as Today's New International Version (TNIV), with changes similar to those in the NRSV.

Some feminist scholars, on the other hand, object to inclusive translations because they think the inclusivity is synthetic: It papers over the Bible's sexism, they argue, and doesn't really change the social reality that women have yet to achieve full equality.

Although theological liberals tend to favor inclusive language and conservatives oppose it, there are exceptions. Some people just like things the way they have always been, a sentiment attested to by the enduring popularity of the beautiful but archaic King James Version (KJV).

If you want to know the extent to which inclusive language has been used in a translation, you will have to read the editor's preface. This information won't be on the cover or the title page. Publishers' Web sites (see the table on page 283–284) can also help you.

Translation as Interpretation

By now, you have probably grasped that translators *interpret* as they translate. Ideas about God differ widely, and Bible translations reflect these differing views. In a circular fashion, the translations then influence beliefs.

Maid or Virgin?

If you are curious about the ways in which religious doctrines can influence translation, here is a good illustration from the book of Isaiah.

In the seventh century BCE, a prophet named Isaiah chastised the ruling class for their evil ways. He predicted that God would send a sign to them: an *almah* would become pregnant, give birth, and call the child Immanuel. Bad things would happen to the nation even before this child grew up (Isa. 7:10–25).

What is an *almah*? *Almah* is the Hebrew word for a young woman of marriageable age. In the version that reflects mainline Protestant values (the NRSV), the passage is translated this way: "Look, the young woman is with child and shall bear a son, and shall name him Immanuel."

On the other hand, the New American Bible (NAB), translated under the authority of the Roman Catholic Church, reads: "the *virgin* shall be with child, and bear a son, and shall name him Immanuel." The NIV, a favorite of Protestant Evangelicals, also uses the word "virgin" in this sentence.

Hebrew has a word for virgin *(bethulah*, which literally means "separated")* but that's not the word used in the original Hebrew texts.

Virgin or young woman, what's the difference? The distinction is small but significant, because Christians later interpreted Isaiah's prophecy as referring to Jesus of Nazareth, whose mother was said to have been a virgin. For both Catholics and conservative Protestants, the doctrine of the Virgin Birth—that the mother of Jesus was impregnated by the Holy Spirit and remained a virgin although she gave birth—is critically important. It is less central to the belief and practice of liberal Protestants. Jewish translators also rendered *almah* as "young woman" (JPS).

By translating *almah* as "virgin," Isaiah's words become a small but crucial piece of a larger theological dispute about the validity and significance of the doctrine of Virgin Birth, and whether it has the authority of scripture behind it. Translation, interpretation, belief, and doctrine are intertwined. That's why comparing different versions of the same passage is so helpful—and so fascinating.

So Many Versions, So Little Time

The table on page 279–280 lists the major, in-print English versions, notes whether they are "literal" (word-for-word) translations or "dynamic" (thought-for-thought), and identifies their theological orientation.

After you decide which version to purchase, the next decision is whether you want a Bible with the Apocrypha/Deuterocanonical books, which are accepted as authoritative by some Christian denominations but not by others. (And no Jewish group accepts them, even though they were part of the Hebrew Bible when it was translated into Greek at the end of the first millennium BCE.)

If you want the most complete collection, look for a Bible that says "With Apocrypha/Deuterocanonical Books," or "Catholic Edition." Versions commissioned by the Roman Catholic Church that carry its *imprimatur* (the New American Bible, Jerusalem Bible, and New Jerusalem Bible), or editions published for the Orthodox Christian community won't necessarily say that the Deuterocanonical books are included because they're just assumed to be part of the package. With other versions, you have a choice.

Eve's Bible refers to passages from the Apocrypha/Deuterocanonical books, so it would be good to have access to those works, even if you choose as your primary Bible a Jewish version that does not include them.

A Shopper's Guide to Buying a Bible

Okay, you've decided which version to use and whether or not to include those "extra" books. Now things get *really* complicated. Publishers package and market Bibles like any other commodity, and the trend in recent years has been to put out special editions for increasingly smaller niche markets such as campus athletes or African-American women. Most of these editions, however, fit into one of the seven categories described in the chart on pages 281–282.

For our purposes, a study Bible (also called an annotated Bible) is the best use of your money. These have copious amounts of reference materials

Table A2.1: English Versions of the Bible

Translation	Date	Translation Method	Theological Perspective
American Standard Bible (ASB)	1901	literal; first revision of KJV	Evangelical, conservative
Amplified Bible	1964; 1987	literal, with amplifications added in parentheses	Evangelical, conservative
Contemporary English Version (CEV)	1995	dynamic; contemporary language	Evangelical, conservative, mainline
English Standard Version (ESV)	2001	literal; revision of RSV without gender-neutral language	Evangelical, conservative
God's Word	1995	dynamic; uses simple, common language	Evangelical, conservative
Good News Translation (GNT), formerly called Today's English Version (TEV)	1976	dynamic; uses simple, common language	Conservative; accepted by Roman Catholics
Holman Christian Standard Bible (HCSB)	2004	dynamic; contemporary language	Evangelical, conservative (Southern Baptist)
King James Version (KJV)	1611	literal; Elizabethan English	Anglican (Church of England)
The Living Bible		paraphrase of American Standard Version (1901)	Conservative
The Message	2002	paraphrase from original languages	Evangelical, conservative
New American Bible (NAB)	1970; NT revised 1986	1970: dynamic; 1986: literal	Roman Catholic
New American Standard Bible (NASB)	1971; updated 1995	literal	Evangelical, conservative

(continued)

Table A2.1: (continued)

Translation	Date	Translation Method	Theological Perspective
New Century Version (NCV)	1991	dynamic	Evangelical, conservative
New English Bible (NEB)	1970	dynamic; British English	British Protestant
New International Version (NIV)	1978, 1983	literal with dynamic balance	Evangelical, conservative
New International Reader's Version (NIrV)	1996, 1998	literal and dynamic; simple language for new readers	Evangelical, conservative
New Jerusalem Bible (NJB)	1985	literal with dynamic balance	Roman Catholic
New King James Version (NKJV)	1982	literal; revision of KJV with some modern language	Conservative
New Living Translation (NLT)	1996, 2004	dynamic; uses contemporary language	Evangelical, conservative
New Revised Standard Version (NRSV)	1990	literal; uses gender-neutral language	Mainline Protestant
Revised Standard Version (RSV)	1952	literal	Mainline Protestant; accepted by Roman Catholic and Orthodox
Stone Edition Tanach	1996	dynamic	Jewish
Tanakh (JPS)	1985	dynamic	Jewish
Today's New International Version (TNIV)	2001, 2005	revision of NIV with updated and gender-neutral language	Evangelical

in addition to the text. Footnotes explain unusual terms and wordplay, provide historical background, and refer you to other relevant passages. Each separate book has an introduction of several pages to orient you to its contents. Some editions include maps and indices to help you cross-reference topics.

The quality and type of supporting materials in study Bibles varies with the publisher; the theological slant of the notes usually coincides with the orientation of the Bible version. My favorite study Bibles are published by Oxford University Press (*The New Oxford Annotated Bible,* third edition, and *The Jewish Study Bible*) and HarperSanFrancisco (*The HarperCollins Study Bible*). They all have informative notes, essays, and auxiliary materials; the Oxford editions also include essays on topics such as biblical interpretation and the cultural context of biblical writings.

Table A2.2: Seven Types of Bibles

Study	Designed for students and readers who want historical background and explanations of unfamiliar words or circumstances. Includes introductory essays to each book.
Reference	Provides multiple references to other passages with a similar topic or keyword. (These may or may not have a bearing on the original passage.)
Life Application/ Devotional	Includes essays and stories designed to deepen the reader's Christian faith. Commentaries on various passages help readers make connections between the text and modern life, and to apply what they read to their own lives.
Parallel	Parallel columns of type on each page carry the text of two or more versions. Available in many different combinations, including multiple languages.
Children's, 'Tween, Teen, Young Adult	Children's Bibles usually are collections of selected, paraphrased stories or the full text of an easy-to-read version with illustrations, cartoon characters, and lots of explanations. "Teen," "'tween," or "young adult" usually are complete texts with commentaries, notes, and "life application" essays geared towards those age groups.

(continued)

Table A2.2: (continued)

Topical	Not Bibles per se but complications of Bible verses grouped according to topics.
Readers' Editions	Just the text with nothing but chapter divisions and verses added. Denominational publishing houses often print these in very low-cost formats.

Before I knew very much about the Bible, I picked up a nice hardbound copy on sale, intending to make a serious effort to read it. Unwittingly, I had purchased the *Scofield Reference Bible* and it killed my interest in the Bible for many years afterward.

C. I. Scofield, a nineteenth-century fundamentalist Protestant, had—how shall I say this?—*unique* ideas about salvation. He postulated that time is divided into seven "dispensations," each of which is characterized by a distinctive relationship between God and humankind. Time itself will end in the "Kingdom Age," when Christ establishes his dominion, the Jewish kingdom is restored, Jews are converted to Christ, and all creation is redeemed.

While most reference and study Bibles have updated their materials over the years, Scofield's notes remain intact and are now published with the New King James Version (NKJV) and NIV, among other versions. His dispensational theology has gained many adherents over the years.

A Shopping Checklist

Now it's time to pay attention to those bells and whistles. By answering the following questions, you'll narrow down your choices.

- What kind of binding do you want? Bibles are among the few books still bound in leather, but you'll find cloth and paper bindings as well. My paperbound study Bibles (called "college" or "student" editions) have proven surprisingly durable.
- How do you want the text to appear on the page? Many editions print the text in columns, usually two to a page, while others format the text like an ordinary book and run it across the page. You can also choose

whether you want text printed with or without subheadings. The subheadings are not part of the original documents, and they reflect the theological orientation of the editors.

- Do you want to travel with your Bible? Pocket, compact, trimline, or slimline editions are lightweight Bibles printed on very fine paper without extended notes or introductions.

- What size type is comfortable to read? You don't need to put up with microscopic print; Bibles are printed with a range of fonts, styles, and sizes. You can also purchase large-print Bibles.

- Do you want the Bible in digital form? Most publishers now produce Bibles on CD-ROM and for PDF downloads. You can also find fully searchable versions online for free.

Table 2.3: Publishers of Bibles and their Web sites

Shopping online is one of the best ways to sort through the huge variety of Bible editions and narrow your choices, even if you eventually purchase your Bible from a bookstore. Here is a list of publishers that either carry a wide array of Bibles or have created a unique version. Some are publishing arms of religious denominations; others are independent publishers. See the table on pages 279–280 for an explanation of the abbreviations.

Augsburg Fortress	CEV, KJV, NIV, NRSV	www.augsburgfortress.org
Broadman & Holman Publishers	HCSB	www.broadmanholman.com
Cambridge University Press	NIV, KJV, RSV, NRSV, NASB, NEB	www.cambridgebibles.com
Catholic Book Publishing Co.	NAB	www.catholicbookpublishing.com
Good News Publishers/ Crossway Books & Bibles	ESV	www.gnpcb.org
Jewish Publication Society	Tanakh	www.jewishpub.org
Logos Research Systems	digital resources	www.logos.com

(continued)

Table 2.3: (continued)

Mesorah	*Stone Edition Tanach*	www.mesorah.com
NavPress	*The Message*	www.navpress.com
Oxford University Press–U.S.A.	KJV, NRSV, RSV, NAB; Scofield KJV, NKJV, NIV	www.oup-usa.org/bibles
Thomas Nelson	KJV, NKJV, NCV, NASB, NAB, NRSV	www.thomasnelson.com
Tyndale House Publishers	NLT, KJV, NIV, iLumina	www.tyndale.com
Zondervan	Amplified, KJV, NASB, NIV, NIRV, TNIV, NRSV	www.zondervan.com/bibles

Your Reference Toolkit

I have a small box of tools tucked under the seat of my truck—just in case. In a similar fashion, it's helpful to build up a collection of reference books for when the notes in your study Bible don't satisfy your curiosity.

- The most used item in my toolkit is a *Bible dictionary.* From Aaron to Zurishaddai, if you need to get the Big Picture or don't know what a word means, chances are you'll find it explained in a Bible dictionary. My favorite is the *HarperCollins Bible Dictionary* (1996), published under the sponsorship of the Society of Biblical Literature and edited by Paul J. Achtemeier.

- The Bible assumes you have an intimate knowledge of Near Eastern geography, but it's unlikely that you do, so a *Bible atlas* can come in handy. Your study Bible will have a few basic maps, but the *HarperCollins Concise Atlas of the Bible* (1997), by James B. Pritchard, contains not only great maps and nifty graphics but excellent background on the history behind the texts.

- *Commentaries* are an entire book dedicated to examining a biblical book in detail, usually from the commentator's theological perspective. One-volume *Bible commentaries,* on the other hand, contain essays by various authors on each book of the Bible. A notable example of the latter is *HarperCollins Bible Commentary—Revised Edition* (2000), edited by James L. Mays. A must-have reference for anyone interested in women and the Bible is *The Women's Bible Commentary—Expanded Edition* (1998), edited by Carol A. Newsom and Sharon H. Ringe. Its essays by women scholars provide a perspective not found in many other places.

WHICH BIBLE ARE WE
TALKING ABOUT?

We talk about "the Bible" as if we all knew what that meant. But "the Bible" means different things to different people depending on their religious affiliation.

Table A3.1 lists the contents of four biblical collections. Here's how the differences came about.

The Tanakh

The Jewish Bible is a collection of twenty-four books divided into three sections: the Law, the Prophets, and the Writings. For this reason, it is popularly called the Tanakh, an acronym derived from the first letter of the Hebrew words for each of the three sections—the Law (*Torah*), Prophets (*Nevi'im*) and the Writings (*Kethuvim*). Additionally, the Tanakh designates the books of Joshua, Judges, Samuel, and Kings as part of the Prophets.

All biblical collections have the first five books—called Torah by Jews—in common. Scholars call these books the Pentateuch, Greek for "five." Some people call them "the five books of Moses" because they believe that Moses, who figures prominently in them, also wrote them. (He did not.)

Christian Bibles

To complete *their* Bible, Christians added the "New" Testament, twenty-seven books that originally were written in Greek during the first and second centuries CE. But their "Old Testament" is not identical to the Tanakh. Some Christian denominations designate as scripture writings not included in the Jewish Bible. Christian Bibles are also ordered differently from the Tanakh and from one another.

Where Did Those Extra Books Come From?

Toward the end of the first millennium BCE, the increasing number of Greek-speaking Jews necessitated translating Jewish Scripture into their language. The most influential Greek translation originated in the third century BCE in Alexandria, Egypt, and circulated throughout the Eastern Mediterranean.

This version is called the Septuagint, Greek for "seventy," because it is said that the Egyptian pharaoh sent for six representatives from each of the twelve tribes of Israel to come to Alexandria and translate the Bible. In just seventy-two days, these seventy-two scholars translated, compared drafts, and agreed upon a final Greek version.

It's a lovely story with a touch of the miraculous about it. In fact, the Greek translations were completed over a period of many years by various translators. Sometimes Septuagint is abbreviated as LXX, the Roman numerals for seventy.

This Bible in Greek contained writings that were removed from the Jewish canon in the first century CE, but the "extra" books were accepted by some Christians to varying degrees.

The Apocrypha and Deuterocanonical Books

The Christian denomination that has come to be called Greek Orthodox simply adopted the Septuagint as their Bible, give or take a few items. The

Russian Orthodox Bible uses the collection that was translated long ago from the Greek into Old Slavonic.

The Roman Catholic Church, on the other hand, relied upon the collection of books translated from Hebrew and Greek into Latin in the fourth century CE by a scholar-monk named Jerome. Jerome translated the "extra" books of the Septuagint, but wrote a preface to them, noting their questionable origin. Subsequently, however, Christian copyists frequently transmitted the entire Latin translation without his notes. The "extra" books got mixed in with the others and were generally accepted as scripture.

At the time of the Protestant Reformation in the sixteenth century CE, the Roman Catholic Church decreed that certain books not in the official Jewish canon were, indeed, scripture. They were placed in the Christian "Old Testament" in much the same order as in the Septuagint. The Roman church called these works Deuterocanonical, a Greek term meaning "second law," which points to their late acceptance as authoritative.

As Protestant reformers translated the Bible from Latin into the vernacular, they generally downgraded the collection of "extra" books to the status of "holy writings" that could be read for edification—but only after a thorough study of the canonical books. The few Protestants who know they exist generally do not consider them scripture. (The first authorized English translation, the King James Version, however, followed the Roman Church, which is why Anglicans include them in their Bibles.)

Protestants labeled this collection the Apocrypha, which literally means "hidden things" and suggests their uncertain status.

Different Sequence, Different Message

Jewish and Christian Bibles also arrange their contents differently to convey two markedly distinct messages.

The narrative arc of the three-part Tanakh follows the Israelites, God's chosen people, through good times and bad to restoration in their homeland (albeit as a colony of the Persians), at the end of Chronicles, the final book of the Writings.

Christians see events through a different lens. They divide the Hebrew scriptures into four sections: the Pentateuch, the historical books, wisdom literature and the psalms, and, finally, the prophets. How does that change the picture? First, the restoration of Israel is deemphasized. Second, the final prophetic book, Malachi, concludes by foretelling the return of the prophet Elijah. Christians interpret this as heralding the coming of Jesus of Nazareth, or, at the very least, the prophet John the Baptist, who preached about Jesus.

Same books + alternate sequence = unique theological point.

Table A3.1: Order of Books
in the Tanakh, Septuagint, and Old Testament

Hebrew Bible	Septuagint	Roman Catholic/ Orthodox	Protestant
TORAH	PENTATEUCH	PENTATEUCH	PENTATEUCH
Bereshith *(Genesis)*	Genesis	Genesis	Genesis
Shemoth *(Exodus)*	Exodus	Exodus	Exodus
Wayiqra *(Leviticus)*	Leviticus	Leviticus	Leviticus
Bemidbar *(Numbers)*	Numbers	Numbers	Numbers
Debarim *(Deuteronomy)*	Deuteronomy	Deuteronomy	Deuteronomy
NEVI'IM (PROPHETS)	HISTORICAL BOOKS	HISTORICAL BOOKS	HISTORICAL BOOKS
Yehoshua *(Joshua)*	Joshua	Joshua	Joshua
Shofetim *(Judges)*	Judges	Judges	Judges
	Ruth	Ruth	Ruth
Shemuel *(1 & 2 Samuel)*	1 & 2 Regnorum *(1 & 2 Samuel)*	1 & 2 Kings *(1 & 2 Samuel)*	1 & 2 Samuel
Melakim *(1 & 2 Kings)*	3 & 4 Regnorum *(1 & 2 Kings)*	3 & 4 Kings *(1 & 2 Kings)*	1 & 2 Kings
	1 & 2 Paralipomenon *(1 & 2 Chronicles)*	1 & 2 Paralipomenon *(1 & 2 Chronicles)*	1 & 2 Chronicles
	1 Esdras (Ezra)	1 & 2 Esdras *(Ezra-Nehemiah)*	Ezra
	2 Esdras *(Nehemiah)*		Nehemiah

(continued)

Table A3.1: *(continued)*

Hebrew Bible	Septuagint	Roman Catholic/ Orthodox	Protestant
Melakim (*1 & 2 Kings*) (*continued*)	Esther Judith Tobit 1, 2, 3, 4 Maccabees	Tobias (*Tobit*) Judith Esther (w/ additions) 1 & 2 Maccabees	Esther
	POETRY AND WISDOM Psalms Odes Proverbs Ecclesiastes Song of Songs Job Wisdom of Solomon Sirach (*Ecclesiasticus*) Psalms of Solomon	POETRY AND WISDOM Job Psalms Proverbs Ecclesiastes Canticle of Canticles (*Song of Solomon*) Wisdom of Solomon Ecclesiasticus (Wisdom of Jesus ben Sirach)	POETRY AND WISDOM Job Psalms Proverbs Ecclesiastes Song of Solomon

LATTER PROPHETS
Yeshayahu (Isaiah)
Yirmevahu (Jeremiah)
 	
Yehezqel
 	
Book of the Twelve
    (Hosea)
    (Joel)
    (Amos)
    (Obadiah)
    (Jonah)
    (Micah)
	PROPHETIC BOOKS
	
	Hosea
	Amos
	Micah
	Joel
	Obadiah
	Jonah
		PROPHETIC BOOKS
		Isaias (*Isaiah*)
		Jeremias (*Jeremiah*)
		Lamentations
		Baruch + Epistle
		of Jeremias
		Ezechiel (*Ezekiel*)
		Daniel + additions
		
		Osee (Hosea)
		Joel
		Amos
		Abidas (*Obadiah*)
		Jonas (*Jonah*)
		Micheas (*Micah*)
			PROPHETIC BOOKS
			Isaiah
			Jeremiah
			Lamentations
			
			Ezekiel
			Daniel
			
			Hosea
			Joel
			Amos
			Obadiah
			Jonah
			Micah

Hebrew Bible	Septuagint	Roman Catholic/ Orthodox	Protestant
(Nahum)	Nahum	Nahum	Nahum
(Habakkuk)	Habakkuk	Habucuc (*Habakkuk*)	Habakkuk
(Zephaniah)	Zephaniah	Sophonias (*Zephaniah*)	Zephaniah
(Haggai)	Haggai	Aggeus (Haggai)	Haggai
(Zechariah)	Zechariah	Zacharias (*Zechariah*)	Zechariah
(Malachi)	Malachi	Malachias (*Malachi*)	Malachi
KETHUVIM (WRITINGS)	Isaiah		
Tehillim (*Psalms*)	Jeremiah		
Iyyob (*Job*)	Baruch		
Mishle (*Proverbs*)	Lamentations		
Ruth	Epistle of Jeremiah		
Shir Hashirm (*Song of Songs*)	Ezekiel		
Qoheleth (*Ecclesiastes*)	Susanna		
Ekah (*Lamentations*)	Daniel		
Ester (*Esther*)	Bel and the Dragon		
Daniel			
Ezra-Nehemyah (*Ezra-Nehemiah*)			
Dibre Hayamin (*1 & 2 Chronicles*)			

NOTES

1. Beginning the Journey

1. Karen Baker-Fletcher, "Anna Julia Cooper and Sojourner Truth: Two Nineteenth-Century Black Feminist Interpreters of Scripture," in *Searching the Scriptures: A Feminist Introduction*, vol. 1, ed. Elisabeth Schüssler Fiorenza (New York: Crossroad, 1993), 47–48.

2. Frances D. Gage, "Soujourner Truth: On Women's Rights," in *Up Against the Wall, Mother . . .* , ed. Elsie Adams and Mary Louise Briscoe (Beverly Hills, CA: Glencoe Press, 1971), 327.

2. Histories: Pious Frauds and Sacred Truths

1. William G. Dever, *What Did the Biblical Writers Know and When Did They Know It?: What Archaeology Can Tell Us About the Reality of Ancient Israel* (Grand Rapids, MI: Wm. B. Eerdmans Publishing Co., 2001), 131–34.

2. Israel Finkelstein and Neil Asher Silberman, *The Bible Unearthed: Archaeology's New Vision of Ancient Israel and the Origin of Its Sacred Texts* (New York: The Free Press, 2001), 141–42.

3. Richard Elliot Friedman, *Who Wrote the Bible?* 2nd ed., reprint, OP1987 (New York: HarperSanFrancisco, 1997), 87.

4. Finkelstein and Silberman, *The Bible Unearthed*, 235–38.

5. Friedman, *Who Wrote The Bible?* 161–206.

3. *Putting Women Back into Sacred History*

1. Judith Plaskow, *Standing Again at Sinai: Judaism from a Feminist Perspective* (San Francisco: Harper & Row, 1990), 25.

2. Claudia V. Camp, "1 and 2 Kings," in *The Women's Bible Commentary*, ed. Carol A. Newsom and Sharon H. Ringe (Louisville, KY: Westminster/John Knox Press, 1992), 104–5.

3. Elisabeth Schüssler Fiorenza, *But She Said: Feminist Practices of Biblical Interpetation* (Boston: Beacon Press, 1992), 73.

4. In Genesis, genealogies help to establish the book's chronology of events. Elsewhere, they confirm a monarch's right to rule, distinguish the various priesthoods and their relative status, reinforce the authority of Moses, place specific personages in a numerically significant position (seventh, usually), and clarify Israel's relationships with other tribes and nations. Genealogies may be boring to read, but they were indispensable tools for the Bible's authors.

5. Naomi Steinberg, "The Genealogical Framework of the Family Stories in Genesis," *Semeia* 46 (1989): 43.

6. Susan Niditch, "Genesis" in *The Women's Bible Commentary,* ed. Carol A. Newsom and Sharon H. Ringe (Louisville, KY: Westminster/John Knox Press, 1992), 16.

7. Camp, "1 and 2 Kings," 98.

8. Susan Ackerman, *Warrior, Dancer, Seductress, Queen: Women in Judges and Biblical Israel,* The Anchor Bible Reference Library (New York: Doubleday, 1998), 153–54.

9. Ibid., 144.

10. Tamara Cohn Eskenazi, "Ezra-Nehemiah," in *The Women's Bible Commentary,* ed. Carol A. Newsom and Sharon H. Ringe (Louisville, KY: Westminster/John Knox Press, 1992), 119.

11. Tamara Cohn Eskenazi, "Out from the Shadows: Biblical Women in the Post-Exilic Era," in *A Feminist Companion to Samuel and Kings*, Athalya Brenner, Feminist Companion to the Bible (Sheffield, England: Sheffield Academic Press, 1994), 269.

12. Daniel C. Snell, *Life in the Ancient Near East* (New Haven: Yale University Press, 1997), 53.

13. Alice L. Laffey, "1 and 2 Chronicles," in *The Women's Bible Commentary*, ed. Carol A. Newsom and Sharon H. Ringe (Louisville, KY: Westminster/John Knox Press, 1992), 112.

4. Stories: Telling Tales Behind God's Back

1. Phyllis Trible, *God and the Rhetoric of Sexuality,* Overtures to Biblical Theology (Philadelphia: Fortress Press, 1978), 113.

2. Esther Fuchs, *Sexual Politics in the Biblical Narrative: Reading the Hebrew Bible as a Woman,* JSOT Supplement Series (London: Sheffield Academic Press, 2003), 139.

3. Phyllis Trible, *Texts of Terror: Literary-Feminist Readings of Biblical Narratives,* Overtures to Biblical Theology (Philadelphia: Fortress Press, 1984), 2.

4. Robert Alter, *The Art of Biblical Narrative* (New York: Basic Books, 1981), 51.

5. Fuchs, *Sexual Politics*, 63.

6. Ibid., 124.

7. Jon D. Levenson, "Genesis, Introduction and Notes," in *The Jewish Study Bible,* ed. Adele Berlin and Marc Zvi Brettler (Oxford: Oxford University Press, 1999), 43, n. 12.

8. Levenson, "Genesis," 42.

9. There's even more to this play on words than the English version reveals. "Isaac" literally means "laughter," a name Sarah gave him, saying "God has brought laughter for me; everyone who hears will laugh with me" (Gen. 21:6). This symbolic name harks back to Sarah laughing when she overheard three of Yhwh's messengers promising Abraham a son by her, despite her advanced age (Gen. 18:1–15). Sarah's name for Isaac also points forward to Sarah's expulsion of Hagar and Hagar's son

by Abraham, Ishmael. In that episode, Sarah sees Ishmael "playing with her son Isaac" (Gen. 21:9) prompting her to demand of Abraham that Ishmael never inherit along with Isaac. The Hebrew translated as "playing with" in Gen. 21 actually means "making him laugh," another pun on Isaac's name. This brings us back to the adultery story in Gen. 26 in which Isaac is caught fondling his own wife. In addition to catching the play on the words involving "Isaac" and "fondling," audience members who knew the Ishmael–Isaac story would have appreciated the additional joke that whenever The Laugher plays around, there are consequences for everyone involved.

5. How to Read a Story in the Bible

1. Renita J. Weems, "The Hebrew Women Are Not Like the Egyptian Women: The Ideology of Race, Gender and Sexual Reproduction in Exodus 1," *Semeia* 59 (1992): 26.
2. Weems, "Hebrew Women," 28–29.
3. Ibid., 29.
4. Shimon Bar-Efrat, *Narrative Art in the Bible,* trans. Dorothea Shefer-Vanson, reprint, 1989, Journal for the Study of the Old Testament Supplement Series (Sheffield, England: Sheffield Academic Press, 2000), 93.
5. Victor H. Matthews and Don C. Benjamin, *Old Testament Parallels: Laws and Stories from the Ancient Near East,* 2nd ed. (Mahwah, NJ: Paulist Press, 1997), Annals of Sargon I, CD-ROM.
6. Stephanie Dalley, *Myths from Mesopotamia: Creation, the Flood, Gilgamesh, and Others,* rev. ed. (Oxford: Oxford University Press, 2000), 21.
7. Ibid., 18.
8. Ibid., 30.

6. Biblical Law Codes: Who Let the Lawyers In?

1. Mary Douglas, *Purity and Danger: An Analysis of the Concepts of Pollution and Taboo,* reprint, 1966 (New York: Routledge &. Kegan Paul, Ltd., 1984), 2

2. Carolyn Pressler, "Wives and Daughters, Bond and Free: Views of Women in the Slave Laws of Exodus 21.2–11," in *Gender and Law in the Hebrew Bible and the Ancient Near East,* ed. Victor H. Matthews, Bernard M. Levinson, and Tikva Frymer-Kensky (Sheffield, England: Sheffield Academic Press, 1998), 147–72.

3. Victor H. Matthews, "Honor and Shame in Gender-Related Legal Situations in the Hebrew Bible," in *Gender and Law in the Hebrew Bible and the Ancient Near East,* ed. Victor H. Matthews, Bernard M. Levinson and Tikva Frymer-Kensky. (Sheffield, England: Sheffield Academic Press, 1998), 98–100.

4. Tikva Frymer-Kensky, "Virginity in the Bible," in *Gender and Law in the Hebrew Bible and the Ancient Near East,* ed. Victor H Matthews, Bernard M. Levinson, and Tikva Frymer-Kensky (Sheffield, England: Sheffield Academic Press, 1998), 84–85.

5. Bernard M. Levinson, "Deuteronomy: Introduction and Notes," in *The Jewish Study Bible,* ed. Adele Berlin and Marc Zvi Brettler (Oxford: Oxford University Press, 2003), 417.

6. Frymer-Kensky, "Virginity," 94.

7. Ellen Frankel, *The Five Books of Miriam: A Woman's Commentary on the Torah,* reprint, 1996 (New York: HarperSanFrancisco, 1998), 168.

8. Tikva Frymer-Kensky, "Deuteronomy," in *The Women's Bible Commentary,* ed. Carol A. Newsom and Sharon H. Ringe (Louisville KY: Westminster/John Knox Press, 1992), 54.

7. Blood, Fire, and Promises: Further Legal Affairs

1. Nancy Jay, *Throughout Your Generations Forever: Sacrifice, Religion, and Paternity* (Chicago: University of Chicago Press, 1992), 40.

2. George E. Mendenhall and Gary A. Herion, "Covenant," in *Anchor Bible Dictionary,* vol. 1, ed. David Noel Freedman (New York: Doubleday, 1992), 1179.

3. See for example Catherine Keller, *From a Broken Web: Separation, Sexism, and Self* (Boston: Beacon Press, 1986).

4. Stephen L. Harris, *Understanding the Bible,* 5th ed. (Mountain View CA: Mayfield Publishing Company, 2000), 128–29.

5. Bernard M. Levinson, "Deuteronomy: Introduction and Notes," in *The Jewish Study Bible*, ed. Adele Berlin and Marc Zvi Brettler (Oxford: Oxford University Press, 2003), 429.

6. Norman K. Gottwald, *The Hebrew Bible—A Socio-Literary Introduction* (Philadelphia: Fortress Press, 1985), 184–87.

8. Poetry: Love, Lament, Triumph, and Thanksgiving

1. Robert Alter, *The Art of Biblical Poetry* (New York: Basic Books, 1985), 10.

2. Walter Brueggemann, "Psalms and the Life of Faith: A Suggested Typology of Function," in *The Poetical Books*, ed. David J. A. Cline, reprint, OP 1980 JSOT 17) (Sheffield, England: Sheffield Academic Press, 1997), 62.

3. Nancy Schreck, OSF, and Maureen Leach, OSF, *Psalms Anew: In Inclusive Language* (Winona, MN: Saint Mary's Press, 1986), 78–79.

4. Alicia Ostriker, "A Holy of Holies: The Song of Songs as Countertext," in *The Song of Songs,* ed. Athalya Brenner and Carole A. Fontaine, A Feminist Companion to the Bible, Second Series, vol. 6 (Sheffield, England: Sheffield Academic Press, 2000), 38.

5. Carole R. Fontaine, "The Voice of the Turtle: Now It's *My* Song of Songs," in *The Song of Songs*, ed. Athalya Brenner and Carole R. Fontaine, A Feminist Companion to the Bible, Second Series, vol. 6 (Sheffield, England: Sheffield Academic Press, 2000), 180.

6. J. Cheryl Exum, "Ten Things Every Feminist Should Know About the Songs of Songs," in *The Song of Songs*, ed. Athalya Brenner and Carole R. Fontaine, A Feminist Companion to the Bible, Second Series, vol. 6 (Sheffield, England: Sheffield Academic Press, 2000), 30–31.

7. Ostriker, "A Holy of Holies: The Song of Songs as Countertext," 43.

8. Exum, "Ten Things Every Feminist Should Know About the Songs of Songs," 30.

9. Ibid., 35.

10. Fontaine, "The Voice of the Turtle," 178.

11. Frank Moore Cross, Jr., *Studies in Ancient Yahwistic Poetry*, 2nd ed. OP 1975 (Grand Rapids and Livonia, MI: William B. Eerdmans Publishing Co., Dove Booksellers, 1997), 3.

12. Susan Ackerman, *Warrior, Dancer, Seductress, Queen: Women in Judges and Biblical Israel*, The Anchor Bible Reference Library (New York: Doubleday, 1998), 58–59.

13. Susan Niditch, "Eroticism and Death in the Tale of Jael," in *Gender and Difference in Ancient Israel*, ed. Peggy L. Day (Minneapolis, MN: Fortress Press, 1989), 52.

14. Ackerman, *Women in Judges*, 42.

15. Kathleen M. O'Connor, "Lamentations," in *The Women's Bible Commentary*, ed. Carol A. Newsom and Sharon H. Ringe (Louisville, KY: Westminster/John Knox Press, 1992), 179–80.

16. Alice Bach, "With a Song in Her Heart: Listening to Scholars Listening for Miriam," in *Women in the Hebrew Bible*, ed. Alice Bach (New York: Routledge, 1999), 421.

17. Bach, "Song in Her Heart," 419.

18. Ibid., 420.

19. Gary I. Schulman and Mary Hoskins, "Perceiving the Male Versus the Female Face," *Psychology of Women Quarterly* 10, no. 2 (June 1986): 141–154.

9. *Prophecy: The Spirit Pouring Out*

1. Esther Fuchs, "Prophecy and the Construction of Women: Inscription and Erasure," in *Prophets and Daniel*, ed. Athalya Brenner, A Feminist Companion to the Bible, Second Series (Sheffield, England: Sheffield Academic Press, 2001), 54.

2. Fuchs, "Prophecy," 59.

3. Diana Edelman, "Huldah the Prophet—of Yahweh or Asherah?" in *Feminist Companion to Samuel and Kings*, ed. Athalya Brenner, The Feminist Companion to the Bible, vol. 5 (Sheffield, England: Sheffield Academic Press, 1994), 248–51.

4. Rosemary Radford Ruether, *Sexism and God-Talk: Toward a Feminist Theology* (Boston: Beacon Press, 1983), 27.

5. Ruether, *Sexism and God-Talk*, 24.

10. *Lewdness, Whoring, and "Womb Love": A Lexicon of Prophetic Speech*

1. Susan Ackerman, "'And the Women Knead Dough': The Worship of the Queen of Heaven in Sixth-Century Judah," in *Gender and Difference in Ancient Israel*, ed. Peggy L. Day (Minneapolis, MN: Augsburg Fortress, 1989), 110.

2. Phyllis Trible, *God and the Rhetoric of Sexuality*, Overtures to Biblical Theology (Philadelphia: Fortress Press, 1978), 45.

11. *Wisdom: The Listening Heart*

1. Victor H. Matthews and Don C. Benjamin, *Old Testament Parallels: Laws and Stories from the Ancient Near East*, 2nd ed. (Mahwah, NJ: Paulist Press, 1997), CD-ROM.

2. Ibid., otp56.htm.

3. Claudia V. Camp, "The Female Sage in Ancient Israel and in the Biblical Wisdom Literature," in *The Sage in Israel and the Ancient Near East*, ed. John G. Gammie and Leo G. Perdue (Winona Lake, IN: Eisenbrauns, 1990), 194.

4. Carol A. Newsom, "Woman and the Discourse of Patriarchal Wisdom: A Study of Proverbs 1–9," in *Gender and Difference in Ancient Israel*, ed. Peggy L. Day (Minneapolis MN: Fortress Press, 1989), 157.

5. Pamela M. Eisenbaum, "Sirach," in *Women's Bible Commentary, Expanded Edition*, ed. Carol A. Newsom and Sharon H. Ringe (Louisville KY: Westminster/John Knox Press, 1998), 304.

6. Sarah J. Tanzer, "The Wisdom of Solomon," in *Women's Bible Commentary, Expanded Edition*, ed. Carol A. Newsom and Sharon H. Ringe (Louisville KY: Westminster/John Knox Press, 1998), 296.

7. Michael V. Fox, "Proverbs," in *The Jewish Study Bible*, ed. Adele Berlin and Marc Zvi Brettler (Oxford: Oxford University Press, 2004), 1497–98.

8. Camp, "Female Sage," 188.

9. The six iterations of The Teacher's advice are Eccl. 2:24–26, 3:12–13, 3:22, 5:17–19, 8:15, 9:7–10.

10. Elsa Tamez, *When the Horizons Close: Rereading Ecclesiastes,* trans. Margaret Wilde (Maryknoll, NY: Orbis Books, 2000), 25.

12. *The Other Half of History*

1. Philip J. King and Lawrence E. Stager, *Life in Biblical Israel,* Library of Ancient Israel (Louisville, KY: Westminster John Knox Press, 2001), 73.

2. Ibid., 75.

3. Ibid., 68, 77.

4. Ibid., 38.

5. Carol L. Meyers, "Everyday Life: Women in the Period of the Hebrew Bible," in *The Women's Bible Commentary,* ed. Carol A. Newsom and Sharon H. Ringe (Louisville, KY: Westminster/John Knox Press, 1992), 248.

6. Carol Meyers, *Discovering Eve: Ancient Israelite Women in Context* (Oxford: Oxford University Press, 1988), 187.

7. Michelle Zimbalist Rosaldo, "Woman, Culture, and Society: A Theoretical Overview," in *Woman, Culture, and Society,* ed. Michelle Zimbalist Rosaldo and Louise Lamphere (Stanford, CA: Stanford University Press, 1974), 21, n. 2. Rosaldo is quoting M. G. Smith, *Government in Zazau* (London: 1960), 18–19.

8. Ibid., 21. Rosaldo is quoting M. G. Smith, *Government in Zazau* (London: 1960), 18–19.

9. Ibid., 21.

10. Ibid., 21.

11. Carol L. Meyers, "Everyday Life," 250–51.

12. Tamara Cohn Eskenazi, "Out from the Shadows: Biblical Women in the Post-Exilic Era," in *A Feminist Companion to Samuel and Kings,* ed. Athalya Brenner, Feminist Companion to the Bible (Sheffield, England: Sheffield Academic Press, 1994), 263.

13. Ibid., 270.

14. Phyllis A. Bird, "The Harlot as Heroine: Narrative Art and Social Presupposition in Three Old Testament Texts," in *Missing Persons and Mistaken Identities: Women and Gender in Ancient Israel,* Overtures to Biblical Theology (Minneapolis, MN: Augburg Fortress, 1997), 200–1.

15. Phyllis A. Bird, " 'To Play the Harlot': An Inquiry into an Old Testament Metaphor," in *Missing Persons and Mistaken Identities: Women and Gender in Ancient Israel* (Minneapolis, MN: Augsburg Fortress, 1997), 224.

16. Phyllis A. Bird, "The Harlot as Heroine," 205.

17. Susan Ackerman, *Warrior, Dancer, Seductress, Queen: Women in Judges and Biblical Israel,* The Anchor Bible Reference Library (New York: Doubleday, 1998), 227–28.

18. Phyllis A. Bird, "The Harlot as Heroine," 217–18.

19. Phyllis A. Bird, " 'To Play the Harlot,' " 234.

20. Phyllis Bird, "The Place of Women in the Israelite Cultus," in *Ancient Israelite Religion: Essays in Honor of Frank Moore Cross,* ed. Patrick D. Miller, Jr., Paul D. Hanson, and S. Dean McBride (Philadelphia: Fortress Press, 1987), 408–10.

21. Ibid., 100.

22. Nancy R. Bowen, "The Daughters of Your People: Female Prophets in Ezekiel 13:17–23," *Journal of Biblical Literature* 118, no. 3 (1999): 426.

23. Ibid., 422.

24. Tikva Frymer-Kensky, *In the Wake of the Goddesses: Women, Culture and the Biblical Transformation of Pagan Myth* (New York: The Free Press, 1992), 159.

25. Othmar Keel and Christoph Uehlinger, *Gods, Goddesses, and Images of God in Ancient Israel,* trans. Thomas H. Trapp, reprint, 1992 (Minneapolis, MN: Fortress Press, 1998), 325–29.

26. Frymer-Kensky, *In the Wake of the Goddesses,* 161.

13. *God, Gods, and Goddesses*

1. William Morris, ed., *The American Heritage Dictionary of the English Language* (New York: American Heritage Publishing Co., 1969), 615.

2. Stephen L. Harris, *Understanding the Bible*, 5th ed. (Mountain View, CA: Mayfield Publishing Company, 2000), 10.

3. Mark S. Smith, *The Early History of God: Yahweh and the Other Deities in Ancient Israel,* The Biblical Resource Series (Grand Rapids, MI: William B. Eerdmans Publishing Company, 2002), 20–24.

4. Ibid., 41.

5. Ibid., 8–9.

6. Adele Berlin and Marc Zvi Brettler, eds., *The Jewish Study Bible* (Oxford: Oxford University Press, 2004), n. 8, 441.

7. M. Dietrich, O. Loretz, and J. Sanmartin, *Keilalphabetischen Texte Aus Ugarit* (Kevelaer and Neukirchen-Vluyn, 1976), 1.114.

8. Dietrich, Loretz, and Sanmartin, *KTU*, 1.23.

9. John Day, "Baal," in *The Anchor Bible Dictionary*, ed. David Noel Freedman (New York: Doubleday, 1992), I 545.

10. Mark S. Smith attributes this typology to Frank Moore Cross. Smith, *Early History of God*, 80.

11. Ibid., 103–104.

12. Andre Lemaire, "'House of David' Restored in Moabite Inscription," *Biblical Archaeology Review,* May/June 1994, 33.

13. Henry O. Thompson, "Yahweh," in *The Anchor Bible Dictionary,* ed. David Noel Freedman (New York: Doubleday, 1992), VI. 1011.

14. The Lost Goddesses

1. Tikva Frymer-Kensky, *In the Wake of the Goddesses: Women, Culture and the Biblical Transformation of Pagan Myth* (New York: The Free Press, 1992), 85.

2. Stephanie Dalley, *Myths from Mesopotamia: Creation, the Flood, Gilgamesh, and Others,* rev. ed. (Oxford: Oxford University Press, 2000), 255, 257.

3. Othmar Keel and Christoph Uehlinger, *Gods, Goddesses, and Images of God in Ancient Israel,* trans. Thomas H. Trapp, reprint, 1992 (Minneapolis MN: Fortress Press, 1998), 226.

4. John Day, "Asherah," in *The Anchor Bible Dictionary*, David Noel Freedman (New York: Doubleday, 1992), vol. I 484–85.

5. Ibid., I 486.

6. Keel and Uehlinger, *Gods, Goddesses*, 237.

7. Mark S. Smith, *The Early History of God: Yahweh and the Other Deities in Ancient Israel*, The Biblical Resource Series (Grand Rapids, MI: William B. Eerdmans Publishing Co., 2002), 133.

8. Keel and Uehlinger, *Gods, Goddesses*, 131.

9. Ibid., 182.

10. Frymer-Kensky, *In the Wake of the Goddesses*, 5.

11. Ibid., 86.

12. Ibid., 116.

13. Ibid., 106.

14. Ibid., 165.

15. Ibid., 178.

16. Ibid., 38, 167.

17. Miriam Robbins Dexter, *Whence the Goddesses: A Source Book*, The Athene Series (New York: Teachers College Press, 1990), 6.

18. Keel and Uehlinger, *Gods, Goddesses*, 273.

Appendix 1. *How to Read the Bible: A Travel Guide*

1. Tammi J. Schneider, *Sarah: Mother of Nations* (New York: Continuum, 2004), 70–73.

BIBLIOGRAPHY

Ackerman, Susan. "'And the Women Knead Dough': The Worship of the Queen of Heaven in Sixth-Century Judah." In *Gender and Difference in Ancient Israel*, edited by Peggy L. Day, 109–24. Minneapolis, MN: Augsburg Fortress, 1989.

———. *Warrior, Dancer, Seductress, Queen: Women in Judges and Biblical Israel*. The Anchor Bible Reference Library. New York: Doubleday, 1998.

Alter, Robert. *The Art of Biblical Narrative*. New York: Basic Books, 1981.

———. *The Art of Biblical Poetry*. New York: Basic Books, 1985.

Bach, Alice. "With a Song in Her Heart: Listening to Scholars Listening for Miriam." In *Women in the Hebrew Bible*, edited by Alice Bach, 419–28. New York: Routledge, 1999.

Baker-Fletcher, Karen. "Anna Julia Cooper and Sojourner Truth: Two Nineteenth-Century Black Feminist Interpreters of Scripture." In *Searching the Scriptures: A Feminist Introduction*, vol. 1, edited by Elisabeth Schüssler Fiorenza, 41–51. New York: Crossroad, 1993.

Bar-Efrat, Shimon. *Narrative Art in the Bible*. Translated by Dorothea Shefer-Vanson. 1989. *Journal for the Study of the Old Testament* Supplement Series. Sheffield, England: Sheffield Academic Press, 2000.

Berlin, Adele, and Marc Zvi Brettler, eds. *The Jewish Study Bible*. Oxford: England: Oxford University Press, 2004.

Bird, Phyllis A. "The Harlot as Heroine: Narrative Art and Social Presupposition in Three Old Testament Texts." In *Missing Persons and Mistaken Identities: Women and Gender in Ancient Israel*. Overtures to Biblical Theology. Minneapolis, MN: Augburg Fortress, 1997.

———— "The Place of Women in the Israelite Cultus." In *Ancient Israelite Religion: Essays in Honor of Frank Moore Cross,* edited by Patrick D. Miller, Jr., Paul D. Hanson, and S. Dean McBride. Philadelphia: Fortress Press, 1987.

————. "'To Play the Harlot': An Inquiry into an Old Testament Metaphor." In *Missing Persons and Mistaken Identities: Women and Gender in Ancient Israel,* 219–36. Minneapolis, MN: Augsburg Fortress, 1997.

Bowen, Nancy R. "The Daughters of Your People: Female Prophets in Ezekiel 13:17–23." *Journal of Biblical Literature* 118, no. 3 (1999): 417–33.

Brueggemann, Walter. "Psalms and the Life of Faith: A Suggested Typology of Function." In *The Poetical Books,* edited by David J. A. Cline. OP 1980 JSOT 17, 35–66. Sheffield, England: Sheffield Academic Press, 1997.

Camp, Claudia V. "1 and 2 Kings." In *The Women's Bible Commentary,* edited by Carol A. Newsom and Sharon H. Ringe, 96–109. Louisville, KY: Westminster/John Knox Press, 1992.

———— "The Female Sage in Ancient Israel and in the Biblical Wisdom Literature." In *The Sage in Israel and the Ancient Near East,* edited by John G. Gammie and Leo G. Perdue, 185–203. Winona Lake, IN: Eisenbrauns, 1990.

Coogan, Michael D. *The New Oxford Annotated Bible*. 3rd ed. Oxford: Oxford University Press, 2001.

Cross, Frank Moore, Jr. *Studies in Ancient Yahwistic Poetry*. 2nd ed. OP 1975. Grand Rapids and Livonia, MI: William B. Eerdmans Publishing Co., Dove Booksellers, 1997.

Dalley, Stephanie. *Myths from Mesopotamia: Creation, the Flood, Gilgamesh, and Others.* Rev. ed. Stephanie Dalley. Oxford: Oxford University Press, 2000.

Day, John. "Asherah." In *The Anchor Bible Dictionary,* David Noel Freedman, I 483–87. New York: Doubleday, 1992.

———. "Baal." In *The Anchor Bible Dictionary,* edited by David Noel Freedman, I 545–49. New York: Doubleday, 1992.

Dever, William G. *What Did the Biblical Writers Know and When Did They Know It?: What Archaeology Can Tell Us About the Reality of Ancient Israel.* Grand Rapids, MI: William B. Eerdmans Publishing Co., 2001.

Dexter, Miriam Robbins. *Whence the Goddesses: A Source Book.* The Athene Series. New York: Teachers College Press, 1990.

Douglas, Mary. *Purity and Danger: An Analysis of the Concepts of Pollution and Taboo.* 1966. New York: Routledge & Kegan Paul, Ltd., 1984.

Edelman, Diana. "Huldah the Prophet—of Yahweh or Asherah?" In *Feminist Companion to Samuel and Kings,* edited by Athalya Brenner. The Feminist Companion to the Bible 5, 231–50. Sheffield, England: Sheffield Academic Press, 1994.

Eisenbaum, Pamela M. "Sirach." In *Women's Bible Commentary, Expanded Edition,* edited by Carol A. Newsom and Sharon H. Ringe, 298–304. Louisville, KY: Westminster/John Knox Press, 1998.

Eskenazi, Tamara Cohn. "Ezra-Nehemiah." In *The Women's Bible Commentary,* edited by Carol A. Newsom and Sharon H. Ringe, 116–23. Louisville, KY: Westminster/John Knox Press, 1992.

———. "Out from the Shadows: Biblical Women in the Post-Exilic Era." In *A Feminist Companion to Samuel and Kings,* edited by Athalya Brenner. The Feminist Companion to the Bible, 252–71. Sheffield, England: Sheffield Academic Press, 1994.

Exum, J. Cheryl. "Ten Things Every Feminist Should Know About the Songs of Songs." In *The Song of Songs,* edited by Athalya Brenner and Carole R. Fontaine. A Feminist Companion to the Bible, Second Series, vol. 6, 24–35. Sheffield, England: Sheffield Academic Press, 2000.

Finkelstein, Israel, and Neil Asher Silberman. *The Bible Unearthed: Archaeology's New Vision of Ancient Israel and the Origin of Its Sacred Texts.* New York: The Free Press, 2001.

Fontaine, Carole R. "The Voice of the Turtle: Now It's *My* Song of Songs." In *The Song of Songs,* edited by Athalya Brenner and Carole R. Fontaine. A Feminist Companion to the Bible, Second Series, vol. 6, 169–85. Sheffield, England: Sheffield Academic Press, 2000.

Fox, Michael V. "Proverbs." In *The Jewish Study Bible,* edited by Adele Berlin and Marc Zvi Brettler, 1447–98. Oxford: Oxford University Press, 2004.

Frankel, Ellen. *The Five Books of Miriam: A Woman's Commentary on the Torah.* 1996. New York: HarperSanFrancisco, 1998.

Friedman, Richard Elliot. *Who Wrote the Bible?* 2nd ed. OP1987. New York: HarperSanFrancisco, 1997.

Frymer-Kensky, Tikva. "Deuteronomy." In *The Women's Bible Commentary,* edited by Carol A. Newsom and Sharon H. Ringe, 52–62. Louisville, KY: Westminster/John Knox Press, 1992.

———. *In the Wake of the Goddesses: Women, Culture and the Biblical Transformation of Pagan Myth.* New York: The Free Press, 1992.

———. "Virginity in the Bible." In *Gender and Law in the Hebrew Bible and the Ancient Near East,* edited by Victor H Matthews, Bernard M. Levinson, and Tikva Frymer-Kensky, 78–96. Sheffield, England: Sheffield Academic Press, 1998.

Fuchs, Esther. "Prophecy and the Construction of Women: Inscription and Erasure." In *Prophets and Daniel,* edited by Athalya Brenner. A Feminist Companion to the Bible, Second Series, 54–69. Sheffield, England: Sheffield Academic Press, 2001.

———. *Sexual Politics in the Biblical Narrative: Reading the Hebrew Bible as a Woman.* JSOT Supplement Series. London: Sheffield Academic Press, 2003.

Gottwald, Norman K. *The Hebrew Bible—Socio-Literary Introduction.* Philadelphia: Fortress Press, 1985.

Harris, Stephen L. *Understanding the Bible.* 5th ed. Mountain View, CA: Mayfield Publishing Co., 2000.

Jay, Nancy. *Throughout Your Generations Forever: Sacrifice, Religion, and Paternity.* Chicago: University of Chicago Press, 1992.

Keel, Othmar, and Christoph Uehlinger. *Gods, Goddesses, and Images of God in Ancient Israel.* Translated by Thomas H. Trapp. 1992. Minneapolis, MN: Fortress Press, 1998.

Keller, Catherine. *From a Broken Web: Separation, Sexism, and Self.* Boston: Beacon Press, 1986.

King, Philip J., and Lawrence E. Stager. *Life in Biblical Israel.* Library of Ancient Israel. Louisville, KY: Westminster John Knox Press, 2001.

Lemaire, Andre. "'House of David' Restored in Moabite Inscription." *Biblical Archaeology Review,* May/June 1994, 30–37.

Levenson, Jon D. "Genesis, Introduction and Notes." In *The Jewish Study Bible,* edited by Adele Berlin and Brettler Marc Zvi, 8–101. Oxford: Oxford University Press, 1999.

Levinson, Bernard M. "Deuteronomy: Introduction and Notes." In *The Jewish Study Bible,* edited by Adele Berlin and Marc Zvi Brettler, 417. Oxford: Oxford University Press, 2003.

Matthews, Victor H. "Honor and Shame in Gender-Related Legal Situations in the Hebrew Bible." In *Gender and Law in the Hebrew Bible and the Ancient Near East,* edited by Victor H. Matthews, Bernard M. Levinson, and Tikva Frymer–Kensky, 97–112. Sheffield, England: Sheffield Academic Press, 1998.

Matthews, Victor H., and Don C. Benjamin. *Old Testament Parallels: Laws and Stories from the Ancient Near East.* 2nd ed. Mahwah, NJ: Paulist Press, 1997. CD-ROM.

Mendenhall, George E., and Gary A. Herion. "Covenant." In *Anchor Bible Dictionary,* edited by David Noel Freedman, 1179–1202. New York: Doubleday, 1992.

Meyers, Carol L. *Discovering Eve: Ancient Israelite Women in Context.* Oxford: Oxford University Press, 1988.

———. "Everyday Life: Women in the Period of the Hebrew Bible." In *The Women's Bible Commentary,* edited by Carol A. Newsom and Sharon H. Ringe, 244–51. Louisville, KY: Westminster/John Knox Press, 1992.

Morris, William, ed. *The American Heritage Dictionary of the English Language*. New York: American Heritage Publishing Co., 1969.

Newsom, Carol A. "Woman and the Discourse of Patriarchal Wisdom: A Study of Proverbs 1–9." In *Gender and Difference in Ancient Israel*, edited by Peggy L. Day, 142–60. Minneapolis, MN: Fortress Press, 1989.

Niditch, Susan. "Eroticism and Death in the Tale of Jael." In *Gender and Difference in Ancient Israel*, edited by Peggy L. Day, 43–57. Minneapolis, MN: Fortress Press, 1989.

O'Connor, Kathleen M. "Lamentations." In *The Women's Bible Commentary*, edited by Carol A. Newsom and Sharon H. Ringe, 178–82. Louisville, KY: Westminster/John Knox Press, 1992.

Ostriker, Alicia. "A Holy of Holies: The Song of Songs as Countertext." In *The Song of Songs*, edited by Athalya Brenner and Carole A. Fontaine. A Feminist Companion to the Bible, Second Seriesvol, vol. 6. Sheffield, England: Sheffield Academic Press, 2000.

Plaskow, Judith. *Standing Again at Sinai: Judaism from a Feminist Perspective*. San Francisco: Harper & Row, 1990.

Pressler, Carolyn. "Wives and Daughters, Bond and Free: Views of Women in the Slave Laws of Exodus 21.2–11." In *Gender and Law in the Hebrew Bible and the Ancient Near East,* edited by Victor H. Matthews, Bernard M. Levinson, and Tikva Frymer-Kensky, 147–72. Sheffield, England: Sheffield Academic Press, 1998.

Rosaldo, Michelle Zimbalist. "Woman, Culture, and Society: A Theoretical Overview." In *Woman, Culture, and Society*, edited by Michelle Zimbalist Rosaldo and Louise Lamphere, 17–42. Stanford, CA: Stanford University Press, 1974.

Ruether, Rosemay Radford. *Sexism and God-Talk: Toward a Feminist Theology*. Boston: Beacon Press, 1983.

Schneider, Tammi J. *Sarah: Mother of Nations*. New York: Continuum, 2004.

Schreck, Nancy, OSF, and Maureen Leach, OSF, *Psalms Anew: In Inclusive Language*. Winona, MN: Saint Mary's Press, 1986.

Schüssler Fiorenza, Elisabeth. *But She Said: Feminist Practices of Biblical Interpetation*. Boston: Beacon Press, 1992.

Smith, Mark S. *The Early History of God: Yahweh and the Other Deities in Ancient Israel*. The Biblical Resource Series. Grand Rapids, MI: William B. Eerdmans Publishing Co., 2002.

Snell, Daniel C. *Life in the Ancient Near East*. New Haven: Yale University Press, 1997.

Steinberg, Naomi. "The Genealogical Framework of the Family Stories in Genesis." *Semeia* 46 (1989): 41–50.

Tamez, Elsa. *When the Horizons Close: Rereading Ecclesiastes*. Translated by Margaret Wilde. Maryknoll, NY: Orbis Books, 2000.

Tanzer, Sarah J. "The Wisdom of Solomon." In *Women's Bible Commentary, Expanded Edition,* edited by Carol A. Newsom and Sharon H. Ringe, 293–97. Louisville, KY: Westminster/John Knox Press, 1998.

Thompson, Henry O. "Yahweh." In *The Anchor Bible Dictionary,* edited by David Noel Freedman, VI 1011–12. New York: Doubleday, 1992.

Trible, Phyllis. *God and the Rhetoric of Sexuality*. Overtures to Biblical Theology. Philadelphia: Fortress Press, 1978.

———. *Texts of Terror: Literary-Feminist Readings of Biblical Narratives*. Overtures to Biblical Theology. Philadelphia: Fortress Press, 1984.

Weems, Renita J. "The Hebrew Women Are not Like the Egyptian Women: The Ideology of Race, Gender and Sexual Reproduction in Exodus 1." *Semeia* 59 (1992): 25–35.

INDEX